GUIDE TO

FOREIGN AND

INTERNATIONAL

LEGAL CITATIONS

ASPEN PUBLISHERS

GUIDE TO

FOREIGN AND

INTERNATIONAL

LEGAL CITATIONS

Second Edition

New York University School of Law
Journal of International Law and Politics

Wolters Kluwer
Law & Business

AUSTIN   BOSTON   CHICAGO   NEW YORK   THE NETHERLANDS

Aspen Publishers
Attn: Permissions Department
76 Ninth Avenue, 7th Floor
New York, NY 10011-5201

To contact Customer Care, e-mail CUSTOMER.CARE@ASPENPUBLISHERS.COM, call 1-800-234-1660, fax 1-800-901-9075, or mail correspondence to:

Aspen Publishers
Attn: Order Department
PO Box 990
Frederick, MD 21705

Printed in the United States of America.

1 2 3 4 5 6 7 8 9 0

ISBN 978-0-7355-7979-8

Library of Congress Cataloging-in-Publication Data

Guide to foreign and international legal citations. — 2nd ed.
    p. cm.
"New York University School of Law, Journal of international law and politics."
    Includes bibliographical references and index.
    ISBN 978-0-7355-7979-8
    1. Citation of legal authorities. 2. Comparative law — Legal research. 3. International law — Legal research. I. New York University. School of Law. II. Title: Foreign and international legal citations.
K89.G85 2009
341.072 — dc22

                                                                          2009004042

About Wolters Kluwer Law & Business

Wolters Kluwer Law & Business is a leading provider of research information and workflow solutions in key specialty areas. The strengths of the individual brands of Aspen Publishers, CCH, Kluwer Law International and Loislaw are aligned within Wolters Kluwer Law & Business to provide comprehensive, in-depth solutions and expert-authored content for the legal, professional and education markets.

CCH was founded in 1913 and has served more than four generations of business professionals and their clients. The CCH products in the Wolters Kluwer Law & Business group are highly regarded electronic and print resources for legal, securities, antitrust and trade regulation, government contracting, banking, pension, payroll, employment and labor, and healthcare reimbursement and compliance professionals.

Aspen Publishers is a leading information provider for attorneys, business professionals and law students. Written by preeminent authorities, Aspen products offer analytical and practical information in a range of specialty practice areas from securities law and intellectual property to mergers and acquisitions and pension/benefits. Aspen's trusted legal education resources provide professors and students with high-quality, up-to-date and effective resources for successful instruction and study in all areas of the law.

Kluwer Law International supplies the global business community with comprehensive English-language international legal information. Legal practitioners, corporate counsel and business executives around the world rely on the Kluwer Law International journals, loose-leafs, books and electronic products for authoritative information in many areas of international legal practice.

Loislaw is a premier provider of digitized legal content to small law firm practitioners of various specializations. Loislaw provides attorneys with the ability to quickly and efficiently find the necessary legal information they need, when and where they need it, by facilitating access to primary law as well as state-specific law, records, forms and treatises.

Wolters Kluwer Law & Business, a unit of Wolters Kluwer, is headquartered in New York and Riverwoods, Illinois. Wolters Kluwer is a leading multinational publisher and information services company.

Contents

INTRODUCTION
AND HOW TO USE THIS GUIDE

The *Guide to Foreign and International Legal Citations* provides standards for citing country-specific constitutions, legislation, and jurisprudence in the style of the source jurisdiction's own citation system. In addition, the Guide provides standards for citing treaties and documents from international organizations as well as from regional and hybrid courts.

The Guide serves three primary purposes.

- First and most important, it provides a system of citation whereby foreign sources can be cited properly in U.S. legal journals. (Users should consult U.S. citation guides for the styling/formatting of standard materials such as books and periodicals.) Foreign citation standards have been altered in the Guide where they do not conform to the standards of U.S. legal journals. This applies particularly to citation standards for countries that do not use the Roman alphabet. The standards of the People's Republic of China, for example, are altered simply because Chinese characters are not used in this Guide.
- Second, the Guide allows persons unfamiliar with foreign and international citation standards to understand and interpret the importance of such standards in the native terms of that jurisdiction or forum. With this comes the ability, for example, to understand basic information such as the type and place in the hierarchy of the court that renders a particular decision, or the type of code that contains a certain law.
- Third, on a more practical level, with this information, scholars, judges, and practicing lawyers are able more easily to identify and locate the source from the source jurisdiction according to its own, more familiar citation norms.

Given the breadth of material in this Guide, it is simply not possible to provide complete citation standards for every country and every international legal forum. If the coverage of a jurisdiction does not include citation standards for a particular type of source, either no standard exists or it has not yet been discovered by the editors of the Guide.

The *Guide to Foreign and International Legal Citations* attempts to respect the idiosyncrasies among academic citation traditions of the various jurisdictions. A paragraph at the beginning of each section notes whether the country's or jurisdiction's citation formats are or are not recognizably standardized. Keep in mind that the standards of many jurisdictions are not as rigorous as are those of the United States. Moreover, even in countries that have more standardized citation systems, the standards are neither absolute nor etched in stone. In many countries, vernacular forms prevail over formal citation standards. This Guide captures the plasticity of citations in actual practice by laying out a general citation rule and following the rule with examples of citations that correspond to the rule or that deviate from it in particular ways.

Finally, two cautionary notes. First, users should keep in mind that particular courts may have their own citation requirements; when submitting documents to courts, lawyers should not rely exclusively on the Guide. Second, while the editors of the Guide have provided URLs current as of sending the book to press, web pages may change, move, or be deleted.

Conventions of This Guide

- The citation instructions contain both source content instructions, noted in square brackets, and formatting instructions, noted in parentheses.
- English translations of many foreign words in citations are placed within parentheses of explanatory text, though translations are not placed in the citations unless the foreign standard itself offers translations. Common practice in the United States is to place English translations within square brackets after foreign words in the original citation.
- If the country of origin of the source may not be clear to the audience, the writer may provide the country name, in parentheses, at the end of the citation.
- Similarly, if citing outside the country in question, the writer may provide the country name, in parentheses, at the end of the citation.

ACKNOWLEDGMENTS

Publication of the *Guide to Foreign and International Legal Citations* (G.F.I.L.C.) would not have been possible without the help of countless individuals and institutions over the past several years.

First, we would like to thank the numerous LL.M. students who took time out of their studies at New York University to provide guidance on the citation standards used in their home countries.

Second, we would like to thank past Journal of International Law and Politics (JILP) Boards and staff editors who contributed their time and thoughts to the production of this Guide.

Third, we would like to thank the past G.F.I.L.C. editors who labored over the years to compile this vast array of material. Special gratitude is extended to Genevieve Beyea for her efforts in preparing this Guide for publication.

Finally, we would like to thank the administration of New York University School of Law for its patience and financial support, which have made this endeavor possible.

Jesse D. Infeld
G.F.I.L.C. Editor, 2008-2009
Clay H. Kaminsky
JILP Editor-in-Chief, 2008-2009

GUIDE TO

FOREIGN AND

INTERNATIONAL

LEGAL CITATIONS

PART

COUNTRY CITATION

GUIDES

A R G E N T I N A

Republica Argentina (Argentine Republic)

I. COUNTRY PROFILE (CIVIL LAW)

Argentina is a federal, democratic republic composed of 23 provinces (*provincias*) and one autonomous district (Federal Capital, Buenos Aires). It is a civil law system primarily influenced by Italy, Spain, France, and Germany. The official language is Spanish.

The Constitution, adopted in 1853 and most recently amended in 1994, provides for a tripartite government with executive, legislative, and judicial branches. The provinces and the City of Buenos Aires enjoy autonomy and choose their own authorities. Each province as well as the City of Buenos Aires enacts its own constitution; each provincial constitution provides for municipal autonomy and the scope of its own institutional, political, administrative, economic, and financial powers.

The President is the head of state and exercises the executive power. The Constitution requires that the President be elected directly by the people every four years and not serve more than two consecutive terms, with the ability to serve a third term or more after an interval of at least one term. Except for the Supreme Court Justices, the President has to select each federal judge from a list of three candidates that is prepared by the Judiciary Council (*Consejo de la Magistratura*). The President appoints the Supreme Court Justices and the other federal court judges with the consent of the Senate. Lower court federal judges are appointed by the Senate from a list of three candidates that is prepared by the Judiciary Council (*Consejo de la Magistratura*), which is made up of members of Congress, the Supreme Court, and professional organizations. Judges hold tenure during good behavior.

The legislative power is vested in the Congress (*Honorable Congreso de la Nación*), which is composed of the Senate (*Cámara de Senadores*) and the Chamber of Deputies (*Cámara de Diputados*). A supermajority is needed in both houses to overcome a presidential veto. The Chamber of Deputies consists of 256 members, distributed on the basis of proportional representation. By direct vote, the people of the provinces and those of the City of Buenos Aires elect representatives to the Chamber of Deputies and the Senate. Deputies are elected for four years and may be reelected. The Senate consists of three senators from each province, and three from the City of Buenos Aires; among the three

3

senators, two represent the majority party and the remaining senator represents the minority party. Senators serve for six years and can be reelected indefinitely.

The judicial power in Argentina is divided into federal and provincial courts, each of which consists of supreme courts, courts of appeal, and lower courts. The courts are further divided in accordance with their areas of specialty. The National Supreme Court (*Corte Suprema de Justicia de la Nación*) possesses the supreme judicial power and has nine members appointed by the President. It has exclusive and original jurisdiction in cases that involve ambassadors, public ministers, and consuls; cases in which a province is a party; cases between one province and the inhabitants of another province; cases between the inhabitants of different provinces; and cases between one province or the inhabitants thereof against a foreign state or citizen. Lower courts, both at the appellate level and the first instance level, have their own specialties such as civil, criminal, labor, administrative, family, or commercial. A list of federal courts is provided in Part 3.2 below. The provincial court system has a structure similar to that of the federal court system. The jurisdiction of the provincial courts includes all matters that do not fall under federal jurisdiction. The provincial court system is divided into three main types of courts — civil, criminal, and labor. The number and the name of the provincial courts vary, depending on the province. A list of typical provincial courts is provided in Part 3.2 below. In addition to the federal and provincial courts, the autonomous City of Buenos Aires has its own courts as listed in Part 3.2.

Internet Resources:

The President	http://www.presidencia.gov.ar
Minister of Justice	http://www.jus.gov.ar
Judiciary	http://www.pjn.gov.ar
National Supreme Court	http://www.csjn.gov.ar

II.   CITATION GUIDE

In Argentina, there is no uniform national citation manual. There are, however, some accepted practices, although they are not followed by all authors.

1.0 Constitution

Cite to the abbreviation of the Constitution ("Const. Nacional," or sometimes "CN," for *Constitución Nacional*), preceded by the article (Art.):

Art. 23, Const. Nacional (Arg.).

1.1 State Constitution

Cite state constitutions with the abbreviation "Const. Prov." followed by the name of the province, both preceded by the article (Art.):

Art. 23, Const. Prov. Córdoba.

2.0 Legislation

2.1 Statutes, Laws, and Decrees

Cite statutes and decrees by the law number, the name of the reporter, the volume number, and the page number:

Ley No. 23098, A.D.L.A., XLIV-D, 3733.

The official gazette, *Boletín Oficial* (B.O.), publishes laws and decrees. Citations should include date and page in the B.O. if possible.

Reporters containing national law, resolutions of the Executive, and provincial legislation, respectively, are:

Anales de Legislación Argentina: A.D.L.A.
El Derecho — Legislación Argentina: E.D.L.A.
Anuario de Legislación de Jurisprudencia Argentina: A.L.J.A.

2.2 Codes

Cite codes by the number of the article followed by the abbreviated title of the code:

Art. 954, Cod. Civ.

The abbreviations of major Codes are:

Código Civil (Cod. Civ.)
Código de Comercio (Cod. Com.)
Código Penal (Cod. Pen.)
Código Procesal Civil y Comercial de la Nación (Cod. Proc. Civ. y Com. Nac.)
Código Procesal Penal de la Nación (Cod. Proc. Pen. Nac.)

3.0 Jurisprudence

Cite cases by the parties' names (plaintiff's and defendant's last name and, optionally, first initial), separated by "c/" in quotation marks, the court (including the section, "sala," if appropriate; for provincial courts add the name of the province), the name of the report, volume, year, and page referenced. If the volume number contains the year, it need not be repeated:

"Peroni c/ Gomez" CNCiv., sala B, LL, 1997-D, 123.

3.1 Reports

The official report of judicial decisions is *Colección Oficial de Fallos de la Corte Suprema de Justicia de la Nación* (abbreviated as "Fallos"). It only contains federal Supreme Court decisions and is cited by abbreviated name, volume number, and page referenced:

Fallos: 45:967.

Authors and practitioners mainly use unofficial reports, including *Revista Jurídica Argentina — La Ley* (LL); *El Derecho* (ED); and *Jurisprudencia Argentina* (JA). All of them report both federal and provincial cases:

LL, 1976-E, 658.

3.2 Courts

The abbreviations of Federal Courts are:

National Supreme Court: *Corte Suprema de Justicia de la Nación* (CSJN)

National Criminal Court: *Cámara Nacional de Casación Penal* (CNCP)

Federal Court of Appeals for Social Security: *Cámara Federal de Apelaciones de la Seguridad Social* (CFASS)

Court of Appeals for Criminal–Economic Matters: *Cámara Nacional de Apelaciones en lo Penal Económico* (CNPenal Económico)

Court of Appeals for Civil and Commercial Matters: *Cámara Nacional de Apelaciones en lo Civil y Comercial Federal* (CN Civ. y Com. Fed.)

Court of Appeals for Administrative Matters: *Cámara Nacional de Apelaciones en lo Contencioso Administrativo Federal* (CN Cont. Adm. Fed.)

Court of Appeals for Criminal and Correctional Matters: *Cámara Nacional de Apelaciones en lo Criminal y Correccional Federal* (CN Crim. y Corr. Fed.)

Federal Court of Appeals: *Cámara Federal de Apelaciones* (Cfed.), of which there are 15: *de Bahía Blanca; de Comodoro Rivadavia; de Córdoba; de Corrientes; de General Roca; de La Plata; de Mar del Plata; de Mendoza; de Paraná; de Santa Fe; de Misiones; de Resistencia; de Salta; de San Martín; de Tucumán.*

Lower Federal Courts: *Juzgado Federal* (Juzg Fed.)

Courts of Ordinary Jurisdiction for the District of Buenos Aires (and their abbreviations) include:

Court of Appeals for Civil Matters: *Cámara Nacional de Apelaciones en lo Civil* (CNCiv.)

Court of Appeals for Commercial Matters: *Cámara Nacional de Apelaciones en lo Comercial* (CNCom.)

Court of Appeals for Labor Matters: *Cámara Nacional de Apelaciones del Trabajo* (CNTrab.)

Court of Appeals for Criminal and Correctional Matters: *Cámara Nacional de Apelaciones en lo Criminal y Correccional* (CNCrim. y Corr.)

Lower Courts of Ordinary Jurisdiction: *Juzgado Nacional de Primera Instancia* (1a Inst.)

Provincial Courts (and their abbreviations) include:

Corte de Justicia (CJ)
Suprema Corte (SC)
Tribunal Superior (TS)
Tribunal Superior de Justicia (Trib. Sup.)
Superior Tribunal (ST)
State Court of Appeals for Civil and Commercial Matters: *Cámara de Apelaciones en lo Civil y Comercial* (CApel. CC)
State Court of Appeals for Criminal Matters: *Cámara de Apelaciones en lo Penal* (CApel. Penal)
State Court of Appeals for Labor Matters: *Cámara del Trabajo* (CTrab.)
State Lower Courts of Ordinary Jurisdiction: *Juzgado de Primera Instancia* (1a Inst.)

III.   SELECTED REFERENCES

ENRIQUE R. AFTALION, INTRODUCCIÓN AL DERECHO (Abeledo Perrot 1999).

GERMAN J. BIDART CAMPOS, THE ARGENTINE SUPREME COURT: THE COURT OF CONSTITUTIONAL GUARANTEES (Hein & Company 1982).

GERMAN J. BIDART CAMPOS, DERECHO CONSTITUCIONAL DEL PODER (Ediar 1967).

EDUARDO COUTIVE, INTRODUCCIÓN DERECHO PROCESAL CIVIL (Depalma 1988).

JULIO B.J. MAIER, DERECHO PROCESAL PENAL (Rústica 1999).

A U S T R A L I A

I. COUNTRY PROFILE (COMMON LAW)

Australia is a federal state governed by bicameral legislatures at both levels of government — Commonwealth and state. Its head of state is the British Sovereign, represented in Australia by the Governor-General, and the head of government is the Prime Minister.

Australia's government is based upon representative democracy through a federal system. The Commonwealth is composed of six states and ten territories. The territories are generally governed by the Commonwealth, although the two mainland federal territories, the Northern Territory and the Australian Capital Territory, have responsibilities similar to the states through self-governing arrangements. English is the official language.

The Constitution provides for separate executive, legislative, and judicial branches. As in other parliamentary systems, the executive branch, including the Prime Minister and cabinet ministers, is elected by members of the party or parties that control the Parliament. Following the Westminster system of separation of powers, Parliament is responsible for establishing law and has the sole power to pass Acts, the Executive is charged with enforcing the law and has the power to make rules and regulations necessary to implement Parliamentary Acts, and the Judicial branch is responsible for interpreting the law.

The Commonwealth and each state are governed by elected Parliaments. The Commonwealth Parliament is formally headed by the Sovereign royal of Great Britain. The Commonwealth Senate is made up of 76 Senators, 12 Senators from each of the six states, and two Senators each from the Northern Territory and the Australian Capital Territory. Senators serve a term of approximately six years (Parliamentary elections occur at least every three years or whenever the Prime Minister's party loses control of Parliament), with half of the Senators from each state or self-governing territory being elected during the general Parliamentary election. The Constitution requires that the number of Representatives be "as nearly as practicable" twice the number of Senators, with the number from each state depending upon its relative proportion to the overall population. Representatives serve for the length of the current Parliament, generally three years.

Laws are made by the federal, state, and territorial parliaments in generally the same way. A member of either house may introduce legislation, which must be voted on and approved by both houses by a majority vote. The Governor-General then signs the legislation, giving it royal assent and making it an Act of

Parliament and thus law. Whenever a federal law conflicts with a state law, the federal law prevails.

The Australian Constitution, which took effect on January 1, 1901, establishes the powers of the Commonwealth (the federal government), with all undesignated powers being reserved to the states and self-governing territory governments.

The Constitution vests the judicial power of the Commonwealth in the High Court of Australia as the Federal Supreme Court. The High Court is vested with both original and appellate jurisdiction. Original jurisdiction applies in cases involving treaties, suits between states or between persons suing or being sued by or on the behalf of a state, suits in which the Commonwealth of Australia is a party, and matters involving writs of mandamus or prohibition. Appellate jurisdiction applies to appeals from decisions of High Court original jurisdiction, Federal Courts, Federal Magistrates Service, courts exercising federal jurisdiction, and State Supreme Courts. The High Court has discretion in deciding which appeals to hear. It must consider, however, whether the issues on appeal involve questions of law of public importance, differences among lower court decisions, or an issue that "in the interests of the administration of justice" should be considered by the High Court.

The Federal Court of Australia was created by the *Federal Court of Australia Act* of 1976. It is an appellate court with jurisdiction over single-judge rulings of the Federal Court, Australian Territory Supreme Courts (except the Northern Territory), and State Supreme Courts when they have exercised federal jurisdiction. Other federal courts include the Family Court of Australia, the Industrial Relations Court of Australia, and the Federal Magistrates Service. The Family Court was established by the *Family Law Act* of 1975 to deal with dissolution of marriage, child welfare and custody, maintenance, and property settlement issues. More recently its federal jurisdiction has been expanded to include bankruptcy, administrative law, and taxation appeals. The Industrial Relations Court was established in 1994 as an independent court designed to deal with industrial relations matters, but such issues were transferred to the jurisdiction of the Federal Court in 1997. Finally, the Federal Magistrate Court, established by the *Federal Magistrates Act* of 1999, is an independent federal court dealing with family law and child support, administrative law, bankruptcy law, and consumer protection. The Federal Magistrate Court's jurisdiction is shared with the Federal Court, Family Court, and some state courts.

Courts in Australian States and Territories have original jurisdiction in matters involving state or territorial law and where the Commonwealth Parliament has specifically conferred jurisdiction for some federal matters. Most criminal matters are handled by state or territory courts. With the exception of the Australian Antarctic and Jervis Bay Territories, each state and inhabited territory has a Supreme Court and local courts of summary jurisdiction. In addition, most jurisdictions have intermediate courts known as a district or county court.

Specialist courts, limited by subject matter, have also been established in some states to deal with issues such as the environment, compensation, and local government issues.

Internet Resources:

Attorney General's Dept.	http://www.ag.gov.au
Capital	http://www.act.gov.au
Federal Gov't	http://www.fed.gov.au
New South Wales	http://www.nsw.gov.au
Northern Territories	http://www.nt.gov.au
Queensland	http://www.qld.gov.au
South Australia	http://www.sa.gov.au
Tasmania	http://www.tas.gov.au
Victoria	http://www.vic.gov.au
Western Australia	http://www.wa.gov.au

II. CITATION GUIDE

There is no official guide to legal citations in Australia. The following merely reflects accepted practices and suggestions as put forward in the comprehensive *Australian Guide to Legal Citation*.

1.0 Constitution

Cite the Australian Constitution as "Australian Constitution" (italicized), followed by the section referenced:

Australian Constitution s 19.

2.0 Legislation and Other Non-Judicial Sources

2.1 Statutes

Cite acts by short title or, if there is no short title, full title (italicized), year, abbreviated name of the jurisdiction (in parentheses), and subdivision referenced:

Copyright Act 1970 (Cth) s 52.

For federal legislation, cite to the abbreviation for Commonwealth (Cth). For state legislation, cite to the abbreviated name of the state.

Australian Capital Territory (ACT)
New South Wales (NSW)

Northern Territories (NT)
Queensland (QLD)
South Australia (SA)
Tasmania (TAS)
Victoria (VIC)
Western Australia (WA)

2.2 Bills

Cite bills in the same way as acts. The name of a bill before parliament is not italicized:

CLERP Bill 1998 (Cth).

3.0 Jurisprudence

Cite cases by parties' name [first plaintiff and defendant (separated by "v" and italicized)], year of decision, volume, reporter, first page of the case, and page referenced:

Croome v. Tasmania (1997) 191 CLR 119, 125 (Brennan CJ, Dawson and Toohey JJ).

If appropriate, the author(s) of the judgment may be identified in parentheses after the page referenced. The year is cited in square brackets if the case appears in a report whose volumes are organized by year.

Generally, court names are not included in a citation. However, if deemed necessary, they can be added to the end of the citation (in parentheses):

Mueller & Co v. Commonwealth (2004) 109 FCR 156, 157 (Federal Court of Australia).

3.1 Reports

Major official reports series (and their abbreviations) include:

Commonwealth Law Reports (CLR)
Federal Court Reports (FCR)
Victorian Reports (VR)
New South Wales Law Reports (NSWL)

The unofficial reports series (and their abbreviations) include:

Australian Law Reports (ALR)
Australian Law Journal Reports (ALJR)
Federal Law Reports (FLR)

4.0 Official Publications

Cite Parliamentary Debates by jurisdiction, title (italicized), assembly name, date of debate, page referenced, and full name of the speaker and, where applicable, the speaker's position in government or opposition ministry (in parentheses):

> Commonwealth, *Parliamentary Debates*, House of Representatives, 23 May 1992, 3121 (Paul Keating, Prime Minister).

Cite Parliamentary papers by jurisdiction, title (italicized), number ("Parl Paper No [ ]"), year (in parentheses), and page referenced:

> Commonwealth, *Department of Foreign Affairs Annual Report 1975*, Parl Paper No 142 (1976) 5.

Cite Law Reform Commission Reports by Name of the Law Reform Commission, title (italicized), Report/Discussion Paper number ("Discussion Paper No [ ]"), year (in parentheses), and page referenced:

> Victorian Law Reform Commission, *Homicide Report*, Report No 40 (1991) 7.

III.   SELECTED REFERENCES

AUSTRALIAN GUIDE TO LEGAL CITATION (Melbourne University Law Review Association Inc. ed., 2d ed. 1998).

COLIN FONG, AUSTRALIAN LEGAL CITATIONS: A GUIDE (Prospect 1998).

COLIN FONG & ALAN EDWARDS, AUSTRALIAN AND NEW ZEALAND LEGAL ABBREVIATIONS (Australian Law Libraries Group 1995).

A U S T R I A

Republik Österreich (Republic of Austria)

I. COUNTRY PROFILE (CIVIL LAW)

Austria is a federal, democratic Republic consisting of nine provinces (*Bundesländer*), including the federal capital province of Vienna. The official language is German. The Constitution of 1920 (*Bundesverfassungsgesetz*), reinstated in 1945, distributes authority between the relatively autonomous provinces, which have their own constitutions (*Landesverfassungsgesetz*) and parliaments (*Landtag*), and the federal government (*Bund*). The provinces are further divided into administrative subunits (*Gemeinden*).

The head of state is the President of the Republic, who is elected directly by the people for a six-year term. The President formally represents the Republic internationally and is constitutionally authorized to conclude international agreements. Furthermore, the Constitution vests (in theory) considerable powers in the President, such as the power to dissolve the National Council, to appoint or dismiss the Prime Minister, and on the latter's proposal to appoint as well as dismiss the other members of the government; he is also designated as Chief of the Army. Nonetheless, the office is generally perceived as ceremonial.

The main executive organ is the government (*Bundesregierung*), which consists of the Federal Chancellor (*Bundeskanzler*) and the Ministers (*Bundesminister*). The Federal Chancellor is appointed by the party or parties that form a majority (through a process of political negotiation) of the National Council. The Ministers are appointed on the basis of the Prime Minister's proposal.

The bicameral Parliament consists of a National Council (*Nationalrat*) and a Federal Council (*Bundesrat*). They together form the National Assembly (*Bundesversammlung*). The 183 members of the National Council are elected directly by the people every four years. The Federal Council consists of 58 members who serve as delegates representing the separate provinces; its members are elected by the provincial parliaments. All laws are published in the Federal Legal Gazette (*Bundesgesetzblatt*), which covers all forms of legislation, regulatory enactments, and treaties.

Austria is a civil law country. The judiciary, which is within the exclusive competency of the federal government, consists of civil and criminal courts. There are no state courts. The lowest courts are the *Bezirksgerichte*, for smaller claims, and the *Landesgerichte*, for matters of greater importance. Appeals are generally brought before the *Oberlandesgerichte*. Appellate decisions can be further appealed to the

Supreme Court (*Oberster Gerichtshof*). Specialized courts exist in Vienna as well: two commercial courts (*Handelsgericht* and *Bezirksgericht für Handelssachen*) and one labor court (*Arbeits- und Sozialgericht*). While the *Arbeits- und Sozialgericht* has the same competence as a *Landesgericht*, the two commercial courts equal the structure of the normal courts. There are four *Oberlandesgerichte*, which as courts of appeals have competence over every subject matter—both criminal and civil law. There is only one Supreme Court, which hears all matters.

Although administrative procedures (regulations and decisions) do not per se fall under the judiciary branch, as a last resort they may be challenged before an administrative tribunal (*Verwaltungsgerichtshof*). Additionally, Austria has implemented independent quasi-judicial tribunals (*Unabhänginge Verwaltungssenate*) within the federal provinces as appellate tribunals for administrative matters. The Constitutional Court (*Verfassungsgerichtshof*) has the authority to test the constitutionality of legislation and administrative acts. Individuals who claim a violation of their fundamental rights must exhaust all possible remedies before bringing the claim before the Constitutional Court.

Internet Resources:

Austrian Press & Information Service:	http://www.austria.org
Legal Information System of the Republic of Austria (RIS):	http://www.ris.bka.gv.at
Parliament:	http://www.parlament.gv.at
Federal Chancellery:	http://www.bka.gv.at

II. CITATION GUIDE

Abkürzungs- und Zitierregeln der österreichischen Rechtssprache und europarechtlicher Rechtsquellen (AZR) [Abbreviation and citation rules of Austrian legal terminology and European sources of law] (Gerhard Friedl et al. eds., 2001) (6th ed. is forthcoming), a widely recognized standard system of citation elaborated and compiled on behalf of the Austrian Law Congress (*Österreichischer Juristentag*), can be considered semi-official.

The standardized form is commonly used in practice. However, while the standardized form calls for full source names and English abbreviations (if appropriate), the use of abbreviated source names and German abbreviations remains common.

1.0 Constitution

Cite the Constitution by subdivision(s) referenced ("Art.", "Abs.", etc.) followed by the Constitution's abbreviation ("B-VG"):

Art. 14 Abs. 3 B-VG.

1.1 State Constitutions

Use the same format as used with the federal Constitution, using instead the name *"Landes-Verfassungsgesetz"* or the abbreviation "L-VG" of the state constitutions and including the abbreviated name of the state in parentheses at the end of the citation.

§ 35 L-VG (Stmk).

2.0 Legislation

2.1 Regulations and Statutes

The standard abbreviated citation for statutes and regulations is referenced by subdivision(s) [section (§), paragraph (Abs.), letter (Z.) or (lit.) and clause (S.) if applicable], followed by an abbreviation of the regulation's name:

§ 15 EF-G.

For a full citation, include the type of statute, date, law gazette number, number of the statute/year, page number (if available), and complete name:

BG vom 28,2,2001 BGBl. I Nr. 12/2001 Bundesgesetz über die Einrichtung eines Allgemeinen Entschädigungsfonds für Opfer des Nationalsozialismus und über Restitutionsmaßnahmen (Entschädigungsfondsgesetz).

2.2 Codes

Cite codes by subdivision(s) referenced, followed by the code's abbreviation:

§ 879 Abs. 2, Z. 3 ABGB.

The abbreviations of major codes are:

Constitution: *Bundesverfassungsgesetz* (B-VG)
General Civil Code: *Allgemeines Bürgerliches Gesetzbuch* (ABGB)
Commercial Code: *Handelsgesetzbuch* (HGB)
Civil Procedural Code: *Zivilprozeßordnung* (ZPO)
Criminal Code: *Strafgesetzbuch* (StGB)
Criminal Procedural Code: *Strafprozeßordnung* (StPO)
General Administrative Code: *Allgemeines Verwaltungsverfahrensgesetz* (AVG)

Jurisdictional abbreviations are:

Burgenland (Bgld)
Körnten (Krnt)

Niederösterreich (Nö)
Oberösterreich (Oö)
Salzburg (Sbg)
Steiermark (Stmk)
Tirol (Tir)
Voralerg (Vlbg)
Wien (Wien)

2.3 Gazettes

Federal laws and statutes as well as treaties are published in the Federal Law Gazette (BGBl. *Bundesgesetzblatt*), while state laws are published in the state gazettes (LgBl. *Landesgesetzblatt*). Since 1997 the federal gazette has been divided into three parts: BGBl. I contains laws and statutes, BGBl. II contains decrees, and BGBl. III contains treaties.

3.0 Jurisprudence

Cite case law by abbreviated court name, date [day.month.year], docket number, and reporter:

OGH 11.1.1972, 6 Ob 207/72 SZ 46/3.

Where a case is known by a given key word, place the word between the docket number and the reporter, set off by dashes:

OGH 14.5. 1963, 8 Ob 75/63 — Bananen — Arb 7747.

3.1 Unreported Cases

Cite unreported case law by the abbreviated title of the issuing authority, date, and docket number:

VwGH, 13.5.1982, 82/06/0034.

3.2 Courts

Austrian courts (and abbreviations) include:

Supreme Court: *Oberster Gerichtshof* (OGH)
Constitutional Court: *Verfassungsgerichtshof* (VfGH)
Administrative and Tax Court: *Verwaltungsgerichtshof* (VwGH)
Second Court of Appeals: *Oberlandesgericht* (OLG [jurisdiction])
Trial and Appeals Court (in state capitals): *Landesgericht* (LG [jurisdiction])

Trial and Appeals Court for labor and social insurance matters: *Arbeits- und Sozialgericht* (ASG)
Trial and Appeals Court for commercial matters: *Handelsgericht* (HG)
Supreme Court for cartels: *Kartellobergericht* (KOG)
Trial Court for cartels: *Kartellgericht* (KartG)

Note: Jurisdictional abbreviations can be found in Section 2.2 above.

3.3 Reports

Austrian law reports (and abbreviations) include:

OGH Report for civil matters: *Entscheidungen des OGH in Zivilsachen* (SZ)

OGH Report for criminal matters: *Entscheidungen des OGH in Strafsachen* (SSt)

VfGH Report for constitutional matters: *Erkenntnisse und Beschlüsse des Verfassungsgerichtshofes* (VfSlg)

VwGH Report for administrative or tax matters: *Erkenntnisse und Beschlüsse des Verwaltungsgerichtshofes, Neue Folge* (VwSlg A for administrative matters, VwSlg F for fiscal matters)

ASG Report for labor matters: *Sammlung Arbeitsrechtlicher Entscheidungen* (ArbSlg)

ASG Report for social insurance matters: *Sozialversicherungsrechtliche Entscheidungen* (SVSlg)

HG Report for commercial matters: *Handelsrechtliche Entscheid*

BELGIUM

Koninkrijk België/Royaume de Belgique
(Kingdom of Belgium)

I. COUNTRY PROFILE (CIVIL LAW)

Belgium is a constitutional, parliamentary monarchy. The country's three official languages are Dutch, French, and German. The country is composed of a federal government, three Communities (the Flemish, French, and German Communities), three Regions (the Flemish, Walloon, and the Brussels-Capital Regions), and ten Provinces. The Communities handle cultural affairs, education, and health, and the Regions manage economic affairs.

The federal government's power is limited by Article 35 of the Constitution to those powers that the Constitution and quasi-constitutional laws (special type of laws adopted by special majorities) formally confer upon it. Legislation implementing Article 35, however, has not yet been enacted. Until it is, the Regions and Communities hold only those powers expressly conferred upon them by the Constitution and quasi-constitutional laws, while the federal government continues to hold all residual powers. Belgium has a bicameral Parliament composed of a Senate (*Senaat* in Flemish, *Sénat* in French) and a House of Representatives (*Kamer van Volksvertegenwoordigers* in Flemish, *Chambre des Députés* in French). Because the importance of the Senate has been reduced over time, the system is no longer fully bicameral. The King, the Chamber of Representatives, and the Senate collectively exercise the legislative power. The King's role, however, is primarily ceremonial. The Prime Minister is formally appointed by the King and approved by Parliament.

The Constitution vests the judicial power in the courts. There is the Court of Cassation (*Hof van Cassatie* in Flemish or *Cour de Cassation* in French). The Court of Cassation is the highest court of appeals in its areas of competency. It consists of bilingual Chambers specializing in civil cases, labor cases, and criminal cases. Its judges are appointed for life by the King. The Constitutional Court (*Grondwettelijk Hof/Cour constitutionelle*, whose old name *Arbitragehof* was changed in May of 2007) has the power to annul and suspend laws, decrees, and ordinances. The Council of State (*Raad van State/Conseil d'Etat*) gives advice concerning proposed laws and regulations and is the highest administrative court. The government appoints and dismisses the officials of the public prosecutor's office.

The five courts of appeals in Belgium are the Brussels court, whose jurisdiction includes the provinces of Walloon Brabant, Flemish Brabant, and the Region of Brussels-Capital; the Ghent court, whose jurisdiction includes the provinces of

West-Flanders and East-Flanders; the Antwerp court, whose jurisdiction includes the provinces of Antwerp and Limburg; the Liège court, whose jurisdiction includes the provinces of Liège, Namur, and Luxembourg; and the Mons court, whose jurisdiction includes the province of Hainaut. Courts with limited jurisdiction include commercial courts and labor courts, which are governed by special laws.

Internet Resources:

Belgian Federal Portal:	http://www.belgium.be
Belgian Judicial Portal:	http://www.cass.be
Constitutional Court:	http://www.arbitrage.be
Abbreviations for Belgian Law	
Journals:	http://www.rechtsaf.be
Further useful links:	http://www.rechtslinks.be

II. CITATION GUIDE

There are two guides available for Belgian citations, one in Dutch (*Juridische verwijzingen en afkortingen*, Kluwer Rechtswetenschappen, 2007) and one in French (*Guides des citations, références et abréviations juridiques*, Kluwer/Bruylant, 2002). Authors should follow these guidelines. The Interuniversitaire Commissie Juridische Verwijzingen en Afkortingen has published a short guide in Flemish available at http://www.law.kuleuven.be/lib/v_en_a/v_en_a.pdf.

1.0 Constitution

Cite the Constitution by article referenced and the abbreviation "GW" (for *Grondwet* in Dutch) or "Const. coord." (for *Constitution coordonné* in French):

Art. 2 GW.

Art. 3 Const. coord.

2.0 Legislation

2.1 Statutes, Laws, and Decrees

Cite statutes, laws, and decrees by date and title, reference to the official journal "*Belgisch Staatsblad*" (abbreviated "*BS*") or "*Moniteur Belge*" in French (abbreviated "*MB*"), journal's date, and page referenced:

Art. 1 K.B. 19 maart 2004 tot wijziging van het koninklijk besluit van 26 februari 1981 houdende uitvoering van de Richtlijnen van de Europese

Gemeenschappen betreffende de goedkeuring van motorvoertuigen en aanhangwagens daarvan, landbouw- of bosbouwtrekkers op wielen, hun bestanddelen alsook hun veiligheidsonderdelen, *BS* 21 maart 2004, p. 16205.

Wet 10 April 1995 tot aanvulling van de Nieuwe Gemeentewet met bepalingen betreffende de gemeentelijke volksraadpleging, *BS* 21 april 1995, 10.134.

Decr. Fr. 30 mei 1994 houdende wijziging van het Decreet van de Franse Gemeenschap van 18 juni 1990 houdende regeling van het toezicht over de Franse Gemeenschapscommissie, *BS* 23 augustus 1994, 21.255.

Art. 19, § 3 wet 26 juni 1990 betreffende de bescherming van de persoon van de geesteszieke, *BS* 27 juli 1990.

The official journal *Belgisch Staatsblad* or *Moniteur Belge* is now available *only* in electronic form at http://www.ejustice.just.fgov.be/cgi/welcome.pl.

2.2 Codes

Major codes are commonly abbreviated in the following way so that it is not necessary to cite to the official journal:

Code civil (C. civ.)/*Burgerlijk Wetboek* (BW)
Code pénal (C. pr. pén.)/*Strafwetboek* (Sw)
Code de commerce (C. comm.)/*Wetboek van Koophandel* (WKh)

Cite codes by article followed by abbreviated name of the Code:

Art. 248 Sw

Art. 577-2, § 9, 3de lid BW.

3.0 Jurisprudence

Cite cases by name of Court or Tribunal and date of decision, followed by reference to the law review in which the decision is published [title, year, volume, and page referenced]:

Cass. 30 januari 1973, *Pas.* 1973, I, 524.

3.1 Reports

For the judgments of the Grondwettelijk Hof/Cour Constitutionelle, see the official publication *Belgisch Staatsblad* or *Moniteur Belge* (available at http://www.ejustice.just.fgov.be/cgi/welcome.pl or http://www.arbitrage.be/).

The judgments of the Court de Cassation/Hof van Cassatie are published in the official publication *Arrêts de la Cour de Cassation/Arresten van het Hof van*

Cassatie, abbreviated as "Arr. Cass." A reference to this publication is preferable. Also consult the court's website: http://www.cass.be.

The Conseil d'Etat/Raad van State publishes its judgments on the Internet at http://www.raadvst-consetat.be.

Judgments of other courts and tribunals are not officially reported but can be found in a number of different law reviews. The citation guides mentioned above contain a list of abbreviations of titles of law reviews where you will find the judgments. Alternatively, a fairly comprehensive list of abbreviations can be found on the Internet at http://www.law.kuleuven.ac.be/lib/afkortingen/index.phtml.

III. SELECTED REFERENCES

C. CAMBIER, PRINCIPES DU CONTENTIEUX ADMINISTRATIF (Bruxelles 1961).

JOHN H. CRABB, THE CONSTITUTION OF BELGIUM AND THE BELGIAN CIVIL CODE (AS AMENDED TO SEPTEMBER 1, 1982 IN THE MONITEUR BELGE) (F.B. Rothman 1982).

FRANCIS DELPEREE, LA CONSTITUTION FEDERALE DU 5 MAI 1993 (Bruxelles 1993).

Books on Belgian Law in English

A. ALEN & B. TILLEMAN, TREATISE ON BELGIAN CONSTITUTIONAL LAW (Kluwer Law & Business 1992).

H. BOCKEN/W. DE BONDT (ed.), INTRODUCTION TO BELGIAN LAW (Bruylant 2001).

VAN BAEL/BELLIS, BUSINESS LAW GUIDE TO BELGIUM (Kluwer Law International 2003).

J. VANDELANOTTE, BELGIUM FOR BEGINNERS (Die Keure 2006).

B R A Z I L

Republica Federativa do Brasil (Federative Republic of Brazil)

I. COUNTRY PROFILE (CIVIL LAW)

The Federative Republic of Brazil is a federal republic with 26 states and a federal district (Brasilia). The Republic was first established in 1889, and the original constitution of the Republic — modeled after the U.S. Constitution — was adopted in 1891. New constitutions were adopted in 1934, 1937, 1946, 1967, and 1988, prompted by regimes ranging from authoritarian to democratic. The current Federal Constitution, drafted by the National Constituent Assembly with significant levels of societal participation and adopted on October 5, 1988, is the most democratic constitution in Brazil's history. It grants significant authority to the federal legislative bodies to counter the power of the President. The Constitution has been amended more than 25 times since 1988.

The Constitution grants broad powers to the federal government, which is made up of executive, legislative, and judicial branches. It provides for universal suffrage and equal rights of citizens, and it decentralizes power from the federal government to Brazil's various states and municipalities. Powers not granted to the federal government or denied to the states are left to the states.

The executive branch is headed by the President, who holds office for four years with the right to run for reelection for one additional four-year term. The President functions as both chief of state and head of government, and appoints a cabinet of ministers to head the respective ministries.

The legislature consists of a bicameral National Congress (*Congresso Nacional*), which is composed of the Federal Senate (*Senado Federal*) and the Chamber of Deputies (*Câmara dos Deputados*). The Federal Senate has 81 members. Three members of the majority party are elected from each state or federal district to serve eight-year terms. Elections are staggered such that one-third of the senators are elected in one four-year period and two-thirds are elected in the subsequent four-year period. The Chamber of Deputies has 513 members, who are elected by a proportional system to four-year terms.

The Judiciary is made up of a complex structure of courts of specialized and general jurisdiction. The Supreme Federal Tribunal, situated in the capital city of

25

Brasilia and consisting of 11 tenured judges, is the highest federal court in the country and is the court of ultimate jurisdiction for all constitutional issues rising from both state and federal courts. Regional federal trial and appeals courts are scattered throughout the country. Although Brazil is a civil law country, case law plays a very important role, particularly in public law where American constitutionalism has been influential. The Supreme Federal Tribunal acts as a court of first instance and may strike laws as unconstitutional. Its Justices are nominated by the President, must be approved by a majority of the Senate, and may hold office until the age of 70.

Each of Brazil's states has its own constitution, governor, state legislature, and independent judiciary composed of both superior courts (trial level) and courts of appeal. In addition to these courts of general jurisdiction, there are specialized state courts with jurisdiction over cases related to areas such as labor relations, military crimes, and electoral matters. Besides the Supreme Federal Tribunal (with general jurisdiction over both state and federal issues), the federal court system adjudicates only those cases where the Federation is named as a party. State courts have jurisdiction over all other cases.

Internet Resources:

Federal Senate:	http://www.senado.gov.br
Chamber of Deputies:	http://www.camara.gov.br
President:	http://www.planalto.gov.br
Ministry of Foreign Relations:	http://www.mre.gov.br
Supreme Federal Tribunal:	http://www.stf.gov.br
Superior Tribunal of Justice:	http://www.stj.gov.br

II. CITATION GUIDE

There is no uniform citation manual in Brazil. The following reflects common citation practices.

1.0 Constitution

Cite the Constitution by title (*Constituição Federal*) and year, followed by article referenced (*artigo*):

Constituição Federal de 1988, artigo 102.

The title and date may be abbreviated with "CF 88," in which case there is no comma between the year and the article ("art."):

CF 88 art. 102.

2.0 Legislation

2.1 Statutes, Laws, and Decrees

Cite statutes, laws, and decrees by type (e.g., Complementar, Ordinária, Medida Provisória), serial number of the text as published in the official gazette *Diário Oficial* (using "de"), and date of publication:

Lei Complementar 65, de 15.04.1991.

Lei Ordinária 8.112, de 11.12.90.

Medida Provisória 1515, de 16.10.94.

The citation may be (and often is) abbreviated with a short title, and serial number and date separated by a slash:

LC 65/91.

Lei 8.112/90.

MP 1515/94.

2.2 Codes

Cite codes by abbreviated title and number of the article:

CC art.159.

The abbreviations of major Codes are:

Civil Code: *Código Civil* (CC)
Criminal Code: *Código Penal* (CP)
Civil Procedure Code: *Código Processo Civil* (CPC)
Criminal Procedure Code: *Código Processo Penal* (CPP)
Commercial Code: *Código Comercial* (CCom.)
Tax Code: *Código Tributário Nacional* (CTN)
Labor Code: *Consolidação das Leis Trabalhistas* (CLT)
Consumers' defense rights: *Código de Defesa do Consumidor* (CDC)
Child and Adolescent Statute: *Estatuto da Criança e do Adolescente* (ECA)
Direct Action of Unconstitutionality Act: *Lei da Ação Direta de Inconstitucionalidade* (LADIN)
Criminal Misdemeanors Act: *Lei das Contravenções Penais* (LCP)
Education Guidelines and Framework Act: *Lei de Diretrizes e Bases da Educação* (LDB)
Budgetary Directives Act: *Lei de Diretrizes Orçamentárias* (LDO)
Tax Foreclosure Act: *Lei de Execuções Fiscais* (LDF)
Civil Code Introduction Act: *Lei de Introdução ao Código Civil* (LICC)

2.3 Legal Rules

Some popular names of legal rules and their legal rule numbers are as follows:

Afonso Arinos Act: Act No. 1390, 03.07.51
Darcy Ribeiro Act: Act No. 9394, 20.12.96
Corp. Act (or S.A. Act): Act No. 6404, 15.12.76
Amnesty Act: Act No. 6683, 28.09.79
Press Act: Act No. 5250, 09.02.67
Informatics Act: Act No. 7232, 29.10.84
National Security Act: Act No. 7170, 14.12.83
Software Act: Act No. 7646, 18.12.87
Foreigners Act: Act No. 6815, 1980
Etelvino Lins Act: Act. No. 6091, 15.09.74
Falcão Act: Act No. 6339, 01.07.76
Fleury Act: Act No. 5941, 22.11.73
Kandir Act: Supp. Act. No. 87, 13.09.96
Sarney Act: Act. No. 7505, 02.07.86

2.4 Treaties and Conventions

Cite treaties and conventions as described in Section 1.0 of Part II, on Treaties and Conventions, filling in the source information with the Brazilian treaty source by title ("Coleção de Atos Internacionais") and treaty number:

[Treaty information], Coleção de Atos Internacionais, No. 30, [date of entry, etc.].

3.0 Jurisprudence

Cite cases by type of motion (see list of motions and their abbreviations below), number assigned to the case by the court, deciding court (often the chamber), and publication date:

AI 220.457, 5a. Câmara Cível do TJ/RJ, em 22.09.1990.

3.1 Courts

The most important courts in Brazil (and abbreviations) are:

Constitutional Ct: *Supremo Tribunal Federal* (STF)
High Court: *Superior Tribunal de Justiça* (STJ)
State Courts of Appeals: *Tribunais de Justiça dos Estados* (TJ)
Regional Federal Courts of Appeals: *Tribunais Regionais Federais* (TRF)
High Labor Court: *Tribunal Superior do Trabalho* (TST)
High Electoral Court: *Tribunal Superior Eleitoral* (TSE)
High Military Court: *Superior Tribunal Militar* (STM)

3.2 Motions

The abbreviations for different types of motions and appeals in Brazil are:

Recurso Extraordinário (RE) [only for STF]
Recurso Especial (Resp.) [only for STJ]
Apelação Cível (Ap.) [all state appeals courts]
Agravo de Instrumento (AI) [all high courts]
Medida Cautelar (MC) [all courts]
Mandado de Segurança (MS) [all courts]

III. SELECTED REFERENCES

PAULO BONAVIDES, CURSO DE DIREITO CONSTITUCIONAL (Malheiros 1997).

MARGARIDA CAMARGO, UMA DÉCADA DE CONSTITUIÇÃO (Renovar 1998).

Fabio Konder Comparato, *The Economic Order in Brazilian Constitution of 1988*, 38 AM. J. COMP. L. (1990).

JOSE AFONSO DA SILVA, DIREITO CONSTITUCIONAL POSITIVO (Malheiros 1997).

Jacob Dorlinger, *The Influence of American Constitutional Law on the Brazilian Legal System*, 38 AM. J. COMP. L. (1990).

A PANORAMA OF BRAZILIAN LAW (Jacob Dorlinger et al. eds., University of Miami North-Center 1992).

CANADA

COUNTRY PROFILE (COMMON AND CIVIL LAW)

Canada is a constitutional monarchy. Its monarch (the King or Queen of England) is the official head of state and is represented in Canada by the Governor General, whose functions are merely formal. The powers conferred upon the Monarch have fallen into desuetude and can no longer be exercised. Thus, in effect, Canada is governed by a parliamentary democracy.

Canada is a federation composed of ten provinces and three territories (two are under federal jurisdiction, one has been granted limited autonomy). The federal Parliament has two chambers: the House of Commons, where elected deputies sit; and the Senate, which is composed of individuals nominated by the Prime Minister. The Prime Minister is the head of the government and is not personally elected but rather is the leader of the party that has the most seats in the House of Commons. The government includes members of the House of Commons, the Senate, and the Prime Minister. The legislative function is exercised by both the House of Commons and the Senate. For a bill to be adopted, it must pass both chambers of Parliament and receive royal assent. The Senate, however, rarely refuses to pass a bill. This system of parliamentary democracy is replicated in all of the ten provinces, except that most provinces have abolished their senate. At both levels, elections must be held at least every five years, during which period the Prime Minister or Premier has discretion as to the moment to call the electors to vote.

The division of powers among the federal and the provincial units is provided for in the Constitution. Provinces have jurisdiction over, *inter alia*, administration of justice, hospitals, schools and education, municipalities, incorporation of companies with provincial objects, property and civil rights, and natural resources. They also have taxation powers that they delegate in part to cities and municipalities. Apart from these powers, ad hoc administrative agreements between the federal government and individual provinces can be concluded to modify this distribution. The federal government has jurisdiction over, *inter alia*, currency, military forces, navigation, fisheries, banks, bankruptcy and insolvency, aboriginal peoples, naturalization of aliens, divorce, criminal law, and foreign relations. The federal government also has certain prerogatives such as the power to allocate funds on issues that do not fall under its jurisdiction but that are of national interest; to adopt laws for peace, order, and good government; and to legislate over matters that do not fall within either federal or provincial jurisdiction (residual jurisdiction).

The federative nature of the state is also reflected in the judiciary. The federal government has created common law courts—of first instance and of appeal (Superior Courts and Courts of Appeal)—in each province (except in Quebec). It has also created a Supreme Court of Canada. The Prime Minister nominates justices of the superior courts, courts of appeal of each province, and the Supreme Court of Canada. These justices have lifetime tenure. Moreover, the federal government has created a Federal Court and Tax Court, both of first instance and of appeal, for the better administration of the laws of Canada. The provinces have established their own courts, which deal with most criminal offenses and, in some provinces, with civil cases involving small amounts of money. These provincial courts may also include specialized courts such as youth and family courts. This division, however, does not automatically reflect their jurisdiction, as provincial courts apply federal laws and vice versa.

Most of Canada's legal landscape is of common law tradition. However, by virtue of its jurisdiction over property and civil rights, Quebec has chosen to be governed by a system of civil law. This makes Quebec a hybrid jurisdiction: civil law as regards private relationships and common law for its public law (administrative and criminal). French and English are the official national languages and have de jure an equal status (although this is not true in all provinces).

More and more, ad hoc agreements are concluded between governments and aboriginal peoples to grant them a larger autonomy over matters of concern for them. The types of delegation of powers to aboriginal peoples are too diversified to be expanded on here, but they comprise executive as well as legislative powers.

Internet Resources:

Government of Canada: http://www.canada.gc.ca

Department of Justice: http://canada.justice.gc.ca/en

II.   CITATION GUIDE

Canada has a recognized system of legal citation, which is explained in the "red book": McGill Law Journal, *Canadian Guide to Uniform Legal Citation* (6th ed., Carswell 2006).

1.0 Constitution

Cite the 1867 British North America Act, which serves as Canada's constitution, by name ["British North America Act, 1867" or "Constitution Act, 1867"] (italicized), volume (abbreviated "Vict."), and chapter ("c.") referenced:

British North America Act, 1867, 30 & 31 Vict., c. 3.

Constitution Act, 1867, 30 & 31 Vict., c. 3.

Cite the 1982 Constitution Act and Canada's Charter of Rights and Freedoms by name (italicized) and section ("s.") referenced:

Constitution Act, 1982, s. 92.

Canadian Charter of Rights and Freedoms, Part I of *Constitution Act, 1982*, c. 11.

The Charter name may be abbreviated with "Canadian Charter" or simply "Charter" (italicized), followed by section referenced:

Canadian Charter, s. 11.

2.0 Legislation

Cite laws by title (italicized), volume by year (if possible, cite to the latest Revised Statutes of Canada, abbreviated "R.S.C."), chapter ("c."), section ("s."), paragraph ("par."), and subparagraph ("subpar.") referenced:

Canada Labour Code, R.S.C. 1985, c. L-2, s. 14.

2.1 Provincial Legislation

The same model prevails for provincial statutes, except that the name of the volumes and the year of the last revision will vary (e.g., "R.S.O." for Revised Statutes of Ontario).

2.2 Codes and Common Statute Abbreviations

Some statutes are referred to by accepted abbreviation. The most frequent are:

Criminal Code (C.C.)
Code of Penal Procedure (C.P.P.)
Civil Code of Quebec (C.C.Q.)
Civil Code of Lower Canada (C.C.L.C.)
Code of Civil Procedure (C.C.P.)

2.3 Treaties and Conventions

Cite treaties and conventions as described in Section 1.0 of Part II, on Treaties and Conventions, filling in the source information with the Canadian Treaty Series by year, "Can. T.S.," and treaty number:

[Treaty information], 1950 Can. T.S. No. 1, [date of entry into force, etc.].

3.0 Jurisprudence

Cite cases by the name of the parties separated by "v." (all italicized), year (when the year corresponds to the year of the volume (for most relatively recent cases), the year preceded by a comma and placed in square brackets; when it does not (for older cases), the year is in parentheses and followed by a comma), volume, and, if there is more than one volume in a year, the name of the volume, page on which the case begins, followed by the word "at" and page referenced:

R v. Seaboyer, [1991] 2 S.C.R. 577 at 590.

If the name of the volume does not indicate which court decided the case, the name of the court must be added in an abbreviated form in parentheses after the citation but before the page number of the actual reference:

Delgamuukw v. British Columbia (1991), 79 D.L.R. (4th) 185 (B.C.S.C.).

In all recent cases, there will be a neutral citation attached to the decision by the court. Where the neutral citation is available, it should be appended at the end of the citation.

3.1 Reporters

Main case reporters and abbreviations are:

Supreme Court Reports (S.C.R.)
Canadian Criminal Cases (C.C.C.)
Canadian Criminal Reports (C.C.R.)
Dominion Law Reports (D.L.R.)
Ontario Reports (O.R.)
Recueils de Jurisprudence du Québec (R.J.Q.)

4.0 Official Publications

Cite official publications by jurisdiction (if it does not appear in the title), name of the legislative assembly (if it does not appear in the title), title (italicized), issue (if applicable), date (in parentheses), and the word "at" followed by page referenced:

Nova Scotia, House of Assembly, Debates and Proceedings, No. 85-29 (18 April 1985) at 1343.

III. SELECTED REFERENCES

GÉRALD A. BEAUDOIN & ERROL MENDES, THE CANADIAN CHARTER OF RIGHTS AND FREEDOMS (3d ed., Carswell 1996).

HENRI BRUN, DROIT CONSTITUTIONNEL (3d ed., Yvon Blais 1996).

PETER HOGG, CONSTITUTIONAL LAW OF CANADA (3d ed., Carswell 1992).

C H I N A

Zhonghua Renmin Gongheguo (People's Republic of China)

I. COUNTRY PROFILE (CIVIL LAW)

China is divided into 23 provinces (including the Taiwan Province, which is separately governed by the Republic of Taiwan), five autonomous regions, the Hong Kong Special Administrative Region (HKSAR), the Macau Special Administrative Region (MSAR), and four municipalities directly under the Central Government (Beijing, Shanghai, Tianjin, and Chongqing). The official language is Mandarin.

The Constitution of the People's Republic of China of 1982 (amended in 1988, 1993, 1999, and 2004) established a parliamentary regime, with the Communist Party of China as the permanent ruling party. Under the Constitution, all power belongs to the Chinese people. The organs through which the people exercise state power are the National People's Congress (NPC, *Quanguo Renmin Daibiao Dahui*) and local people's congresses at various levels. The NPC is the highest organ of state power, which, together with its permanent body, the Standing Committee of the NPC (*Quanguo Renmin Daibiao Dahui Changwu Weiyuanhui*), exercises the legislative power of the state. All administrative, judicial, and prosecutorial organs of the state are created by the people's congresses, to which they are responsible and under whose supervision they operate. The NPC is elected for a term of five years. It has the power to supervise the enforcement of the Constitution and to enact and amend basic statutes concerning criminal offenses, civil affairs, state organs, and other matters. The NPC also has the power to elect the head of the nation (the President, or, literally, State Chairman, *Guojia Zhuxi*), the President of the Supreme People's Court (*Zuigao Renmin Fayuan Yuanzhang*), and the Procuratorate-General of the Supreme People's Procuratorate (*Zuigao Renmin Jianchayuan Jianchazhang*). The Standing Committee of the NPC has the power to interpret the Constitution and to supervise its enforcement, to interpret statutes, and to enact and amend statutes with the exception of those that should be enacted by the NPC.

The State Council of the People's Republic of China (*Zhonghua Renmin Gongheguo Guowuyuan*) is the highest organ of state administration. It is vested with power by the Constitution to enact administrative regulations and rules, and to issue decisions and orders in accordance with the Constitution and statutes. The head of the State Council is the Premier (*Zongli*), who has the overall responsibility for the performance of the executive functions of the government.

China is a civil law country. The main sources of law are the Constitution (*Xianfa*), statutes enacted by the NPC or its Standing Committee (*falü*), administrative regulations issued by the State Council (*xingzheng fagui*), administrative rules issued by those departments under the State Council (*bumen guizhang*), local regulations (*difangxing fagui*), and interpretations of laws, including legislative interpretations (*lifa jieshi*), judicial interpretations (*sifa jieshi*), and administrative interpretations (*xingzheng jieshi*). The judicial interpretations of the Supreme People's Court serve an unofficial, quasi-legislative role in China's legal system.

China's courts consist of the Supreme People's Court (*Zuigao Renmin Fayuan*), local people's courts at various levels (*Geiji difang geji renmin fayuan*), military courts (*junshi fayuan*), and other special people's courts (*zhuanmen renmin fayuan*), for example, railway courts (*tielu fayuan*) and maritime courts (*junshi fayuan*).

Internet Resources:

The National People's Congress:	http://www.npc.gov.cn
The Central People's Government:	http://www.gov.cn
The Supreme People's Court:	http://www.court.gov.cn
The Supreme People's Procuratorate:	http://www.spp.gov.cn
Ministry of Foreign Affairs:	http://www.fmprc.gov.cn
Ministry of Commerce:	http://www.mofcom.gov.cn

II. CITATION GUIDE

There is no official legal citation guide in China. The Beijing University Press has published a Proposed Legal Citation System for legal citations in Chinese. The official system for transliterating Chinese names and places into Roman letters is the *Hanyu Pinyin* system.

1.0 Constitution

Cite the Constitution and amendments by abbreviated title (Xianfa), article, section, and year (in parentheses):

Xianfa art. 35, sec. 1 (1982).

The abbreviations of the Constitution and its amendments are:

Constitution of the People's Republic of China of 1982: *Zhonghua Renmin Gongheguo Xianfa*, 1982 (Xianfa (1982)).

Amendment to the Constitution of the People's Republic of China of 1988: *Zhonghua Renmin Gongheguo Xianfa Xiuzhengan*, 1988 (Xianfa Xiuzhengan (1988)).

Amendment to the Constitution of the People's Republic of China of 1993: *Zhonghua Renmin Gongheguo Xianfa Xiuzhengan*, 1993 (Xianfa Xiuzhengan (1993)).

Amendment to the Constitution of the People's Republic of China of 1999: *Zhonghua Renmin Gongheguo Xianfa Xiuzhengan*, 1999 (Xianfa Xiuzhengan (1999)).

Amendment to the Constitution of the People's Republic of China of 2004: *Zhonghua Renmin Gongheguo Xianfa Xiuzhengan*, 2004 (Xianfa Xiuzhengan (2004)).

2.0 Legislation

2.1 Statutes, Regulations, and Rules

Cite statutes, regulations, and rules by title, section (including article and paragraph if appropriate), year of enactment (in parentheses), official publication in which it is published, and page referenced:

Civil Procedure Law of the People's Republic of China, art. 44 (1991), Zhonghua Renmin Gongheguo Falü Huibian, 123.

2.2 Legislative, Administrative, and Judicial Interpretations

Cite legislative, administrative, and judicial interpretations by title, article, year (in parentheses), and official publication in which it is published:

The Supreme People's Court Interpretation on Questions Concerning Foreign Interests, art. 2 (1985), Zuigao Renmin Fayuan Gongbao.

2.2.1 Official Publications

The official publications are:

For statutes: *Zhonghua Renmin Gongheguo Falü Huibian*

For administrative regulations and rules: *Zhonghua Renmin Gongheguo Fagui Huibian*

For local regulations and rules: *Zhonghua Renmin Gongheguo Difangxing Fagui Huibian*

For legislative interpretations: *Quanguo Renmin Daibiao Dahui Changwu Weiyuanhui Gongbao*

For administrative interpretations: *Guowuyuan Gongbao*

For judicial interpretations: *Zuigao Renmin Fayuan Gongbao*

2.3 Treaties and Conventions

Cite treaties and conventions as described in Section 1.0 of Part II, on Treaties and Conventions, filling in the source information with the Chinese Treaty Series by year, series title (Zhonghua Renmin Gongheguo Tiaoyue Ji), and page referenced:

[Treaty information], 1955 Zhonghua Renmin Gongheguo Tiaoyue Ji 1, [date of entry, etc.].

3.0 Jurisprudence

Cite cases by names of parties (separated by a "v."), reporter, year, name of the court and decision date if available (in parentheses) (or alternatively the case number in the reporter), followed by the word "at" and page referenced:

China People's Insurance Corp. v. Foxtort Company Ltd., Renmin Fayuan Anlixuan, 1997 No. 4, at 264.

There is no comprehensive system of official reports of jurisprudence. One preferred, unofficial publication commonly used by practitioners is *Renmin Fayuan Anlixuan* (Selected Cases of People's Courts, edited by China Legal Studies Institute of the Supreme People's Court).

3.1 Courts

Chinese Courts include:

Supreme People's Court: *Zuigao Renmin Fayuan*
High People's Court: *Gaoji Renmin Fayuan*
Intermediate People's Court: *Zhongji Renmin Fayuan*
Basic People's Court: *Jiceng Renmin Fayuan*
Military Courts: *Junshi Fayuan*
Other special people's courts: *Zhuanmen Renmin Fayuan*

3.2 Reports

Reports of jurisprudence include:

Zuigao Renmin Fayuan Gongbao
Anli Xuanbian

III.   SELECTED REFERENCES

WANG CHENGUANG & ZHANG XIANCHU (EDS.), INTRODUCTION TO CHINESE LAW (Sweet & Maxwell Asia 1997).

C.W. CHIU, LEGAL SYSTEM OF THE PRC (Longman Group 1997).

CHRIS HUNTER (ED.), A GUIDE TO THE LEGAL SYSTEM OF THE PRC (Asia Law & Practice 1997).

STANLEY B. LUBMAN, CHINA'S LEGAL REFORMS (Oxford University Press 1996).

C Z E C H   R E P U B L I C

Česká Republika

COUNTRY PROFILE (CIVIL LAW)

The Czech Republic was established on January 1, 1993, as one of the two successor states to the peacefully divided Czechoslovakia. Its capital is Praha (Prague), and its official language is Czech. The Czech Republic is a parliamentary democracy. It is composed of 13 Administrative Regions (*kraje*) and the Capital City (*hlavni mesto*). The legal system is a civil law system based on Austro-Hungarian codes. The Constitution of the Czech Republic explicitly defines civil rights, the relationship between the executive and legislative branches of power, and the independence of the judiciary. The constitutional institutions include the President (Chief of State), the Parliament (comprising the Chamber of Deputies and the Senate), the Government (comprising the Prime Minister, as Head of Government, the Deputy Prime Minister, and Ministers), the Constitutional Court, the system of courts (including the Supreme Court, the Supreme Administrative Court, and superior, regional, and district courts), and others.

The President is elected to a term of five years by the members of both chambers of Parliament; the President may serve a maximum of two successive terms in office. Although presidential power is limited, the President retains the right to veto any bill passed by Parliament, with the exception of constitutional bills. This power is void in times of constitutional or other political crises.

Parliament consists of two chambers: the Chamber of Deputies (*Poslanecká sněmovna Parlamentu České republiky*) and the Senate (*Senát Parlamentu České republiky*). Members of both the Chamber of Deputies and the Senate are directly elected by the people. The Chamber of Deputies consists of 200 deputies who are elected to terms of four years on the basis of proportional representation. Political parties must obtain at least 5 percent of the popular vote in order to gain seats in the Chamber. The President may dissolve the Chamber of Deputies as outlined in Article 35 of the Constitution. The Senate consists of 81 senators elected to six-year terms on the basis of majority vote; every two years, one-third of the Senate's members come up for election. The Senate cannot be dissolved.

Parliament passes all bills and expresses approval of important international treaties. It decides the most important acts of state, such as declaring war or approving the deployment of foreign armies on Czech soil. A resolution by a parliamentary chamber is passed by a clear majority of deputies or senators present. A constitutional bill or an international treaty must be approved by 60 percent of the total number of deputies and senators present. All bills are introduced in the Chamber of Deputies. Individual deputies, groups of deputies, the Senate, the Government, and local or regional cabinet representatives all possess the right of legislative initiative. Once a bill is passed by the Chamber of Deputies, it is sent to the Senate, which has the power to veto it, send it back to the Chamber of Deputies with amendments, or table it.

The Constitutional Court (*Ústavní soud*) is a separate judicial body whose duty is to protect constitutional rights. It consists of 15 Justices who are appointed to ten-year terms by the President with the consent of the Senate. Constitutional Court Justices are bound only by constitutional laws, by international treaties, and by a law designating the proceedings of the Constitutional Court.

The Supreme Court (*Nejvyšší soud České republiky*) is the supreme judicial body in all matters except those within the jurisdiction of the Constitutional Court and the Supreme Administrative Court (*Nejvyšší správni soud České republiky*). Supreme Court Justices are appointed for life by the President. Their decisions are bound only by law, and they are empowered to determine whether other legal regulations are in accordance with the law. The Supreme Court's docket mainly consists of appeals on issues of law arising from appellate court decisions and in recognizing and enforcing decisions of foreign courts.

Internet Resources:

Prague Castle (President):	http://www.hrad.cz
The Czech Republic Government:	http://www.vlada.cz
Parliament — Chamber of Deputies:	http://www.psp.cz
Parliament — Senate:	http://www.senat.cz
The Constitutional Court:	http://www.concourt.cz
The Supreme Court:	http://www.nsoud.cz

II.   CITATION GUIDE

There is no formal uniform code of citation in the Czech Republic and no common practice.

0.1 Common Abbreviations

Common abbreviations and words include number (č.), statute (zákon), constitutional (Ústavni), section (odst.), paragraph (pism.), reporter (Sbírka, abbreviated as Sb.).

1.0 Constitution

Cite the Constitution (*Ústavni zákon České republiky*) by number (č), section (odst.), paragraph (pism.), and other subdivision(s), followed by the abbreviation "Ústavy ČR":

> Č 1.63 odst. 1 pism. a) Ústavy ČR.

There are various other foundational sources of law, including Ústavní zákon o bezpečnosti České republiky (zákon č. 110/1998 Sb.) and Ústavni zákon o změnách státních hranic se Slovenskou republikou (zákon č. 74/1997 Sb.).

2.0 Legislation

2.1 Statutes, Laws, and Decrees

2.1.1 Vernacular Form

In the common form, cite statutes, laws, and decrees by section (odst.), paragraph (pism.), subdivision(s) (if any), and title (often abbreviated):

> § 25 odst. 1 pism. a) AZ.

Legislation is commonly referred to by a short title (e.g., "Autorský zákon" for Copyright Act) or an abbreviated, vernacular form (e.g., "AZ").

2.1.2 Formal Form

In the rarely used standard form, cite statutes, laws, and decrees by the word "Zákon," number (č.) and year (separated by a back slash), the publication in which it is published (Sbírka, abbreviated "Sb.", followed by the publication's name, e.g., "Sb. zákonů"), and full title:

> Zákon č. 121/2000 Sb. o právu autorském, o právech souvisejících s právem autorským a o změně některých zákonů.

2.2 Codes

The abbreviations of major Codes are:

Civil Code: *Občanský zákonik* (OZ)
Commercial Code: *Obchodni zákoník* (ObchZ)
Criminal Code: *Trestní zákon* (TZ or TrZ)

3.0 Jurisprudence

In the common form, cite cases by abbreviated name of the reporter in which the case is published (sometimes with the volume number preceding it),

43

case number, and year (often abbreviated to the final two digits but may be four digits):

R 13/97.

In the rarely used standard form, the reporter's full name is written out (e.g., "Sbírka soudních rozhodnuti a stanovisek"), followed by case number (č.____), and year.

3.1 Reports

The two major reporters are abbreviated by "N" (the Collection of Constitutional Court's decisions and opinions) and "R" (the Collection of Courts' decisions and opinions).

Unreported cases are not cited.

D E N M A R K

Kongeriget Danmark (Kingdom of Denmark)

 I. COUNTRY PROFILE (ELEMENTS OF CIVIL AND COMMON LAW)

The Kingdom of Denmark is a constitutional monarchy. The Constitution was originally adopted in 1849 and was most recently amended in 1953. Formally, the Constitution confers substantial powers on the monarch, but in reality the monarch's functions are largely ceremonial. The monarch appoints the Prime Minister and the Cabinet Ministers, but, apart from one instance in the early twentieth century, the monarch has summarily approved the candidates proposed by the leader of the party or parties who hold a majority of the seats in Parliament (*Folketinget*). Furthermore, the Ministers may be dismissed at any time by a parliamentary vote of no confidence. The state is divided into three branches. The executive power is vested in the Government (*Regeringen*), which is usually composed of members of Parliament; the legislative power is vested in Parliament; and the judicial power is vested in the Judiciary (*Domstolene*).

The state administration is divided between the central administration and the municipal authorities. The central administration, or Government, is headed by the Prime Minister (*Statsministeren*) and 20 Cabinet Ministers (*ressortministre*). Each Cabinet Minister heads a ministry, which is a special area of administration. The ministries are most often organized in departments and directorates. The local administration outside the two old metropolitan areas of Copenhagen and Frederiksberg consists of 14 County Councils (*amtskommuner*) and 275 City or District Councils (*primaerkommuner*). The city and district councils enjoy substantial exclusive powers, conferred on them directly by Section 82 of the Constitution.

The 1953 Constitution establishes a unicameral Parliament, which consists of 179 members, two of whom are from the Faeroe Islands and two from Greenland. Members of Parliament are directly elected by the people. Democracy is safeguarded not only by the Constitution (*Grundloven*) but also by the Parliamentary Election Act of Denmark (*Folketingsvalgloven*), which establishes an electoral system based upon proportional representation. Elections are held every four years, unless Parliament is dissolved by the Prime Minister in the interim. The legislative and the executive powers are balanced against each other in the sense that a parliamentary majority is needed in order to pass bills, and, as noted above, the members of Parliament may overthrow an individual Minister or the entire

Government by a vote of no confidence. On the other hand, the Prime Minister can dissolve the Parliament at any time in the hope of obtaining a more stable majority.

The courts are organized in a hierarchical three-tiered system. At the bottom level, City Courts (*Byretten*) are organized in 82 districts. Above the District Courts are Eastern and Western High Courts (*Landsretten*). The highest court of the country is the Supreme Court (*Hoejesteret*). Among other things, cases involving constitutional or administrative claims are dealt with in these courts. In addition to the ordinary courts, there are courts that deal only with special areas of law, for instance, the Maritime and Commercial Courts. The jury system is only used in cases of capital criminal offenses.

Denmark joined the European Union (EU) in 1973. Legal acts of the EU, which are called Regulations (*forordninger*), are directly applicable to Danish citizens when they have been published in Danish in the Official Journal of the European Union. EU directives, on the other hand, do not bind Danish citizens before they have been given legal force by legislation.

Greenland and the Faeroe Islands are part of the Kingdom of Denmark but are largely self-governing. Legislation formally comes under the Danish Folketing, which includes two representatives from Greenland and the Faeroes, respectively, but, in practical terms, the local governments of Greenland and the Faeroe Islands administer almost all legislative matters in their respective areas.

Internet Resources:

Parliament:	http://www.ft.dk
Prime Minister:	http://www.stm.dk
Judiciary:	http://www.domstol.dk
The Foreign Ministry:	http://www.um.dk

II.   CITATION GUIDE

Denmark has no uniform national citation manual. There are, however, some commonly accepted practices, but they are not followed by all authors. It is general practice to write out the full name of the material cited the first time the source is mentioned, followed by an abbreviation for subsequent citations.

1.0 Constitution

Cite the Constitution by abbreviated name ("Grundloven," "GRL" or "Grl"; the formal name "Danmarks Riges Grundlov" is rarely used), followed by "Lov nr." [law number] and serial number, and date of promulgation:

Grl, Lov nr. 169 af 5.6.1953.

2.0 Legislation

2.1 Statutes, Laws, and Decrees

Cite statutes, laws, and decrees by "Lov nr." [law number] and serial number, followed by "af" [of], date, and, usually, the official title of the law:

Lov nr. 274 af 22.12.1908 om foraeldelse af visse fordringer.

When a law has been amended, the citation should include the original law followed by the citations of the amending law(s) in chronological order (italicized), adding the phrase "som aendret ved" [as changed by]:

Lov nr. 188 af 9.5.1984 om gennemfoerelse af konvention om, hvilken lov der skal anvendes paa kontraktlige forpligtelser m.v. *som aendret ved lov nr. 305 af 16.5.1990.*

When a law has been amended a number of times, an official incorporation of the amendments will be made and a *lovbekendtgoerelse* will be published. If this is the case, cite to the *lovbekendtgoerelse*. In cases of further amendment, the citation should refer to the *lovbekendtgoerelse* and to the amending laws:

Lovbekendtgoerelse nr. 28 af 21.1.1980 om koeb *som aendret ved lov nr. 733 af 7.12.1988, lov nr. 271 af 2.5.1990 og lov nr. 1098 af 21.12.1994* [The Sale of Goods Act].

"L" is sometimes used as an abbreviation for lov [law], followed by the year of adoption and serial number of the legislation (although it is rarely seen):

L 1996 1048.

Lbkg is sometimes used as an abbreviation of *lovbekendtgoerelse*, again followed by the year of adoption and the serial number of the legislation (and other information as appropriate):

Lbkg 1996 612 som aendret ved L 1996 1048, L 1996 1056 og L 1997 456.

2.2 Codes

The abbreviations of major Codes are:

Sale of Goods: *Koebeloven* (Kbl)
Law of Contracts: *Aftaleloven* (Aftl)
Promissory Notes: *Gaeldsbrevsloven* (Gbl)
Corporate Law: *Aktieskelskabsloven* (Asl)
Tort Law: *Erstathingsansvarsloven* (Eal)
Civil/Criminal Procedure: *Retsplejeloven* (Rpl)
Penal Code: *Straffeloven* (Strfl)
Public Administration: *Forvaltningsloven* (Fvl)
Public Discourse: *Offentlighedsloven* (Offl)

Cite codes by title followed by the "§" symbol and the referenced article:

Kbl § 24.

Cite laws that are based on international agreements by article instead of section, using the term "artikel":

EMRK artikel 6 [The European Convention on Human Rights].

2.3 Regulations

Cite regulations by type ("bekendtgoerelser" or "cirkulaerer," abbreviated as "bkg" or "cirk," respectively), serial number, date, and title:

Bekendtgoerelser nr. 232 af 23.11.1933 om udledning af kulbrinte.

Regulations issued under the authority of an adopted law are called *bekendtgoerelser* (not to be confused with *lovbekendtgoerelser* described above). They have the legal effect of laws, and most detailed regulation is found in the *bekendtgoerelser*. Internal regulations by state administration are called *cirkulaerer*. These are important when researching the internal guidelines but cannot confer duties on the citizens of Denmark.

Laws and regulations (*bekendtgoerelser*) are published in *Lovtidende* and internal regulations (*cirkulaerer*) are published in *Ministerialtidende*.

3.0 Jurisprudence

Cite cases by reporter title, year of decision, reporter page, and a reference to the court which decided the case:

UfR 1989.672 H.

Alternatively:

U 83/345 SH.

Cases are published in the Ugeskrift for Retsvaesen ("UfR" or simply "U"), though not all cases are published.

3.1 Courts

The courts are entitled (and abbreviated) as follows:

Supreme Court: *Hoejesteret* (H)
High Court: *Landsretten* (L)
Maritime and Commercial Court: *Soe-og Handelsretten* (SH)
City Courts: *Byretten* (B(R))

Note: For the High Court, sometimes V(L) or OE(L) (or simply VL or OEL) is used to refer to the Eastern or Western High Court, respectively. Decisions from smaller specialized courts are sometimes published in smaller reporters.

III.   SELECTED REFERENCES

HANS GAMMELTOFT-HANSEN ET AL., DANISH LAW: A GENERAL SURVEY (G.E.C. Gads 1982).

E G Y P T

Jumhuriyat Misr al-Arabiyah
(The Arab Republic of Egypt)

I. COUNTRY PROFILE (CIVIL LAW)

The Arab Republic of Egypt is a parliamentary republic with a strong head of state. The official language is Arabic. Egypt is divided into 28 Governorates (*muhafazat*, singular: *muhafazah*), with sub-units of cities and villages. Governors and mayors are appointed by the central government, while local councils are directly elected by the people.

Egyptian law has its roots in the Islamic legal tradition, but the legal system is built on a combination of Sharia and civil law, first introduced during the Napoleonic occupation of Egypt. While Sharia (the uncodified body of Islamic law and practices based on the Qur'an and Sunnah) as interpreted through the teachings of the Hanafi school of thought has recently reemerged as a force in modern Egyptian legal development, the country remains a secular Arab nation. Egypt has elements of both a common and civil law system.

Egypt's Constitution is contained in an act promulgated on September 11, 1971, with amendments ratified in 1980. It establishes Egypt as a secular Arab state and bans religiously based political parties. The Constitution also establishes a parliamentary system but grants the head of state wide powers. The President is head of state and is directly elected to a six-year term by the people, following the approval of his candidacy by the National Assembly. The President may appoint one or more vice presidents, a prime minister, vice prime ministers, and other cabinet ministers, and may dismiss these officers at any time.

General legislative power is vested in the two houses of Parliament: the 454-member People's National Assembly (*Majlis al-Sha'b*) and the 264-member Shura (consultative) Council (*Majlis al-Shura*). Four hundred forty-four members of the People's Assembly are popularly elected, although the Constitution requires that at least half of the Assembly's membership be "workers and peasants," and the President has the right to appoint ten members. Members serve five-year terms, although the President may dissolve Parliament at any time. The Shura Council's role is consultative. One hundred seventy-six of its members are directly elected by the people, and 88 are appointed by the president. Members serve six-year terms. Although legislation

51

is the primary source of law, the writings of the Muslim *Hanafi* school are applicable to matters of family law, and non-Muslim citizens may fall under Christian or Jewish canon law if applicable.

The President and the members of the People's Assembly may propose legislation, although legislation proposed by Assembly members must be referred first to a special committee to assess its suitability for consideration by the Assembly. Acceptable draft laws are referred to a committee of the Assembly for a report. Once legislation is ratified by the People's Assembly, it is submitted to the President, who must approve or veto the legislation within 30 days. A Presidential veto can be overruled by a two-thirds majority of the People's Assembly. If the President neither approves nor vetoes the legislation within 30 days, the legislation becomes law.

The Constitution also establishes the Judiciary and specifies that it shall be independent and subject to no authority but the law. The organization of the State Security Courts, their competencies, and the conditions that must be fulfilled by judges are prescribed by law. A separate administrative court system, the Council of State (*Maglis id-Dowla*), handles cases involving the state. The Supreme Judicial Council, whose members are drawn primarily from the Judiciary, supervises the appointment, promotion, and transfer of judges.

The Supreme Constitutional Court (*Mahkramat al-Naqd*) consists of seven judges appointed by governmental decree. This Court has exclusive jurisdiction over every case concerning the constitutionality of laws, rules, and regulations. The judgments issued by the Court in constitutional cases and its legislative interpretations are published in an Official Gazette.

The lower courts, the Summary Tribunals (*Mahakim Guz'iya*) and the Summary Tribunals of First Instance (*Mahakim Kulliya*), are divided into civil and criminal courts. The Summary Tribunals are tasked with settling minor offenses, minor civil and commercial cases, minor personal status matters, and labor issues. The Summary Tribunals of First Instance hear appeals from the Summary Tribunals and have original jurisdiction over civil and commercial disputes in excess of 250 Egyptian pounds as well as all significant personal status matters. The final court of appeal in both civil and criminal matters is the Court of Cassation, sometimes referred to as the Supreme Court (*Al Maharama al-Dusturiya*). It consists of 30 judges and generally hears appeals in panels of at least five judges from the judgments of the courts of appeal and assize courts on the grounds of violation of the law or grave procedural error. It may reverse the decision of the lower court, and, in certain instances, may decide a case on the merits. Recently, a special Administrative Court was established to deal with certain cases involving the administrative issues.

Internet Resources:

Egypt State Information Service:	http://www.egypt.gov.eg/english/
Political System:	http://www.state.gov/r/pa/ei/bgn/
	5309.htm
	http://www.egypt.gov.eg/english/
	laws/constitution/index.asp
Legal System:	http://www.nyulawglobal.org/
	globalex/Egypt.htm
Cabinet:	http://www.egyptiancabinet.gov.eg

II. CITATION GUIDE

There is no formal citation standard used in Egypt. The following standards are general practice in transliterated English usage.

1.0 Constitution

Cite the Constitution by title followed by a transliteration of the Arabic title (in parentheses), abbreviation (in square brackets), section and article, and the word "In" (underlined) followed by title of the official gazette in which the Constitution is published (abbreviated Egy OG), date, volume, and page referenced:

> Constitution of the Arab Republic of Egypt (*Dustur Juinhuriyat Misr al-Arabiyah*) [Egy const.] of September 11, 1971, sec. II, art. 9. In Egy OG of September 12, 1971, vol. 14th year, no. 36 bis (a), p. 13.

A subsequent shorter form abbreviates the Constitution's name and provides the section and article referenced:

> Egy Const, Sec. II, art. 10.

2.0 Legislation

2.1 CODES

Cite codes by title followed by a transliteration of the Arabic title (in parentheses), abbreviation (in square brackets), and article, and the word "In" (underlined) followed by title of the official gazette in which the code is published (abbreviated Egy OG), date, volume, and page referenced:

> Civil and commercial Procedure code of Egypt (*Qanun al-Murafa at al-Madaniyah wa al-Tjariyah*) [Egy CivComPC] of May 7, 1968, art. 2. In Egy OG of May 9, 1969, no. 19, p. 245.

An abbreviated title of the code may also be used, followed by the article referenced:

> Egy CivComPC, art. 1.

The abbreviations of major Codes are:

Egyptian Civil Code: *al-Qanun al-Madani* (Egy CivC)

Criminal Code: *Qanun al-Ugubat* (Egy CrimC)

Code of Civil and Commercial Procedure: *Qanun al-Murafa at al-Madaniyah wa al-Tjariyah* (Egy CivComPC)

Code of Criminal Procedure: *Qanun al-ijra at al Jina iyah* (Egy CrimPC)

2.2 Statutes, Laws, and Decrees

Cite statutes, laws, and decrees by title followed by a transliteration of the Arabic title (in parentheses) if available, and the word "In" (underlined) followed by title of the official gazette in which the code is published (abbreviated Egy OG), date, volume, and page referenced:

> Law no. 18 of April 16, 1977 on agricultural land tax (*Daribat al-Aradi al-Zira iyah*). In Egy OG of April 21, 1977, no. 16, p. 347.

In subsequent citations, an abbreviated form may be used, by citing to a shortened form of the title, followed by the article referenced:

> Land Tax Law, art. 2.

2.3 Official Publication for Legislation

For any legislation, citations may also be made to the official gazette's name followed by transliteration of the Arabic title (in parentheses) if available, date, volume, and page referenced:

> The official gazette of Egypt (*al-Jaridah al-Rasmiyah*) [Egy OG] of April 14, 1977, no. 15, p. 314.

In subsequent citations, an abbreviated form may also be used, by citing to the official gazette's abbreviation (adding date and volume information if necessary), followed by page referenced:

> Egy OG, p. 313.

3.0 Jurisprudence

Cite cases by case number, decision number, date, deciding court, title of the publication containing the case followed by transliteration of the Arabic title (in parentheses) if available, date, volume, and page referenced:

> Case no. 1635, decision no. 41, of Feb. 14, 1972, Court of Cassation, Criminal Division [Egyptian Judicial review] (*Mahkamat al-Naqd Majmuat al-Ahkam al-Sadirah*

min al-Hay ad al-Ammah lil-mawad al-Jima iyah) Jan.–Mar. 1972,
no. 1, p. 168.

In subsequent citations, cite to case number and decision number:

Case no. 1635/decision no. 41.

E T H I O P I A

Ityop'iya Federalawi Demokrasiyawi Ripeblik
(Federal Democratic Republic of Ethiopia)

I. COUNTRY PROFILE (CIVIL LAW)

The Federal Democratic Republic of Ethiopia is a federal, democratic republic. Ethiopa is made up of nine states and two self-governing, administrative cities (Addis Ababa and Dire Dawa). Addis Ababa is the national capital. Although the Constitution officially recognizes nine ethnic nationalities within the federal state, recent studies show that as many as 99 languages are spoken in Ethiopia. The work of the government, however, is carried out in English and Amharic. Major local languages include Amharic, Tigrigna, and Oromifa.

Ethiopia's Constitution, adopted in 1994, vests federal power in the executive, legislative, and judicial branches. The President of Ethiopia serves as the head of state, and is elected jointly by a two-thirds majority vote of the House of People's Representatives and the House of the Federation, for a six-year term. The Prime Minister of Ethiopia, the chief executive, is selected among members of the Council of People's Representatives by the party in power following legislative elections. The Prime Minister in turn designates, with the approval of the House of People's Representatives, the Ministers who constitute the Council of Ministers.

Ethiopia's bicameral Parliament consists of the House of the Federation or upper chamber, whose 108 members are chosen by state councils and serve five-year terms, and the House of People's Representatives or lower chamber, whose 547 members are directly elected by popular vote from single-member districts and serve five-year terms. The House of the Federation is charged with interpreting the Constitution, addressing questions related to the right to self-determination of the various ethnic nationalities within Ethiopia, and seeking solutions to conflict among Ethiopia's member states. The House of People's Representatives is the country's federal legislative body. Laws passed by this body are submitted to the President for his signature; if he does not sign a law within 15 days, it takes effect without his signature.

Ethiopia is primarily a civil law country. Its major legal codes, drafted and originally adopted primarily in the 1950s and 1960s and amended several times since, are still in effect despite several regime changes. The Constitution provides for the establishment of a Federal Supreme Court. The President and Vice

President of the Federal Supreme Court are appointed by the House of People's Representatives based upon the recommendations of the Prime Minister. Other federal judges on the Supreme Court are selected by the Federal Judicial Administrative Council, and their names are then submitted for appointment to the House of People's Representatives by the Prime Minister. At its discretion, the House of People's Representatives may also establish federal high and first-instance courts. Finally, there is a Council of Constitutional Inquiry, which is composed of the President and Vice President of the Supreme Court, six legal experts, and three members of the House of the Federation. The Council investigates constitutional disputes and submits recommendations to the House of the Federation.

There are also three levels of regional courts within the nine member states: state supreme courts, high courts, and courts of first instance. Religious or customary courts may be given recognition only by the House of People's Representatives or state councils.

Internet Resources:

Parliament:	http://www.ethiopar.net
Ethiopian Embassy:	http://www.ethiopianembassy.org/judiciary.html
Ethiopia on the web:	http://library.stanford.edu/africa/ethio.html
Website of the ministry of Justice (under construction):	http://lcweb2.loc.gov/frd/cs/ettoc.html
Mekelle University Law Faculty:	http://www.mu.edu.et/Academics/FOL/muLaw/muLawIntro.html
Harvard University Law Library:	http://www.law.harvard.edu/library/services/research/guides/international/web_resources/foreignF.php#Ethiopia
Washburn University Law Library:	http://www.washlaw.edu/forint/africa/ethiopia.html

II. CITATION GUIDE

Ethiopia does not have a formal citation standard. Since 1965, the *Journal of Ethiopian Law* has been the most consistent source of Ethiopian legal scholarship, although copies before 1994 are difficult to obtain. The following citation guide is based on the usages prevalent in this journal as of 1994.

1.0 Constitution

Information on the citation of Ethiopia's Constitution was not obtained.

2.0 Legislation and Other Non-Judicial Sources of Law

Cite legislation by title of the Code, article and subdivision (if any) referenced, title of the publication in which the Code is found, and volume [year, volume number]:

> The Maritime Code of Ethiopia of 1960. Article 209, Proclamation No. 164, Negarit Gazeta (extra-ordinary), Year 19, No. 1.

The *Negarit Gazeta* is the official legislative, executive, and administrative law reporter in Ethiopia. It is published in Amharic and English, although not on a regular or periodic basis.

Proclamations, orders, and legal notices appear in the *Negarit Gazeta* under their generic name, number, and year of publication. Laws are published in the *Negarit Gazeta* in short chronological order. There is no index in the individual issue or in the bound volumes for each year. Nor is there a cumulative index of all the bound volumes.

3.0 Jurisprudence

Information on citation of judicial authorities is not available. As a civil law country, Codes continue to be the primary sources of law in Ethiopia.

3.1 Courts

The names of the courts are as follows:

Federal Supreme Court
Federal High Court
Federal First Instance Court
Council of Constitutional Inquiry
State Supreme Courts
High courts
Courts of first instance
Religious or customary courts

F I N L A N D

Suomen Tasavalta (Republic of Finland)

COUNTRY PROFILE (CIVIL LAW)

The Republic of Finland, established on December 6, 1917, is a sovereign republic. Finland (*Suomi*) is subdivided into six provinces and operates under a civil legal system. The two official languages in the country are Finnish and Swedish. All laws are published in both official languages. In addition, the Sámi people of Lapland, the northern region of Finland, hold the constitutionally protected right to publish laws in the Sámi language. Finland entered into membership in the European Union on January 1, 1995.

Finland's Constitution was adopted on March 1, 2000. Prior to that date, the country was governed by four Constitutional Acts: the Constitution Act of Finland (1919), the Parliament Act, and two ministerial liability acts. The Constitution is the supreme law of the land and is the source of all public power. It enshrines the fundamental principle that sovereign power lies with the Finnish people represented by the Parliament.

The state is organized on the basis of a separation of powers between the Government, Parliament, the President, and the courts. Executive power lies with the Government (*valtioneuvosto*), with certain duties carried out by the President (*tasavallan presidentti*). The President is elected directly by majority vote, with a second runoff election held if necessary, for a term of six years. The President must be a native Finnish citizen and is limited to two terms in office. The Prime Minister is elected by Parliament and appointed by the President. Other ministers are appointed by the President based upon nominations by the Prime Minister. The Government or Council of Ministers is made up of the Prime Minister (*Pääministeri*) and a maximum of 17 Ministers (*Ministeri*). The Government, which is the decision-making body for governmental and administrative matters, consists of the Government plenary session and the ministries. Foreign policy is directed by the President in conjunction with the Government. The Government has the authority to forward proposals for legislation to the Parliament for enactment.

The legislative power lies with the Parliament (*eduskunta*). Finland has a unicameral Parliament consisting of 200 seats. Chapter Six of the Constitution provides that the principal duty of Parliament is to enact legislation. Members of Parliament are elected directly by popular vote to four-year terms, although the President, after consulting with Parliament, may order a new election prior to the end of that term if the Prime Minister so advises. Parliament may adopt Acts, which must be submitted to the President for ratification. Following signature by the President, the Act is published in the official statute book. Acts that are not ratified within three months, or that are vetoed by the President, are returned to the Parliament, and they may still enter into force if there is sufficient support in Parliament, provided that no further amendments are made.

Judicial power lies with the Courts (*tuomioistuimet*). Finland has a three-tiered hierarchical system of courts. Sixty-six first-instance District Courts (*käräjäoikeus*) have jurisdiction to hear both civil and criminal matters in territorially limited districts. Their decisions may be appealed to one of six regionally organized Courts of Appeal (*hovioikeus*), which also have first-instance jurisdiction over certain governmental and treason matters. The highest court is the Supreme Court of Finland (*korkein oikeus*). Appeals from decisions of the Courts of Appeal are heard only with leave of the Supreme Court, usually by a panel of five justices. Along with its judicial authority, the Supreme Court of Finland also has the power to request legislation modifying or interpreting current legislation. Administrative law cases are heard by Administrative Courts (*hallinto-oikeus*), appeals from decisions of which may be taken with leave to the Supreme Administrative Court (*korkein hallinto-oikeus*). In addition, Finland has a network of Specialized Courts (*erityistuomioistuin*), arranged by subject matter jurisdiction. These include, *inter alia*, Market Courts (*markkinatuomioistuin*), Labour Courts (*työtuomioistuin*), and Social Insurance Courts (*vakuutusoikeus*) dealing with such matters as entitlement to welfare benefits. The two principal law journals are *Suomen asianajajaliiton äänenkannattaja* and *Lakimies: Suomalaisen lakimiesten yhdistyksen aikakauskirja*.

The Constitution grants the autonomous Åland Islands very liberal executive and legislative powers. Legislative and executive powers are vested in the Provincial Legislative Assembly (*Lagting/Maakuntapäivät*) and the Provincial Government (*Landskapsstyrelse/Maakuntahallitus*). The official language of the Åland Islands is Swedish.

Internet Resource:

Republic of Finland: http://www.om.fi

II. CITATION GUIDE

Finland does not have an official national citation manual. There are, however, citation practices that are widely accepted and used.

1.0 Constitution

Cite the Constitution by title (*Suomen perustuslaki*), chapter number followed by the word *"luku,"* and section number:

Suomen perustuslaki, 1 luku, § 1.

Note: The Constitution is also assigned an official Statute Book number: 731/1999, and may technically be cited like other legislation. It is rarely, however, cited in any way other than by its official title.

2.0 Legislation

Cite statutes and decrees by serial number and year [serial number/year], typically followed by the official title of the law:

562/1995 Laki kalastuslain muuttamisesta.

All officially promulgated laws, including the Constitution, Acts of Parliament, and Governmental and Ministerial Decrees are published in the Official Statute Book of Finland (*Suomen säädöskokoelma*). The FINLEX database, accessible on the Internet at http://www.finlex.fi/english/index.html, is a free databank of the texts of all legislation contained in the Statute Book, decisions of the Finnish Supreme Court and Supreme Administrative Court, and all proposed legislation.

Note: The commercial publishers, Kauppakaari Oyj, publish a two-volume series of the Law of Finland (*Suomen Laki I-II*) on an annual basis, which uses a different system of citation.

3.0 Jurisprudence

3.1 The Supreme Court

Cite Supreme Court cases by abbreviated name of the Supreme Court ("KKO"), year, and case number (all separated by colons):

KKO:2001:118.

For cases prior to 1987, also indicate the volume (I or II) in which the case was published after the year and between hyphens:

KKO:1986-I-1.

KKO:1986-II-1.

Cases of the Supreme Court are published twice yearly in the yearbook *Korkeimman oikeuden ratkaisuja*, published by Edita Oyj. The cases are also available on the Internet from the FINLEX database, as well as the Supreme Court of Finland's website: http://www.kko.fi/ennakkoratkaisut.

3.2 The Supreme Administrative Court

Cite Supreme Administrative Court cases by date of the decision [day.month. year], and case number:

> 11.09.2001/2122.

Only a selection of those cases deemed by the court to be of pertinent use in the guidance of future disputes is published in the yearbook of the court, *Korkein hallinto-oikeuden vuosikirja* (abbreviated "KHO"). Those selected cases are also available from the FINLEX database as well as from the website of the Supreme Administrative Court: http://www.kho.fi/tietop.html.

Those cases selected for publication in the yearbook may also be cited according to the Supreme Court format:

> KHO:1993-B-505.

3.3 Lower Courts

Decisions of lower courts are rarely published or cited. The majority of cases that are published may be found in the leading law journals. Cite lower courts cases by date and case number.

3.4 Specialized Courts

Since 1947, selected Labour Court decisions have been published in the court's yearbook, the *Työtuomioistuimen vuosikirja*. The Market Court also publishes a yearbook containing selected decisions since 1979.

III. SELECTED REFERENCES

THOMAS H. REYNOLDS & ARTURO A. FLORES, FOREIGN LAW: CURRENT SOURCES OF CODES AND BASIC LEGISLATION IN JURISDICTIONS OF THE WORLD (3d ed. 1989).

F R A N C E

République Française (French Republic)

I. COUNTRY PROFILE (CIVIL LAW)

France is a civil law country with extensive codification, where legislation is the main source of law. The Constitution of the Fifth Republic of 1958 is characterized by a semi-presidential regime. It incorporates human rights through references to the 1789 Declaration of the Rights of the Man and the Citizen and the preamble of the 1946 Constitution.

The executive is led by the President (*Président de la République*) and Prime Minister (*Premier Ministre*). Elected by a direct universal suffrage for a five-year term, the President guarantees the national independence and the integrity of the territory, is the chief of the army, ensures that the Constitution is respected, and presides over the Council of Ministers. The President appoints the Prime Minister, who then designates other members of the government. The President may take emergency measures in times of crisis under strict conditions pursuant to Article 16 of the Constitution. During this time, the National Assembly, however, cannot be dissolved, and the Constitution cannot be amended. The Prime Minister leads the administration, and determines and conducts national policy.

The legislative power is held by a bicameral Parliament, consisting of the National Assembly (*Assemblée Nationale*) and the Senate (*Sénat*). Unlike the National Assembly, which is elected by a direct universal suffrage, the Senate is elected by indirect universal suffrage by locally elected representatives. All laws must be approved by both chambers. The Parliament exercises control over executive government action through a formal process of opening investigations. It may also contest the mandate of the government. The Constitution grants the legislative branch extensive power to enact statutes and also provides for a possibility of enlargement of the powers of this branch. All other areas are left to the executive branch, which has the power to enact regulations.

The Constitutional Council (*Conseil Constitutionnel*) is responsible for ensuring that referenda and the election of the President and Parliament are fair. It performs mandatory reviews of the constitutionality of the laws, treaties, and parliamentary standing orders prior to ratification. The Council does not review the decisions of lower courts for constitutionality on appeal. Instead, it is called to action through petitions by the President, the Prime Minister, or the President of the National Assembly or President of the Senate, or by a vote of 60 senators or Assembly members. The term of office of its nine members is nine years, and the term is nonrenewable. Three members are appointed by the President, three by the President of the National Assembly, and three by the President of the Senate. One-third of the Constitutional Council's members are appointed every three years. Former Presidents of the Republic are members "ex officio."

The judicial system is divided into a judiciary body, combining civil and criminal courts, and an administrative body of various administrative courts. The former body is headed by the Court of Cassation (*Cour de Cassation*), the latter by the Council of State (*Conseil d'État*). The Tribunal of Conflicts arbitrates cases of conflict of jurisdiction or decisions between the two; it is composed of an equal number of judges from the Court of Cassation and the Council of State.

The Court of Cassation consists of three civil chambers: a commercial chamber, a social chamber, and a criminal chamber. It decides whether the lower courts have correctly interpreted and applied the rule of law and the rules of procedure. It does not usually overrule a lower court's judgment but instead quashes it and remits the case for rehearing by a Court of Appeal (*Cour d'Appel*) other than the one that originally heard the case. Important controversial cases may be decided in plenary session. The Courts of Appeal deal with both civil and criminal matters. In civil matters, the trial courts are the Tribunals of Great Instance (*Tribunaux de Grande Instance*), or the Tribunals of Instance for small claims (*Tribunaux d'Instance*). In criminal matters, the Tribunal of Police deals with minor offenses, the Criminal Tribunal with crimes, and the Assises Courts (*Cours d'Assises*) with the most serious offenses. The Assises Courts are the only courts that utilize a jury system. The decision of one Assises Court can be appealed to another. The Court of Cassation can also consider appeals on criminal matters. The hierarchy of the administrative courts in decreasing seniority is as follows: the Council of State, the administrative Courts of Appeal, and the administrative tribunals.

Internet Resources:

National Assembly:	http://www.assemblee-nat.fr
Senate:	http://www.senat.fr
President:	http://www.elysee.fr
Prime Minister:	http://www.premier-ministre.gouv.fr
Constitutional Council:	http://www.conseil-constitutionnel.fr
Court of Cassation:	http://www.courdecassation.fr
Council of State:	http://www.conseil-etat.fr
Official Journal:	http://www.journal-officiel.gouv.fr
Legislation:	http://www.legifrance.gouv.fr

II. CITATION GUIDE

France does not have a uniform national citation manual. There are some accepted practices, but they are not followed by all authors.

1.0 Constitution

Cite the Constitution (*La Constitution du 4 octobre 1958*) by the abbreviation "Const." followed by "Art." and article number:

Const., Art. 18.

2.0 Legislation

2.1 Statutes, Laws, and Decrees

Cite statutes and decrees by type (e.g., "L. const.," "Loi," "ord.," or "Décret"), followed by n° and reference number [last two digits of the year in which the law was enacted-serial number], and then "du" followed by the date [day, month (spelled out), year]. Some statutes are cited by the name of the senator or deputy who introduced the bill, e.g., loi Royer, loi Badinter:

L. const. n° 95-880 du 4 août 1995.

Loi n° 67-1828 du 27 juillet 1967.

Ord. n° 59 2 du 2 janvier 1959

Décret n° 56-1128 du 9 novembre 1956.

2.1.1 Official Gazette

Laws and decrees are published in the official gazette, the *Journal Officiel de la République francaise* (abbreviated "J.O."). Cite laws and decrees published in the official gazette by the above standard, followed by "J.O. du" and date of the gazette, and page referenced:

Loi n° 67-1828 du 27 juillet 1967, J.O. du 27 juillet 1967, p. 1234.

2.2 Codes

Cite codes by "Art." and article number, followed by abbreviated title of the code. A letter may precede the article number: "L" if it is a parliamentary law (*loi*), "D" if it is a decree (*décret*), "R" if it is a regulation (*règlement*):

Art. 2012 C. civ.

Art. 223 N.C.P.C.

Art. L. 311-11 C. org. jud.

The abbreviations of major Codes are:

Civil Code: *Code civil* (C. civ.)
Criminal Code: *Code pénal* (C. pén.)

Commercial Code: *Code de commerce* (C. com.)
Criminal Procedure: *Code de Procédure Pénale* (C. pr. pén.)
New Civil Procedure Code: *Nouveau Code de procédure civile* (nouv. C. pr. civ. (or N.C.P.C.))
Employment Code: *Code du Travail* (C. trav.)
Judicial Code: *Code de l'organisation judiciaire* (C. org. Jud).

2.3 Treaties and Conventions

Cite treaties and conventions using source information, as described in Section 1.0 of Part II, on Treaties and Conventions, with at least two treaty sources — the Journal Officiel (J.O.) and one other source:

> [Treaty information], J.O., 21 feb. 2001, p. 220; 2001 Recueil des traités, No. 4, [date of entry, etc.].

2.3.1 French Treaty Sources

French Treaty Sources, and their citation formats, are:

Journal Officiel: "J.O.", [date of publication], [page referenced].
Recueil des traités et accords de la France: [year], "Recueil des traités," [treaty number].
Recueil des traités de la France: [volume], "Recueil des traités," [page referenced].

3.0 Jurisprudence

Cite cases by name of the parties (optional), court (by abbreviated title, placing the city or regional name after the court name for city or regional courts), chamber (if appropriate), date and title of the reporter, volume, page referenced, and name of the commentator (optional).

Example of a citation in an official report:

> Civ. 1ère, 14 déc. 1983, Bull civ. I, n° 295.

Example of a citation in unofficial reports:

> C.A. Aix-en-Provence, 16 oct. 1962, JCP 1962. II. 12923, note Level.

> Com. 30 juill. 1952, D. 1952. 724.

3.1 Courts

Chambers of the Court of Cassation and their abbreviations include:

Assemblée plénière (Ass. Plén.)
Chambres réunites (Ch. Réuns.)
Chambre mixte (Ch. Mixte)
Première chambre civile (Civ. 1ère)
Deuxième chambre civile (Civ. 2ème)
Troisième chambre civile (Civ. 3ème)
Chambre commerciale et financière (Com.)
Chambre criminelle (Crim.)
Chambre sociale (Soc.)

Regional Courts include:

Cours d'Appel (C.A.)
Tribunaux de Grande Instance (T.G.I.)
Cours d'Assises
Tribunaux d'Instance (Trib. inst.)

3.2 Reports

There is no comprehensive system of official reports of judicial decisions. There are some common reports, including the judgments of the Cour de Cassation, published in part only in the *Bulletin des arrêts de la Cour de cassation rendus en matière criminelle* or *civile* (cited Bull. crim. and Bull. civ., respectively); and the decisions of the Conseil constitutionnel, published in the *Recueil des décisions du Conseil constitutionnel.*

Some unofficial reports are commonly used by authors and practitioners:

La Semaine Juridique (JCP)
Recueil Dalloz (D.)
Gazette du Palais (Gaz. Pal. or G.P.)
Recueil des arrêts du Conseil d'État statuant au contentieux (Rec. Lebon or Lebon)

III.   SELECTED REFERENCES

René David, French Law: Its Structure, Sources, and Methodology (Michael Kindred trans., Louisiana State University Press 1972).

C. DEBBASCH ET AL., DROIT CONSTITUTIONNEL ET INSTITUTIONS POLITIQUES (2d ed., P.U.F. 1986).

FRANÇOISE DREYFUS & FRANÇOIS D'ARCY, LES INSTITUTIONS POLITIQUES ET ADMINISTRA-TIVES DE LA FRANCE (2d ed., Economica 1987).

M. GOUNELLE, INTRODUCTION AU DROIT PUBLIC, INSTITUTIONS-FONDEMENTS-SOURCES (2d ed., Montchretien 1989).

H. PINSSEAU, L'ORGANISATION JUDICIAIRE FRANÇAISE (La Documentation Française 1978).

T. RENOUX, LE CONSEIL CONSTITUTIONNEL ET L'AUTORITE JUDICIAIRE (Economica 1984).

G E R M A N Y

Bundesrepublik Deutschland
(Federal Republic of Germany)

I. COUNTRY PROFILE (CIVIL LAW)

Germany is a democratic, federal republic made up of 16 States (*Länder*) whose legal system is based on a civil law tradition. The German Constitution, the Basic Law (*Grundgesetz*) of 1949, was intended as a provisional Constitution to serve until a permanent one for Germany as a whole could be adopted. It lost its "temporary" status on October 3, 1990, when the five states of the former German Democratic Republic (*Deutsche Demokratische Republik*) and East Berlin joined the unified German Federation.

In Germany's federal structure most of the legislative power is concentrated at the national level, while administrative, judicial, and enforcement functions are exercised principally at the state level. Executive responsibilities on the federal level lie principally with the Federal Government (*Bundesregierung*), which is headed by the Chancellor (*Bundeskanzler*). The Chancellor is elected by the Bundestag. The Federal President (*Bundespräsident*), the official head of state, is elected for a five-year term — with the possibility of reelection for a consecutive term — by a Federal Convention (*Bundesversammlung*) consisting of equal numbers of members of the Lower House of Parliament (*Bundestag*) and members elected by the parliaments of the individual states. The President's duties are primarily ceremonial.

The Constitution vests the legislative power in a bicameral parliament, consisting of the Lower House of Parliament, whose members are directly elected by the people every four years, and the Senate (*Bundesrat*), which is composed of members of the state governments. Most federal law is initiated by the Federal Government and later voted upon and passed into law, first by the *Bundestag* and then the *Bundesrat*. The *Bundesrat*, however, has only suspensive veto power over most legislation. Thus, with the important exception of bills relating to the administrative responsibilities of the states, the *Bundesrat* can only delay legislation rather than veto it outright.

The 16 *Länder* have their own constitutions, each of which establishes a unicameral State Legislature (generally called *Landtag*). The State Legislature elects the state's Prime Minister (generally called *Ministerpräsident*), who heads the State's Government (*Landesregierung* or *Staatsregierung*).

Judicial power is exercised by the Federal Constitutional Court, the federal courts, and the courts of the States. Judicial functions pertaining to the federal constitution are performed exclusively by the Federal Constitutional Court (*Bundesverfassungsgericht*). State constitutional matters are generally adjudicated by State Constitutional Courts (*Landesverfassungsgericht*). In contrast to some other federative countries, Germany's state and federal courts are integrated in a single court system, organized both hierarchically and by subject matter. The courts are grouped into five categories: Ordinary Courts (*Ordentliche Gerichtsbarkeit*), Labor Courts (*Arbeitsgerichtsbarkeit*), Administrative Courts (*Verwaltungsgerichtsbarkeit*), Social Courts (*Sozialgerichtsbarkeit*), and Fiscal Courts (*Finanzgerichtsbarkeit*). The federation can establish special courts as well, like the Federal Court for Patent Matters. The Ordinary Courts are responsible for criminal matters, civil matters (such as matrimonial or family proceedings and disputes arising under private law such as sale or lease agreements, as well as commercial and corporate law), and non-contentious legal proceedings, which include bequests, probate, and guardianship matters. There are four levels: local courts, regional courts, regional courts of appeals (all administered on the state level), and the Federal Court of Justice (*Bundesgerichtshof*). In criminal cases, one of the first three courts has original jurisdiction, depending on the nature of the crime. In civil proceedings, jurisdiction is vested in either the local or regional court.

The Labor Courts handle disputes arising from employment contracts and industrial relations, including collective bargaining agreements. There are three levels: labor courts, labor courts of appeals (both administered on the state level), and the Federal Labor Court (*Bundesarbeitsgericht*). The Administrative Courts also have three levels: the administrative courts and administrative courts of appeals, both on the state level, and, finally, the Federal Administrative Court (*Bundesverwaltungsgericht*). They handle proceedings under administrative law that do not fall within the jurisdiction of the social courts, the finance courts, the ordinary courts (e.g., cases of official liability), or the constitutional courts. The Social Courts rule on all disputes concerned with social security. They also have three levels: local, appellate, and the Federal Social Court (*Bundessozialgericht*). Finally, the fiscal courts (*Finanzgerichtsbarkeit*), which consist of only one level of state courts and the Federal Finance Court (*Bundesfinanzhof*), deal with taxation and related matters.

Internet Resources:

Federal Government: http://www.bundesregierung.de
Lower Chamber of Federal
  Government: http://www.bundestag.de
Higher Chamber of Federal
  Government: http://www.bundesrat.de

Federal President:	http://www.bundespraesident.de
Constitutional Court:	http://www.bundesverfassungsgericht.de
Federal Courts:	http://www.bundesgerichtshof.de
	http://www.bundesarbeitsgericht.de
	http://www.bundessozialgericht.de
	http://www.bverwg.de
	http://www.bundesfinanzhof.de
Federal Patent Court:	http://www.bpatg.de
Attorney General:	http://www.generalbundesanwalt.de
Federal Ministry of Justice:	http://www.bmj.bund.de
Federal Law:	http://bundesrecht.juris.de/bundesrecht
	http://www.jura.uni-muenster.de
	http://www.jura.uni-sb.de
Federal Gazette:	http://www.bundesgesetzblatt.de

II. CITATION GUIDE

Citation is quite uniform, although there are neither binding rules regarding citation nor a national citation manual in Germany. Möllers, "Juristische Arbeitstechnik und wissenschaftliches Arbeiten," 3 *Aufl. München* 2005 could serve as a guideline. The relevant chapter has been made available online by the University of Augsburg at http://www.jura.uni-augsburg.de/prof/moellers/downloads/arbeitstechnik_jur/richtiges_zitieren.pdf.

0.1 Common Abbreviations

Common abbreviations in German citation practice include Article ("Artikel," or "Art."), paragraph ("Absatz" or "Abs."), and clause ("Satz" or "S."). The "Abs." and "S." symbols are optional (i.e., "Art. 1 Abs. 1 S. 1" = "Art. 1/1").

1.0 Constitution

Cite the Constitution (*Grundgesetz der Bundesrepublik Deutschland*) by subdivision referenced (see Part 0.1 above), followed by abbreviated title ("GG"):

Art. 1 Abs. 3 GG.

Art. 1 Abs. 1 S. 1 GG.

Art. 1/1 GG.

2.0 Legislation

2.1 Statutes, Laws, and Decrees

Cite statutes, laws, and decrees by passage referenced, full title, short title (in parentheses), date [day.month.year], followed by abbreviated title of the official gazette in which it is published (e.g., "BGBl."), volume, year, and page referenced:

> § 1 Gesetz über die politischen Parteien (Parteiengesetz) v. 31.1.1994, BGBl. I 1994, 149.

2.1.1 Federal Gazette

The Federal Gazette (*Bundesgesetzblatt*) is cited BGBl. Before 1945, it was called *Reichsgesetzblatt* (cited RGBl.). State gazettes are generally called *Gesetz- und Verordnungsblatt* (cited GVBl.).

2.2 Codes

Cite Codes by subdivision referenced (see Section 0.1 above), followed by abbreviated title of the Code:

> § 812 Abs. 1 S. 1 BGB.

> § 812/1 BGB.

The abbreviations of major Codes are:

Law on the Organization of the Judiciary:*Gerichtsverfassungsgesetz* (GVG)
Code of Civil Procedure: *Zivilprozeßordnung* (ZPO)
Code of Criminal Procedure: *Strafprozeßordnung* (StPO)
Code of Administrative Procedure: *Verwaltungsverfahrensgesetz* (VwVfG)
Civil Code: *Bürgerliches Gesetzbuch* (BGB)
Commercial Code: *Handelsgesetzbuch* (HGB)
Criminal Code: *Strafgesetzbuch* (StGB)
Code of Social Law: *Sozialgesetzbuch* (SGB)

Many Federal Statutes can be found on the website of the Federal Ministry of Justice (http://bundesrecht.juris.de/bundesrecht). Links to many federal and state laws are available at http://www.jura.uni-muenster.de and http://www.jura.uni-sb.de (under "Recherche" and then "Jura-Links").

2.3 Treaties and Conventions

Cite treaties and conventions as described in Section 1.0 of Part II, on Treaties and Conventions, filling in the source information preferably with either the federal gazette (BGBl. II) or Germany's treaty series (*Verträge der Bundesrepublik Deutschland*) by volume, title, series (in parentheses), and treaty number:

[Treaty information], 5 Verträge der Bundesrepublik Deutschland (ser. A), No. 1, [date of entry, etc.].

3.0 Jurisprudence

Cite cases published in official reporters by abbreviated title of the reporter, volume, first page of the decision, and page referenced:

BGHZ 126, 105, 107.

Cite other cases by abbreviated name of the court, location of the court (unless citing to federal courts or unique state courts like BayObLG, KG), date (optional and unusual), official registration number (optional and unusual), abbreviated name of the periodical in which the decision is published, year, first page of the decision, and page referenced:

OLG Köln, Urteil v. 13.12.1996 (6 U 191/96), NJW 1997, 3179.

OLG Köln, NJW 1997, 3179.

BGH NJW 1994, 831, 835.

3.1 Court Abbreviations

Courts are normally cited by abbreviation. Federal Courts are referred to simply by their official denomination (e.g., BAG).

All other courts are referred to by level and location (e.g., AG Bonn). Some courts have kept their traditional names and are usually cited by them (e.g., KG or *Kammergericht,* instead of OLG Berlin; HansOLG or *Hanseatisches Oberlandesgericht* instead of OLG Hamburg; BayVGH or *Bayerischer Verwaltungsgerichtshof* instead of VGH München).

The names and abbreviations for courts include:

Federal Constitutional Court: *Bundesverfassungsgericht* (BVerfG)
State Constitutional Court: *Landesverfassungsgericht* (LVerfG)
Federal Court of Justice: *Bundesgerichtshof* (BGH)
BGH's predecessor court: *Reichsgericht* (RG)
BGH, *en banc: Bundesgerichtshof Großer Senat* (BGH GS)
BGH, *en banc,* for civil matters: *Bundesgerichtshof Großer Senat für Zivilsachen* (BGH GS Z)
BGH, *en banc,* for criminal matters: *Bundesgerichtshof Großer Senat für Strafsachen* (BGH GS St)
BGH, united *en banc* panels: *Vereinigte Große Senat*
Common Chamber of Supreme Federal Courts: *Gemeinsamer Senat* (GmS)

Local court (ordinary): *Amtsgericht* (AG)
Regional court (ordinary): *Landgericht* (LG)
Regional court of appeals (ordinary): *Oberlandesgericht* (OLG)
Supreme court of appeals (ordinary) for Bavaria: *Bayerisches Oberstes Landesgericht* (BayObLG)
Local labor court: *Arbeitsgericht* (ArbG)
Labor court of appeals: *Landesarbeitsgericht* (LAG)
Federal Labor Court: *Bundesarbeitsgericht* (BAG)
Local administrative court: *Verwaltungsgericht* (VG)
Administrative court of appeals: *Oberverwaltungsgericht* (OVG) or *Verwaltungsgerichtshof* (VGH)
Federal Administrative Court: *Bundesverwaltungsgericht* (BVerwG)
Local social court: *Sozialgericht* (SG)
Social court of appeals: *Landessozialgericht* (LSG)
Federal Social Court: *Bundessozialgericht* (BSG)
Finance court: *Finanzgericht* (FG)
Federal Finance Court: *Bundesfinanzhof* (BFH)
Federal Court for Patent Matters: *Bundespatentgericht* (BPatG)

3.2 Reports

Official reporters (and abbreviations) are:

Federal Constitutional Court reporter: *Entscheidungen des Bundesverfassungsgerichts* (BVerfGE)

Federal Labor Court reporter: *Entscheidungen des Bundesarbeitsgerichts* (BAGE)

Federal Administrative Court reporter: *Entscheidungen des Bundesverwaltungsgerichts* (BVerwGE)

Federal Social Court reporter: *Entscheidungen des Bundessozialgerichts* (BSGE)

Federal Finance Court reporter: *Sammlung der Entscheidungen und Gutachten des Bundesfinanzhofs* (BFHE)

Federal Court of Justice reporter in civil matters: *Entscheidungen des Bundesgerichtshofs in Zivilsachen* (BGHZ)

The Federal Court of Justice reporter in criminal matters: *Entscheidungen des Bundesgerichtshofs in Strafsachen* (BGHSt)

Reichsgericht reporter in civil matters (now defunct): *Entscheidungen des Reichsgerichts in Zivilsachen* (RGZ)

Reichsgericht reporter in criminal matters (now defunct): *Entscheidungen des Reichsgerichts in Strafsachen* (RGSt)

Some lower level courts also have their own reporters, for example, Decisions of the Bavarian Supreme Court of Appeals in Criminal Matters, *Entscheidungen des Bayerischen Obersten Landesgerichts in Strafsachen* (BayObLGSt), or Decisions of the Court of Appeals in Criminal Matters, *Entscheidungen der Oberlandesgerichte in Strafsachen* (OLGSt).

Parallel citations, especially if the decision was also published in one of the major journals (such as the weekly *Neue Juristische Wochenschrift*, cited NJW) are frequently used, but not required.

III.   SELECTED REFERENCES

DAVID P. CURRIE, THE CONSTITUTION OF THE FEDERAL REPUBLIC OF GERMANY (Chicago University Press 1997).

DONALD P. KOMMERS, THE CONSTITUTIONAL JURISPRUDENCE OF THE FEDERAL REPUBLIC OF GERMANY (2d ed., Duke University Press 1997).

G R E E C E

Elliniki Dhimokratia (Hellenic Republic)

I. COUNTRY PROFILE (CIVIL LAW)

The modern Greek state, officially known as the Hellenic Republic, was established in 1830. Greece is a presidential, parliamentarian democracy. Its legal system is based on the civil law tradition. Greece became a full member of the European Union in 1981.

The Constitution, the fundamental written law of the country, follows the doctrine of separation of powers and provides numerous checks and balances. Executive power is vested in the Greek government, legislative power is vested in Parliament, and judicial powers are vested in the courts.

The President of the Republic is the head of state. Under the Constitution, as amended in 1975 and 1986, the President's role is primarily ceremonial. The President is elected by a two-thirds vote of the Members of Parliament for a term of five years. Executive powers are vested in the Prime Minister and the Ministerial Cabinet. The Prime Minister is usually the head of the political party that achieved a majority of votes during the most recent elections. He or she selects the members of the Ministerial Cabinet. The Cabinet and the Prime Minister must enjoy the support of a majority of the members of the Parliament throughout their term.

Parliament consists of a single body with 300 members. Members of Parliament are directly elected by popular vote every four years.

The Greek legal system is separated into two main categories: public and private. The hierarchy of legal rules includes the Constitution, International Treaties, Laws and Customs, Presidential Decrees, and Administrative Acts. Most important laws are codified by category. Examples include the Civil Code, Commercial Code, Penal Code, Code of Civil Procedure, Code of Criminal Procedure, Code of Private Maritime Law, Code of Public Maritime Law, Code of Administrative Procedure, and Military Penal Code. Jurisprudence, scholars' opinions, and other legal literature are not considered formal sources of law, owing partly to Greece's civil law background. Judicial precedent, however, especially decisions of the Supreme Civil and Criminal Court (*Areios Pagos*), is often reflected in legislative actions and amendments.

Judicial power is vested in civil, criminal, and administrative courts. All judges are appointed for life by the President of the respective court after consultation with a judicial council. The Constitution lays out in detail the procedure for the appointment of judges, their privileged salary scales, and acts and responsibilities deemed incompatible with their judicial functions. It also provides for their independence. Each type of court is divided into courts of first instance and courts of appeal. In addition, the Supreme Court hears appeals of civil and criminal decisions. The Supreme Civil and Criminal Court does not make find-ings of fact; it focuses only on legal issues and the correct interpretation of the applicable law. The Supreme Civil and Criminal Court does not have discretion-ary power to choose the cases it hears.

The Council of State (*Symboulio tis Epikrateias*) is the supreme administrative law court. The Council of State hears appeals from lower court decisions. It also has original jursidiction over cases involving requests for annulment of illegal and harmful administrative decisions and acts. Like the Supreme Civil and Criminal Court, the Council of State does not have discretionary power to choose the cases it hears.

The Audit Court (*Elegktiko Synedrio*) has jurisdiction over matters involving state funds, such as national income, state salaries, and state financial transac-tions. The Audit Court's primary function is to review and consent to any draft of law containing financial provisions before it is voted on in Parliament.

Finally, the Special Supreme Court (*Anotato Eidiko Dikastirio*) is made up of the presidents of the Council of State, the Supreme Court, and the Audit Court, together with four councillors of the Council of State and four judges of the Supreme Civil and Criminal Court who are appointed by ballot every two years. The Special Supreme Court is a permanent court, which hears cases involving the validity of parliamentary elections, and the resolution of contradictory rulings among the three supreme courts or other high courts, especially in matters of national and social importance. Like the Supreme Civil and Criminal Court and the Council of State, this court does not have discretionary power to choose the cases it hears.

Internet Resources:

Athens Bar Association:	http://www.dsa.gr
Greek Parliament:	http://www.parliament.gr
Greek Ministry of Justice:	http://www.ministryofjustice.gr
Greek Ministry of Development:	http://www.ypan.gr

II. CITATION GUIDE

Although there are no binding rules regarding citation, and there is no national citation manual in Greece, citation is quite uniform in legal literature and court cases.

1.0 Constitution

Cite the Constitution by article ("Arthro" or "Ar."), clause (in parentheses), and followed by the word "Syntagma" (Constitution) or its abbreviation "Synt.":

Arthro 4 (2a) Synt.

2.0 Legislation

2.1 Statutes, Laws, and Presidential Decrees

Cite statutes, laws, and decrees by type (either the full word, e.g., "Nomos," or the abbreviated form, e.g., "N."), registered number and year [number/year], the word "Arthro" or "Ar." (Article), and clause (in parentheses):

N. 513/2000 Ar. 16 (5).

PD 663/2001 Ar.15 (6).

YA 54/1999 Ar. 4 (3).

Basic legal rules for titles (and abbreviations) are:

Law or Statute: *Nomos* (N.)
Presidential Decree: *Proedriko Diatagma* (PD)
Ministerial Decision: *Ypourgiki Apofasi* (YA)
Multi-Ministerial Decision: *Diypourgiki Apofasi* (DYA)

2.2 Official Gazette

Citations to legislative sources may refer to the Official Gazette. Cite sources published in the Official Gazette by abbreviated title of the gazette ("FEK"), series ("A," "B," etc.), and number and date of publication [number/day.month.year]:

FEK A' 53/18.06.2003.

FEK B' 12/3.05.2000.

2.3 Codes

Cite codes by "Ar." followed by article number, and abbreviated title:

Ar. 14 AK.

Ar. 9 PK.

The abbreviations for major codes are:

Civil Code: *Astikos Kodikas* (AK)
Penal Code: *Pinikos Kodikas* (PK)

Code of Civil Procedure: *Kodikas Politikis Dikonomias* (KPolD)
Code of Criminal Procedure: *Kodikas Pinikis Dikonomias* (KPD)
Administrative Law Procedure: *Kodikas Diikitikis Dikonomias* (KDD)
Code of Private Maritime Law: *Kodikas Idiotikou Naftikou Dikaiou* (KIND)
Code of Public Maritime Law: *Kodikas Dimosiou Naftikou Dikaiou*
   (KDND)
European Community Treaty: *Synthiki Europaikis Kinotitas* (SynthEK)

3.0 Jurisprudence

Whereas there are no official reporters in Greece, many important cases are
reprinted in major journals, which can be said to function primarily as reporters.
Such journals also include secondary legal materials, such as articles and comments on reprinted cases. Cite cases published in such reporters by abbreviated
title of the reporter, volume number and year [number/year], first page of the
decision, and page referenced:

N.B. 17/2000, 105, 107.

Ell.Dik. 545/1996, 103, 105.

Cite other cases by registration number and year [number/year], abbreviated
court name, and seat of the court and the special jurisprudence, if any (in
parentheses):

657/2003 Mon.Pr. Ath. (Asf. Metra).

345/1980 Trim.Dioik.Prot. Ath.

3.1 Court Abbreviations

Abbreviate court names by the first two or three letters of their names and the
place of their seat, if multiple, and special jurisdiction (in parentheses):

One-Member Court of First Instance in Athens, provisional measures
   jurisdiction (Mon.Pr. Ath. (asf.m.))
Court of Appeals in Patras (Ef. Patrwn)
Council of State: *Symboulio tis Epikrateias* (StE)
Supreme Civil and Criminal Court: *Areios Pagos* (AP)
Audit Court: *Elegktiko Synedrio* (E.S.)
Special Supreme Court: *Anotato Eidiko Dikastirio* (AED)
Administrative Court of Appeals in Thessaloniki (D.Ef. Thes.)

3.2 Reports

Case reporters are not published by the courts but rather by private high academic committees. The names and abbreviations of the reporters are:

For civil cases: *Nomikos Kodikas* (Nom.Kod.)

For civil and commercial cases: *Epitheorisi Emporikou Dikaiou* (E.Emp.D.); *Elliniki Dikaiosini* (Ell.Dik.); *Nomiko Bima* (N.B.)

For public law cases (administrative and constitutional law): *Efarmoges Dimosiou Dikaiou* (Efarmoges D.D.); *Diikitiki Diki* (D.D.); *To Syntagma* (ToS)

For maritime law cases: *Nautiki Dikaiosini* (N.D.); *Peiraiki Nomologia* (P.N.)

III.   SELECTED REFERENCES

N. ANDROULAKIS, POINIKO DIKAIO GENIKO MEROS THEORIA GIA TO EGKLIMA [GENERAL PENAL LAW — CRIME THEORY] (2000).

A. GEORGIADIS, GENIKES ARXES ASTIKOU DIKAIOU [GENERAL PRINCIPLES OF CIVIL LAW] (1997).

K. MAURIAS, SYNTAGMATIKO DIKAIO-THEORIA TOU KRATOUS, POLITEUMA, LEITOURGIES TOU KRATOUS [CONSTITUTIONAL LAW — THE STATE, THE REPUBLIC AND THE STRUCTURE OF THE AUTHORITIES] (2000).

M. P. STATHOPOULOS, GENIKO ENOXIKO DIKAIO [GENERAL PENAL LAW] (1998).

HONG KONG

Xianggang Tebie Xingzhengqu (Hong Kong Special Administrative Region)

I. REGION PROFILE (COMMON LAW)

The People's Republic of China resumed sovereignty over Hong Kong on July 1, 1997. Under the "One Country, Two Systems" principle, China's system and policies are not practiced in the Hong Kong Special Administrative Region (HKSAR), and Hong Kong's existing system is to remain unchanged until 2047. The Chinese government is, however, responsible for Hong Kong's defense and foreign affairs. As a result of Hong Kong's colonial past, the official languages of Hong Kong are both Chinese (a dialect is not specified) and English, and Hong Kong's legal system is based on the Anglo-American common law tradition.

The Basic Law is Hong Kong's primary constitutional document. The Basic Law was adopted on April 4, 1990, by a joint Hong Kong–Mainland drafting committee and formally took effect on July 1, 1997, with the handover of Hong Kong to the People's Republic of China.

Under the Basic Law, the Government of the HKSAR is divided into three branches. Executive power is vested in the Government of Hong Kong, headed by a Chief Executive selected by the Central People's Government. The Executive Council assists the Chief Executive in formulating policy. The Government is organized into the Government Secretariat and several departments. The Government Secretariat formulates policies and initiates legislative proposals, while the Departments implement laws and policies and provide direct services to the public.

Legislative power is vested in the Legislative Council. The Legislative Council enacts legislation, approves public expenditures, and monitors the performance of the Government. The vast majority of statutory law is made locally and is contained in the Laws of Hong Kong. Additionally, a great deal of legislation, known as "subsidiary legislation," is made under delegated powers. Legislation by the Legislative Council must also be reported to the Standing Committee of the People's Congress. The Standing Committee can then return the legislation if it deems it to be in contradiction to the Basic Law, whereupon it is immediately invalidated.

Judicial power is vested in an independent Judiciary. The Judiciary consists of the Court of Final Appeal, the High Court (which comprises the Court of Appeal and the Court of First Instance), the District Court, the Magistrate's Court, the Coroner's Court, and the Juvenile Court. Additionally, there are tribunals that have special jurisdiction to adjudicate disputes concerning specific areas, including, for example, the Lands Tribunal, the Labor Tribunal, the Small Claims Tribunal, and the Obscene Articles Tribunal.

The Court of Final Appeal has the power of final adjudication. The Chief Justice of the Court of Final Appeal is the head of the Judiciary, both in a judicial and an administrative sense. He is assisted on the administrative support side by a Judiciary Administrator. On the judicial side, the courts are presided over by judges with professional legal qualifications and experience from both Hong Kong and other common law jurisdictions. Some senior judges are recruited from among eminent local barristers, while others are promoted from within the Judiciary or from senior posts in the Department of Justice. In addition, there are Registrars and Deputy Registrars who relieve the judges of much "chambers" work (i.e., the work done before, after, or instead of full court proceedings).

Internet Resources:

Legislative Council Annual Report:	http://www.legco.gov.hk/index.htm
Hong Kong Law Reform Commission:	http://www.info.gov.hk/hkreform
The Hong Kong Government:	http://library.ust.hk/guides/legal/hkgazsupp.html
The Hong Kong Government Gazette:	http://www.gld.gov.hk/cgi-bin/gld/egazette/index.cgi?lang=e&agree=0
Archive of Consultation (Green) Papers:	http://www.info.gov.hk/policy_f.htm

II. CITATION GUIDE

There is no uniform code of citation in Hong Kong. The following reflects the citation practice, which is generally followed, of the *Hong Kong Law Journal,* the leading English language scholarly journal on common law in Hong Kong.

1.0 Basic Law

Cite the Basic Law by title (often abbreviated "BL," but also referred to as "Basic Law" or "HK Basic Law"), and subdivision(s) referenced with the basic format of "BL Chapter-Number(Section Number)(Article Number)." Add "[Constitution]" after the title if it is unlikely to be understood that the Basic Law is

Hong Kong's "Constitution." Similarly, add "(H.K.)" at the end if it is unclear what the citation is referencing:

BL 24(2)(4).

Basic Law [Constitution] 24(2)(4) (H.K.).

BL 1(3).

2.0 Legislation and Other Non-Judicial Sources of Law

2.1 Hong Kong Legislation

Cite legislation as originally enacted by reference number and year. If the short title of the ordinance is included in a citation, the reference number and year (in parentheses) should follow the title:

No. 4 of 2000.

Title of Ordinance (No. 4 of 2000).

Cite subsidiary legislation by adding the words "sub leg" (in parentheses):

The Rules of Bankruptcy (sub leg, Cap 6).

2.2 U.K. Legislation

Cite U.K. legislation by title and year (no comma), followed by ("s" or "ss") and section(s) referenced:

Hong Kong Act 1985, ss 9, 10.

2.3 References

Major references to Hong Kong laws include *Annotated Ordinances of Hong Kong* and *Halsbury's Laws of Hong Kong.*

3.0 Jurisprudence

Cite cases by full name of the parties (italicized), separated with a "v.", year (in square brackets if the year of publication is used as a proxy for volume, and in parentheses if a separate volume number exists), volume (if available), abbreviated title of the reporter in which the case is published, first page of the case, and page referenced:

Party-A v. Party-B [1998] 2 ITLJ 545 at 553.

Party (1997) 49 Cr App R 83.

Party (n 1 above), p 84.

3.1 Reports

For *Hong Kong Cases* (HKC) and *Hong Kong Law Reports* (HKLR), the date or the name of the court is not needed:

Eastman Kodak, Inc. v. Seven-Eleven Corp. [1999] 3 HKC 123.

For unreported cases or cases online, include the case number, date, and court:

Eastman Kodak, Inc. v. Seven-Eleven Corp. unrep., Companies Winding-up No. 112 of 1998 (Court of First Instance, 10 May 1999), at 5, http://website.com.

Major law reports are:

The Authorized Hong Kong Court of Final Appeal Reports (HKCFAR)
The Authorized Hong Kong Law Reports & Digest (HKLR)
Hong Kong Cases (HKC)
Hong Kong Inland Revenue Board of Review Decisions
Hong Kong Public Law Reports
Hong Kong Tax Cases

I N D I A

Republic of India

I. COUNTRY PROFILE (COMMON LAW)

India is a sovereign, socialist, secular, democratic republic. The country is composed of 28 states and seven centrally administered union territories. The national language of India is Hindi. English and various languages that are spoken in the various states and territories are, however, recognized as official languages by the Indian Constitution.

The Indian Constitution is an elaborate and comprehensive document containing 395 articles, divided into 22 parts and twelve schedules. It was adopted on January 26, 1950. The head of the Executive branch of government is the President of India. The President's duties, however, are primarily ceremonial. In reality, and as required by the constitution, the President is required to exercise his or her powers on the advice of the Council of Ministers, which is led by the Prime Minister. A special electoral college elects the President. The Vice President is elected by the members of both houses of Parliament assembled at a joint meeting. The President and Vice President are elected to five-year terms. The Prime Minister is nominated by the political party or coalition commanding a parliamentary majority and is appointed by the President. Subordinate ministers are appointed by the President on the advice of the Prime Minister.

Legislative power is vested in a bicameral parliament, consisting of the House of the People (*Lok Sabha*) and the Council of States (*Rajya Sabha*). The *Lok Sabha* includes 552 members of whom 530 represent the states, 20 represent the union territories, and two are appointed by the President. The *Rajya Sabha* includes 233 members elected by the state and union territory legislatures and twelve members appointed by the President. Members of the *Rajya Sabha* serve six-year terms; one-third of the members are elected every two years.

Judicial power is vested in the Supreme Court, high courts, and people's courts (*Lok adalats*). The Supreme Court of India is the court of final appeal. It consists of a Chief Justice and 25 associate justices, all of whom are appointed by the President.

The High Court is the highest court of appeal (for both criminal and civil matters) in each state, and it also heads each state's judicial administration. Each state is divided into judicial districts presided over by a district judge, who is the highest judicial authority in a district. Below the district judge, there are courts of civil jurisdiction, known in different states as *munsifs*, sub-judges, or civil judges.

The criminal courts consist of the sessions courts and the magistrates courts. Family law questions are dealt with according to the religious affiliations of the parties.

Many state legislatures are bicameral, patterned after the national Parliament. The states' Chief Ministers are responsible to the legislatures in the same way that the Prime Minister is responsible to Parliament. Each state also has a presidentially appointed Governor, who may assume certain broad powers when directed by the central government.

Internet Resources:

Government of India:	http://www.nic.in
Judgment Information System:	http://judis.nic.in
Indian Courts:	http://indiancourts.nic.in

II. CITATION GUIDE

India does not have a uniform citation standard, and citation practices vary considerably among authors.

1.0 Constitution

Cite the Constitution by title ("Constitution of India, 1950" or "CONSTUTITION OF INDIA, 1950"), followed by "art." and article referenced. A less official, abbreviated title may also be used:

INDIA CONST. (1950) art. 325.

1.1 Other Foundational Sources of Law

Cite the Government of India Act by title, year (in parentheses), and passage referenced:

Government of India Act, (Year).

Cite Constitutional Assembly Debates by volume, "C.A.D.", and page referenced:

10 C.A.D. 60.

2.0 Legislation

Citation of legislation varies among authors. Typically, cite legislation by section ("s.", "S.", or "Sec."), order ("O."), or rule ("R.") referenced, official title, and year. Alternatively, cite legislation by section ("s.", "S.", or "Sec."), order ("O."), or rule ("R.") referenced, official title, act number, and year:

> s.80 (2), Code of Civil Procedure, 1908.

> R. 2, Code of Civil Procedure, Act No. 5 of 1908

Cite presidential ordinances by passage referenced, official title, and year. If desired, "No." followed by ordinance number and "of" may be inserted between title and year:

> S. 4, Arbitration and Conciliation Ordinance, 1996.

> Sec. 5 (1), Arbitration and Conciliation Ordinance, No. 5 of 1996.

There is no uniform system of referring to delegated legislation in India, and citation forms vary dramatically. Legislation may be cited by abbreviated description of the legislation, title of the law or issuing authority, and publication in which the legislation is contained (Gazette of India, abbreviated GAZ. INDIA, or State Government page) by volume, title, page, and place and date of publication:

> Noti. 3/154, Passport Act, 1968, Ministry of External Affairs, 1072 GAZ. INDIA 246, New Delhi, 24 Dec 1974.

The abbreviations of legislation are:

> Government Order (G.O.)
> Notification (Noti.)
> Special Government Order (S.G.O.)

2.1 Major Laws and Codes

Major compilations of statutes and laws may be divided into Central and State Acts. On occasion the Acts permit the administration to frame regulations under such acts. Some major Central Acts are:

> Arbitration Act 1996
> Code of Civil Procedure 1908
> Code of Criminal Procedure
> Companies Act 1956
> Copyright Act 1957
> Foreign Exchange Management Act (and various foreign exchange regulations framed under the Act)
> Indian Contract Act
> Industrial Disputes Act 1947
> Indian Trade Union Act 1926
> Income Tax Act
> Negotiable Instruments Act 1881
> Payment of Wages Act

Securities and Exchange Board of India Act (and various securities regulations framed under the Act)
Trademark Act 1999
Transfer of Property Act
Workmen's Compensation Act

3.0 Jurisprudence

Typically, cite reported cases by party name [plaintiff or appellant "v." respondent], and reporter in which the case is published by year or volume (in parentheses), abbreviated title, first page of the case, and page referenced:

S. R. Bommai v. Union of India, (1994) (3) S.C.C. 1, 12.

For decisions of the Privy Council, which existed until 1949, cite to the I.A., A.I.R., or India Cases.

For decisions of the Supreme Court or Federal Court between 1937 and 1950, cite to the S.C.R. or to a reporter listed below, which refers to either court.

For a High Court, Supreme Court, Court of the Judicial Commissioner, or Sadar Dewani Adalats, cite to the S.C.C., A.I.R., Indian Decisions, or I.L.R. Indicate the jurisdiction of the court in parentheses after A.I.R. or I.L.R., as there are different series for each state and region:

1991 A.I.R. 20 (Mad.) 83.

3.1 Reporters

Major reporters and their abbreviations include:

All India Reporter (A.I.R.)
Indian Decisions (Ind. Dec.)
Indian Law Reports (I.L.R.)
Supreme Court Reports (S.C.R.)
Supreme Court Journal (S.C.J.)
Supreme Court Cases (S.C.C.)
Supreme Court Almanac (S.C.A.L.E.)

Previous reporters that no longer exist include:

Indian Cases (Indian Cas.)
Law Reports, Privy (I.App.)
Council, Indian Appeals (I.A.)
Federal Court Reports (F.C.R.)
Federal Law Journal (F.L.J.)

There are also several unofficial law reports that cover particular jurisdictions or areas of law.

3.2 Unreported Decisions

Citation formats for unreported cases vary. Typically, cite unreported cases by name of the parties [plaintiff or appellant "v." respondent], abbreviated type of case (see list below), "No. __ of [year]," abbreviated name of the court (listed above), location of the court (if below a high court), and date of the decision:

> Dr. Ajay Kumar Singh v. District Magistrate, Dhanbad, No. 156 of 1996, C.A. H.C. Pat., 15 May 1997.

Types of cases (and abbreviations) include:

Civil Appeal (C.A.)
Criminal Appeal (Cr.A.)
Criminal Case (C.C.)
Civil Suit (C.S.)
Civil Revision Petition (C.R.P.)
Criminal Miscellaneous Petition (Cr.M.P.)
First Appeal (F.A.)
Habeas Corpus Petition (H.C.P.)
Interlocutory Application (I.A.)
Letters Patent Appeal (L.P.A.)
Miscellaneous First Appeal (M.F.A.)
Original Suit (O.S.)
Original Side Appeal (O.S.A.)
Second Appeal (S.A.)
Special Leave Petition (S.L.P.)
Tax Case (T.C.)
Writ Appeal (W.A.)
Writ Petition — Civil (W.P.(C.))
Writ Petition — Criminal (W.P.(Cri.))

3.3 Names and Common Abbreviations of Courts and Jurisdictions

Cite the currently operational courts, the Superior Courts and High Courts, as ([region] H.C.).

There are 20 High Courts in India, with territorial jurisdiction in appellate and constitutional matters over one or more States. Four High Courts have jurisdiction to hear original civil matters. Names (and abbreviations) for these jurisdictions are as follows:

Bombay (Bom.)
Madras (Mad.)
Calcutta (Cal.)

Chhattisgarh (C.G.)
Delhi (Del.)
Andhra Pradesh (A.P.)
Gauhati (Gau.)
Patna (Pat.)
Himachal Pradesh (H.P.)
Sikkim (Sik.)
Kerala (Ker.)
Karnataka (Kant.)
Orissa (Ori.)
Madhya Pradesh (M.P.)
Punjab & Haryana (P. & H.)
Jammu & Kashmir (J. & K.)
Jharkhand (Jhark.)
Allahabad (All.)
Rajasthan (Raj.)
Gujarat (Guj.)

Subordinate Courts include:

District & Sessions Court (D. & S.C.)
Magistrate's Court (M.C.)
Civil Court (C.C.)
Metropolitan Magistrate's Court (M.M.C.)

Quasi-Judicial Forums and Tribunals include:

Income Tax Appellate Tribunal (I.T.A.T.)
Land Reforms Appellate Tribunal (L.R.A.T.)
Sales Tax Appellate Tribunal (S.T.A.T.)
Motor Vehicles Tribunal (M.V.T.)
Rent Recovery Tribunal (R.R.T.)
Monopolies and Restrictive Trade Practices Commission (M.R.T.P.C.)
Central Administrative Tribunal (C.A.T.)
State Administrative Tribunal (S.A.T.)
Joint Administrative Tribunal (J.A.T.)
Central Excise, Gold, Appellate Tribunal (C.E.G.A.T.)
Company Law Board (C.L.B.)
Debt Recovery Tribunal (D.R.T.)
National Human Rights Commission (N.H.R.C.)
Board of Industrial and Financial Reconstruction (B.I.F.R.)

Names (and abbreviations) of places in which High Courts of British India sat, and other defunct High Courts, and Courts of Judicial Commissioners that have since been abolished were located include:

Sindh (Sindh)
Lahore (Lah.)
Goa (Goa)
Oudh (Oudh)
Punjab (Punj.)

Courts no longer in existence or which no longer have jurisdiction over Indian matters include:

Privy Council (P.C.)
Federal Court (F.C.)
Court of the Judicial Commissioner (C.J.C.)
Supreme Court at Calcutta (Calcutta S.C.)
Sadar Dewani Adalat (S.D.)

I R E L A N D

Éire (Republic of Ireland)

I. COUNTRY PROFILE (COMMON LAW)

Ireland is a parliamentary republic. Irish Gaelic (*Gaeilge*) is the official first language, but English is universally spoken; legislation appears in both languages. The modern Irish state was established in 1937. The Republic of Ireland consists of 26 of the 32 counties that make up the island of Ireland. The remaining six counties in the northeast form Northern Ireland, which is part of the United Kingdom. Formal ties with the Commonwealth were ended on April 18 1949, when the 26 southern counties became a republic. The Irish legal system is based on English common law tradition, substantially modified by indigenous concepts.

Legislative power is vested in the bicameral National Parliament (*Oireachtas*). Parliament consists of the President and two houses (Houses of the *Oireachtas*): the Senate (the *Seanad Eireann*) and the House of Representatives (the *Dáil Eireann*). The President is directly elected by the people to a seven-year term and may not serve more than two terms. The President is the constitutional head of state, but this is a largely ceremonial role and does not entail executive authority. All legislation passed by Parliament, however, must be presented to the President for final approval. The President may refer legislation to the Supreme Court if a question of constitutionality arises. The President also dissolves the Parliament on the Prime Minister's (*Taoiseach*'s) advice, although this power is discretionary if the Prime Minister has ceased to retain a majority of Parliament.

The 60 members of the Senate are either nominated or elected as follows: 11 members are nominated by the Prime Minister, six members are elected by the national universities, and 43 members are elected from panels of candidates established on a vocational basis. The 166 members of the House of Representatives are directly elected by universal adult suffrage to a maximum term of five years under a complex system of proportional representation.

Primary legislation is passed through Acts of the Parliament, and subordinate legislation is made by Government Ministers under powers conferred on them by Acts. The vast majority of legislation is formulated in this House. Bills to amend the Constitution and financial legislation can only be initiated in the House of Representatives. The Senate does have the power to delay legislative proposals and is allowed 90 days to consider and amend bills sent to it by the House of

97

Representatives. The Senate, however, may only make recommendations as to financial legislation, and this must be done within 21 days (as opposed to the normal 90).

Executive power is vested in the Government. The Government consists of the Prime Minister and at least six, but not more than 15, cabinet ministers who meet and act as a collective authority. Formally, the Prime Minister and cabinet ministers are appointed by the President, with the approval of or on the nomination of the House of Representatives. Effectively, the Prime Minister is elected by the political party or coalition of parties that holds a majority of the seats in the House of Representatives. Cabinet ministers are nominated by the Prime Minister and approved by the House of Representatives. In addition to exercising executive authority, the Government acts in an administrative and legislative role. The Government is also responsible for managing public finances, and only the Government may introduce financial legislation in the House of Representatives. If the Prime Minister loses the support of the majority of the House of Representatives, the result is either the dissolution of the House of Representatives and a general election, or the formation of a successor Government.

The Irish Constitution (*Bunreacht na Éireann*), enacted in 1937, is Ireland's fundamental legal document. The Constitution describes the main institutions of the state and establishes the legislative, executive, and judicial branches of government. It also recognizes and declares certain fundamental personal rights.

Judicial power is vested in public courts established by law. Judges are appointed by the President on the advice of the Government. The courts consist of the following: The court of first instance is the District Court (*an Chuirt Duiche*), which hears minor cases. More serious cases are heard in the Circuit Court (*an Chuirt Chuarda*). The High Court (*an Ard-Chuirt*) has full original jurisdiction in, and power to determine, all matters and questions, whether of law or fact, civil or criminal. The High Court consists of the President and 35 ordinary judges. When exercising its criminal jurisdiction, the High Court is known as the Central Criminal Court. The jurisdiction of the High Court extends to the question of the constitutional validity of any law (except laws that the President has already referred to the Supreme Court), and no such question may be raised in any court other than the High Court or the Supreme Court. The High Court also hears appeals from decisions of the Circuit Court in civil matters. The High Court additionally has power to review the decisions of all inferior tribunals by the issue of prerogative orders of mandamus, prohibition, and certiorari.

The Supreme Court (*an Chuirt Uachtarach*) consists of the Chief Justice (who is *ex officio* an additional judge of the High Court) and seven ordinary judges. The Supreme Court has final appellate jurisdiction. The Supreme Court also has original jurisdiction to decide whether a bill referred to it by the President is repugnant to the Constitution. If a question of the permanent incapacity of the President arises, it is decided by the Supreme Court.

Internet Resources:

British and Irish Legal Information Institute:	http://www.bailii.org/
CIA World Factbook:	https://www.cia.gov/library/ publications/the-world-factbook/geos/ei.html
Courts Service of Ireland:	http://www.courts.ie
Europa World Yearbook:	http://www.europaworld.com/ entry/ie.dir.2
Government of Ireland:	http://www.irlgov.ie
Irish Law Site at UCC:	http://www.ucc.ie/ucc/depts/law/ irishlaw

II.   CITATION GUIDE

1.0 Constitution

Cite the Constitution by title (either in English, "Constitution of Ireland, 1937," or in Irish, "*Bunreacht na Éireann*, 1937"), preceded or followed by "Art." or "Article" and article number:

Art. 2, Constitution of Ireland, 1937.

Constitution of Ireland, 1937, Article 40.1.

The "Constitution of the Irish Free State, 1922" (*Bunreacht na Saorstát Éireann*) may be cited for the previous Irish Constitution (1922-1937).

2.0 Legislation and Other Non-Judicial Sources of Law

Cite acts by title and year, followed by "Section," "s.", or "Sec." and section referenced (if appropriate):

Limited Liability Act, 1855.

Companies Act, 1963, s.2(i).

Safety Health & Welfare at Work Act, 1989, Section 6(1).

Cite statutory instruments by "S.I.", the S.I. number, and year:

S.I. No. 156 of 1968.

S.I. No. 133 of 1983.

Cite statutory rules and orders (1922-1947) by "S.R. & O," the number, and year:

S.R. & O No. 2081 of 1933.

99

Statutes are compiled in Acts of the Oireachtas (1937-present) and Acts of the Oireachtas (*Saorstát Éireann*) (1922-1937).

2.1 Treaties and Conventions

Cite treaties and conventions as described in Section 1.0 of Part II, on Treaties and Conventions, filling in the source information with the Irish treaty series by year, "Ir. T.S.", and treaty number:

[Treaty information], 1930 Ir. T.S., No. 1, [date of entry, etc.].

3.0 Jurisprudence

Cite cases by name of the parties involved (optional), year (in square brackets), volume, abbreviated title of the reporter in which the case is published, and first page or page referenced. The deciding court may also be parenthetically placed:

Phipps -v- Judge Hogan [2007] IE.S.C. 68 (20 December 2007) (Ireland Supreme Court).

D.P.P.-v- Adam Keane [2007] IE.C.C.A. 119 (19 December 2007) (Ireland Criminal Court of Appeal).

Traffic Group Ltd -v- Companies Acts [2007] IE.H.C. 445 (20 December 2007) (Ireland High Court).

[1990] E.L.R. 155.

[1993] 1 IR 102 (High Court).

3.1 Court Names

Court names (and abbreviations) are as follows:

Supreme Court (IE.S.C.)
High Court (IE.H.C.)
Court of Criminal Appeal (IE.C.C.A.)

3.2 Reports

Major law reporters are entitled and abbreviated as follows (all but those with asterisks are presently defunct):

Employment Law Reports (E.L.R. or ELR)*
Irish Company Law Reports (I.C.L.R. or ICLR)
Irish Reports (I.R. or IR)*
Irish Law Times Reports (I.L.T.R. or ILTR)
Irish Law Reports Monthly (I.L.R.M. or ILRM)*

Irish Law Reports (I.L.R. or ILR)
Irish Jurist Reports (Ir.Jur.Rep.)
Frewen (Frewen)

3.3 Unreported Cases

Cite unreported cases by name of the parties (optional), "Unreported," name of the court, and date of the decision:

Prows v Frendo Unreported Supreme Court 15th December 1977.

4.0 Official Publications

Cite Senate debates by volume, title, column, and date (in parentheses):

99 SEANAD DEB. Col. 555 (Feb. 28, 2000).

Cite House of Representatives debates by volume, title, column, and date (in parentheses):

99 DÁIL DEB. Col. 555 (Feb 28, 2000).

III.   SELECTED REFERENCES

RAYMOND BYRNE & J. PAUL MCCUTCHEON, THE IRISH LEGAL SYSTEM (2d ed., Butterworths 1990).

RICHARD H. GRIMES & PATRICK T. HORGAN, INTRODUCTION TO LAW IN THE REPUBLIC OF IRELAND (Wolfhound Press 1981).

H. MURDOCH, A DICTIONARY OF IRISH LAW (Topaz Publications 1988).

I S R A E L

Medinat Yisrael (State of Israel)

I. COUNTRY PROFILE (COMMON LAW)

The State of Israel was founded on May 14, 1948, as a democratic Jewish state. Israel's legal system is based on the common law tradition. The Israeli structure of government is a parliamentary democracy consisting of a legislative, executive, and judicial branch. Its institutions are the Presidency (Head of State), the Government (Cabinet of Ministers), the *Knesset* (Parliament), and the judiciary.

Legislative power is vested in the *Knesset*, which consists of a single, 120-member chamber. Members of the *Knesset* (MKs) are elected every four years via general elections in which voters elect a party and the *Knesset* seats are assigned in proportion to each party's percentage of the total national vote. Each party chooses its own *Knesset* candidates as it sees fit. The major function of the *Knesset* is to enact laws and revise them as necessary. Additional duties include establishing a government, making policy decisions, reviewing government activities, and electing the President of the State and the State Comptroller. Legislation may be presented by an individual *Knesset* member, a group of *Knesset* members, the government as a whole, or a single Minister from within the government.

Executive power is vested in the government. The President of the State is elected by the *Knesset* in a secret vote and serves in a largely ceremonial capacity for a seven-year term. The President selects the party leader most able to form a government, usually the head of the largest party in the *Knesset*, to serve as Prime Minister. The Prime Minister functions as the head of Government and exercises executive power. Other ministers are appointed by the Prime Minister with the *Knesset*'s approval. These ministers are typically responsible for one or more government ministries but may also serve as a Minister Without Portfolio.

Israel's fundamental law is composed of the Basic Laws. Currently, there are 11 Basic Laws, outlining the fundamental features of the Israeli government. Thus, Israel currently has no formal, single-document constitution. Individual civil rights have been recognized, however, by the Israeli Supreme Court based on two Basic Laws (Human Dignity and Liberty and Freedom of Occupation) as well as other general rights that have been recognized in Israeli jurisprudence.

After independence, the *Knesset* enacted the Law and Administration Ordinance stipulating that laws prevailing in the country prior to statehood would remain in force so long as they did not contradict the principles embodied in the Declaration of the Establishment of Israel or conflict with laws enacted by Parliament. Thus, the legal system includes remnants of Ottoman law, British Mandate laws, elements of Jewish religious law, and some aspects of other systems. The prevailing characteristic of the legal system, however, is the large corpus of independent statutory and case law that has evolved since 1948.

Judicial power is vested in the judiciary, which is divided into two main categories. First, there are general courts of law that have general jurisdiction. The general court of law system is made up of three levels: the Supreme Court, the District Courts, and the Magistrates' Courts. Second, there are tribunals or other authorities of limited jurisdiction. These tribunals include the military courts, the labor courts, the administrative courts, and the religious courts. There are religious courts for the four main religious denominations: Jewish, Muslim, Christian, and Druze. Each of the religious court systems try, on the basis of their respective religious law, cases applying to members of their own religious community who are citizens of the state. The religious courts adjudicate certain matters of family law, with exclusive jurisdiction over some matters (such as marriages and divorces) and with concurrent jurisdiction with the civil courts over other matters. In cases in which secular and religious courts have concurrent jurisdiction, the plaintiff, by choosing the court, determines if religious or state law will be applied. Although Basic Law authorizes the High Court of Justice to review the religious tribunals only on matters concerning their authority, it has expanded its power to intervene in order to liberalize their judgments. There is no jury system. The Supreme Court has supervisory power over all other courts. It is both a court of appeal and a high court of justice, sitting as a court of first instance in constitutional and administrative cases.

Internet Resources:

State of Israel Government Gateway: http://www.info.gov.il
The *Knesset:*   http://www.knesset.gov.il
The Judiciary: http://www.court.gov.il
Israel Ministry of Foreign Affairs: http://www.mfa.gov.il
The State Comptroller and Ombudsman: http://www.mevaker.gov.il
Israel Ministry of Justice: http://www.justice.gov.il
Central Bureau of Statistics: http://www.cbs.gov.il

 CITATION GUIDE

The authoritative source for citing Israeli legal material is a report published in 2006 by the Israel Bar Publishing House, entitled: *Klalei Haizkur Haachid Ba*

Ktiva Hamishpatit. This report is available only in Hebrew and may be accessed in PDF form at: http://www.tau.ac.il/law/izkur/izkur.pdf.

1.0 Constitution

Israel has no formal, single-document constitution. Rather, it has a series of Basic Laws, some of which contain constitutional rights that have been acknowledged by the Israeli Court.

Cite a Basic Law by title, year, official publication ("S.H."), and page referenced:

Basic Law: The Knesset, 1993, S.H. 239.

The existing Basic Laws are:

Basic Law: The Knesset (1958)
Basic Law: Israel Lands (1960)
Basic Law: The President of the State (1964)
Basic Law: The Government (1968 & 2001)
Basic Law: The State Economy (1975)
Basic Law: The Army (1976)

Basic Law: Jerusalem, Capital of Israel (1980)
Basic Law: The Judiciary (1984)
Basic Law: The State Comptroller (1988)
Basic Law: Human Dignity and Liberty (1992)
Basic Law: Freedom of Occupation (1994)

2.0 Legislation and Other Non-Judicial Sources

2.1 Primary or Secondary Legislation

Cite statutes and regulations by title and year in which first promulgated:

The Criminal Act, 1977.

Niarot Erech, 1968.

More formal citations, which include the series in which the statute or regulation is published, are often avoided insofar as such references may create confusion, for example, if the statute has been amended.

Statutes are published in English in the Laws of the State of Israel (L.S.I.). Cite these statutes by volume, "L.S.I.", first page of the statute, and year of publication.

2.2 Legislative Draft Bills

Cite draft legislation by title, year, series in which the legislation is published (*Hatza-ot Hok*, abbreviated H.H.), and first page of the legislation:

Draft Bill Amending the Income Tax Ordinance (No. 21), 1974, H.H., 142.

3.0 Jurisprudence

Cite cases by type of procedure, case number, district, or city in which the court is located if the case was decided by a District or Magistrate Court (in parentheses), name of the parties (in bold, separated by "v."), abbreviated title of the reporter, volume, part (in parentheses), and first page of the case:

Cr. A. 7024/93, **The State of Israel v. Pelach**, P.D. 49 (1) 1.

D. C. A. (T.A.) 780/70, **Iryat Tel-Aviv-Jaffa v. Shulamit Sapir**, P. D. 25 (2) 486.

LC 53/33-3 **Cohen v. Supersal LTD**, PDA 38(1) 39.

3.1 Procedure Types

The two basic procedure types are civil cases (C.C.) and criminal cases (Cr. C.). General motions may be heard in the civil instance as civil motions (C.M.) or in the criminal instance as criminal motions (Cr. M.).

Cases may be heard in a first instance in the Magistrate Court or in the District Court depending on the matter of the case and the amount claimed.

District court cases:

D.C.C. (civil cases as first instance)
D.Cr.C. (criminal cases as first instance)
D.C.M. (general civil motions)
D.Cr.M. (general criminal motions)

Magistrate court cases:

M.C.C. (civil cases)
M.Cr.C. (criminal cases)
M.C.M. (general civil motions)
M.Cr.M. (general criminal motions)

3.2 Districts

If the case is a District Court (D.C.) case, include the abbreviated name of the district in which the court is located (in parentheses) after the type of procedure. The Districts are:

Jerusalem (Jm.)
Tel Aviv (T.A.)
Haifa (Hi.)
Be'er-Sheva (B.S.)
Nazareth (Nz.)

If the case is a Magistrate Court (M.C.) case, include the name of the city in which the court is located (in parentheses) after the type of procedure.

3.3 Other Courts

The highest court of Israel is the Supreme Court (S.Ct.). As a court of first instance, the Supreme Court adjudicates primarily in matters regarding the legality of decisions by state authorities, government decisions, those of local authorities, and decisions by other bodies and persons performing public functions under the law. The Supreme Court has jurisdiction to hear criminal and civil appeals from judgments of the District Courts. Cases that begin in the District Court are appealable, by right, to the Supreme Court. Other matters may be appealed only with the Supreme Court's permission. The Supreme Court has special jurisdiction to hear appeals in matters of *Knesset* elections, rulings of the Civil Service Commission, disciplinary rulings of the Israel Bar Association, administrative detentions, and prisoners' petitions appealed from the District Court. Appeals may be on civil issues (C.A.) or on criminal issues (Cr. A.). Constitutional cases and some administrative cases are heard by the Supreme Court while sitting as the High Court of Justice (H.C.), and the High Court is further a forum for evaluating the legality of the decisions of state authorities.

District Courts (D.C.) are the middle-level courts of the Israeli judiciary. They have jurisdiction in any matter that is not within the sole jurisdiction of another court. In criminal matters, District Courts hear cases where the accused faces more than seven years' imprisonment. In civil cases, District Courts' jurisdiction extends to matters in which more than one million shekels (approximately U.S. $300,000) are in dispute. District Courts also hear cases dealing with companies and partnerships, arbitrations, prisoners' petitions, and appeals on tax matters. These courts hear appeals of judgments of the Magistrates' Courts. Bankruptcy cases are in the jurisdiction of the District Court while sitting as a Bankruptcy Court (Bnk.).

District Courts also serve as the appellate court below the Supreme Court. They may sit either as a civil appeals court (D.C.A.) or as a criminal appeals court (D.Cr.A). The District Courts sit as courts of first instance in any matter not within the jurisdiction of the Magistrate Court or within the sole jurisdiction of another court.

Family cases are in the jurisdiction of Family Courts (Fam.), which are a division of the Magistrate Court.

Labor cases are in the jurisdiction of labor courts. The first instance of the labor court is the Regional Labor Court (L.C.). Cite labor court decisions by adding the initials of the city in which the labor court is located in parentheses after the type of procedure, as provided above. The appellate court for decisions of the Regional Labor Courts is the National Labor Court (N.L.C.).

3.4 Reports

Official Reporters include:

• Supreme Court:

  · PISKE DIN SHEL BET HAMISHPAT HAELYON [Decisions of the Israeli Supreme Court]. Jerusalem, the Israeli Bar, 1948-. KMK18.A2 I87

• District Courts:

  · PESAKIM SHEL BATE HAMISHPAT HA-MEHOZIYIM BE-YISRAEL [Decisions of the District Courts]. Tel Aviv, The Israeli Bar, 1948-. KMK20.A2, P47

• Labor Courts:

  · PISKE DIN AVODA [Decisions of the Labor Courts] LAW ISRAEL 6 Labor.

3.5 Unpublished or Electronically Reported Cases

Cite unpublished cases as if citing a published case but in place of the reporter's name, volume, and page number, put "(not published)."

Cite cases taken from an electronic database similarly to unpublished cases, substituting the phrase "(electronic database)" or the name of the database, e.g., (Takdin), (Dinim), (Pad-Or), etc., for "(not published)":

C.A. 18/94 **Yarom Ahikam v. Roy Shelah** (Takdin).

Bnk. (T-A) 2118/02, **The Trustee v. Rubanenco** (not published).

III. SELECTED REFERENCES

THE LAW OF ISRAEL, A GENERAL SURVEY (Harry and Michael Sacher Institute for Legislative Research and Comparative Law, the Hebrew University of Jerusalem 1995).

AMOS SHAPIRA & KEREN C. DE WITT-ARAR, INTRODUCTION TO THE LAW OF ISRAEL (Kluwer Law International 1995).

ESTHER M. SNYDER, ISRAEL: A LEGAL RESEARCH GUIDE (W.S. Hein & Company 2000).

I T A L Y

Repubblica Italiana (Italian Republic)

I. COUNTRY PROFILE (CIVIL LAW)

Italy is a parliamentary republic consisting of 20 regions (*regioni*). The Italian legal system is based on the civil law tradition. Italy is a Member State of the European Union.

The Italian Constitution was adopted on December 22, 1947, and has been effective since January 1, 1948. The State and the Roman Catholic Church are each declared to be independent and sovereign.

The head of the state is the President of the Republic. The President is elected to a seven-year term by the two Houses of Parliament in joint session and by three delegates of Regional Councils for each region (the exception is *Valle d'Aosta*, which has only one delegate). The President has the power to dissolve one or both Houses after hearing the opinion of the Presidents of each House.

Executive power is vested in the Government. The President appoints the Prime Minister, who is responsible for the Government's general policy. Other Ministers, who are responsible collectively for their acts as a body and individually for their respective government departments, are also appointed by the President on the recommendation of the Prime Minister. The Government must receive an initial vote of confidence by Parliament and holds power until the confidence is revoked or Parliament's term expires. Together, the Prime Minister and the other Ministers make up the Council of Ministers (*Consiglio dei Ministri*). Except in cases of necessity and urgency, the Government may not issue Law Decrees (*Decreti legge*) unless the power to do so is properly delegated by Parliament. Law Decrees must be submitted to Parliament. They lose effect as of the date of issue if they are not converted into law within 60 days of their publication.

Legislative power is vested in Parliament (*Parlamento*). Parliament consists of the Chamber of Deputies (*Camera dei Deputati*) and the Senate of the Republic (*Senato della Repubblica*). Legislation may be introduced by the Government, a Member of Parliament, certain other specified bodies, or 50,000 voters. Ordinarily, legislation is reviewed by committees and then submitted to the Houses. After legislation is passed by both houses and promulgated by the

President, it becomes law and is published in the Official Gazette (*Gazzetta Ufficiale della Repubblica*) and in the Official Statute Book of Laws and Decrees (*Raccolta Ufficiale delle Leggi e dei Decreti*).

Judicial power is vested in the judiciary, which is divided into five categories of jurisdiction: ordinary, administrative, auditing, military, and fiscal. Administrative jurisdiction is exercised by the Regional Administrative Courts (*Tribunali Amministrativi Regionali*, abbreviated TAR) at the local level and by the Council of State (*Consiglio di Stato*) at the national level. Auditing jurisdiction is exercised by the State Auditors' Court (*Corte dei Conti*) through the Public Prosecutor's Office (*Procura della Repubblica*). The Superior Council of the Military Judiciary (*Consiglio Superiore della Magistratura Militare*) administers military judges and military crimes committed by members of the armed forces. Fiscal jurisdiction is exercised by the Provincial Fiscal Commissions (*Commissione Tributaria Provinciale*) and the District Fiscal Commissions (*Commissione Tributaria Distrettuale*).

Ordinary jurisdiction is administered in the ordinary courts by magistrates who act either as a judge (*giudice*) or as a public prosecutor (*pubblico ministero*). The courts and judges include the Justice of the Peace (*Giudice di pace*), which has no criminal jurisdiction; the Tribunal (*Tribunale*), which is a court of first instance for more serious civil and criminal cases and also hears appeals from the Justice of the Peace; the Justice of Surveillance (*Giudice di sorveglianza*), which enforces sentences; the Juvenile Courts (*Tribunale per i minorenni*); the Court of Appeals (*Corte di appello*), which hears appeals from the Tribunals; and the Court of Cassation (*Corte di cassazione*), which is the highest court of appeals. In addition, there are several special courts and a Judge for Preliminary Inquiries (*Giudice per le investigazioni preliminari*), who examines evidence presented by the police in criminal matters and decides whether such evidence is sufficient to bring the accused to trial.

The Italian Constitutional Court is composed of 15 justices, each of whom serves a nine-year term. One-third of the justices are nominated by the President, one-third by Parliament, and one-third by the ordinary and administrative supreme courts. The Constitutional Court hears cases concerning the constitutionality of laws and acts having the force of law emanating from central and regional government, cases concerning the constitutional assignment of powers within the State, between the State and the region, and between regions, and impeachment of the President.

Internet Resources:

Italian Parliament:	http://www.parlamento.it
Minister of Justice:	http://www.giustizia.it
Constitutional Court:	http://www.cortecostituzionale.it

II. CITATION GUIDE

In Italy, there is no uniform national citation manual. There are some accepted practices, but they are not always followed.

1.0 Constitution

Cite the Constitution (*La Costituzione*) by "Art." and article number, followed by the abbreviated title "Cost.":

Art. 3 Cost.

2.0 Legislation

2.1 Statutes, Laws, and Decrees

Cite statutes, laws, and decrees by source (abbreviated form is acceptable), date, and number. Cite statutes, laws, and decrees in simplified form by abbreviated source, number, and year:

Legge 3 Marzo 1999, n. 10.

L. 10/1999.

Decreto Legge 3 Marzo 1999, n. 10.

D.L. 10/1999.

Decreto Legislativo 3 Marzo 1999, n. 10.

D.Lgs. 10/1999.

Common terms include: Statute ("Legge" or "L."), Law Decree ("Decreto Legge" or "D.L."), and Legislative Decree ("Decreto Legislativo" or "D.Lgs.").

Citations to legislative sources may be followed by the number and the date of the *Official Gazette* ("Gazzetta Ufficiale" or "G.U."):

D.L. 10/1999, in G.U. 4 Marzo 1999, n. 54.

D.L. 10/1999, in G.U. 54/1999.

2.2 Codes

Cite codes by "Art." and article number, followed by abbreviated title (Note: "ex art. _____ c.p.c." means "according to art. _____ c.p.c."):

Art. 2043 c.c.

The abbreviations for the Codes are:

Civil Code (c.c. or cod. civ.)
Criminal Code (c.p. or cod. pen.)
Code of Civil Procedure (c.p.c. or cod. proc. civ.)
Code of Criminal Procedure (c.p.p. or cod. proc. pen.)
Navigation Code (cod. nav.)

2.3 Treaties and Conventions

Cite treaties and conventions as described in Section 1.0 of Part II, on Treaties and Conventions, filling in the source information with the Italian treaty source ("Trattati e Convenzioni") by volume, source, and first page:

[Treaty information], 4 Trattati e Convenzioni 3, [date of entry, etc.].

2.3.1 Treaty Sources

Treaties from 1861 to 1945 are published in the *Trattati e Convenzioni fra L'Italia e gli Altri Stati*, abbreviated "Trattati e Convenzioni."

Contemporary treaties are not published until a domestic law is passed that incorporates the treaty, in which case the incorporated treaty text is published in the *Gazzeta Ufficiale* or *Raccolta Ufficiale*.

3.0 Jurisprudence

Cite cases by court, date, and decision number. When citing to a case (except for cases decided by the Court of Cassation), reference should also be made to the law review(s) in which it is published. Cite cases in simplified form by court, decision number, and year:

Cass., 3 Marzo 1999, n. 10.

Cass. 10/1999.

C.A. Milano, 3 Marzo 1999, n. 10.

3.1 Courts

Court abbreviations are:

Court of Cassation: *Corte di cassazione* (Cass.)
Court of Appeals: *Corte d'Appello* (C.A. or App. followed by the city in which it sits)
Tribunal: *Tribunale* (Trib. followed by the name of the city in which it sits)

3.2 Reports

There are no official reports for judicial decisions in Italy.
Abstracts (*massime*) of nearly all decisions of the Court of Cassation are published monthly in the *Massimario* (Mass.), ordered by number.

Moreover, there are secondary sources called *Repertori* (singular: *Repertorio*) in which abstracts (*massime*) of most relevant judicial decisions and references to law review articles are reported by subject.

The two most important *Repertori*, published yearly, (with their abbreviations) are:

> *Repertorio del Foro Italiano* (Rep. Foro it.)
> *Repertorio della Giurisprudenza Italiana* (Rep. Giur. it.)

Furthermore, most law reviews report court decisions both in full text and in abstract. Among the most important, published monthly (with their abbreviations), are:

> *Foro Italiano* (Foro It., or FI)
> *Giurisprudenza Italiana* (Giur. it., or GI)

III. SELECTED REFERENCES

M. CAPPELLETTI ET AL., THE ITALIAN LEGAL SYSTEM: AN INTRODUCTION (Stanford University Press 1967).

T. G. WATKIN, THE ITALIAN LEGAL TRADITION (Ashgate 1997).

J A P A N

Nippon

COUNTRY PROFILE (CIVIL LAW)

Japan is a constitutional monarchy. The official language is Japanese (*Nihongo*). The country is divided into 47 political and administrative prefectures (called either *to* (one), *do* (one), *fu* (two), or *ken* (43)). Each prefecture contains cities (*shi*), towns (*machi*), and villages (*mura*), which are the smallest political and administrative subdivisions of Japan. Japan's legal system is based on the civil law tradition.

The Constitution of Japan (*Nihonkoku Kenpo*), promulgated in 1946 and made effective in 1947, prescribes renunciation of war and the separation of legislative, executive, and judicial powers, and includes a bill of rights. Sovereignty belongs to the people, who are represented by the Dict (*Kokkai*). The Emperor is the symbol of the state and of the unity of the people but has no political powers.

Legislative power is vested in the Diet, which consists of the House of Representatives (*Shugiin*) and the House of Councilors (*Sangiin*). The 480 members of the House of Representatives are directly elected by the people to four-year terms. Their terms may, however, end prematurely if the Prime Minister (*Naikaku Sori Daijin*) dissolves the House of Representatives. The 242 members of the House of Councilors are also directly elected by the people. They serve six-year terms, half of which end every three years.

Executive power is vested in the Cabinet, which consists of the Prime Minister, who is the head of the Cabinet, and other Ministers. The Prime Minister is elected by the Members of the Diet, and is typically the leader of the political party that, by itself or in a coalition with other parties, commands a majority of the seats in the House of Representatives. All other Ministers are appointed by the Prime Minister. The Cabinet is collectively responsible to the Diet.

Judicial power is vested in a single system of courts. The Supreme Court (*Saiko Saibansho*, cited as *Saikosai*) is the court of final appeal. It is composed of a Chief Justice and 14 Justices. The Chief Justice is nominated by the Cabinet and appointed by the Emperor. The other Justices are appointed by the Cabinet. A Justice can, however, be removed by a majority in a popular referendum at the first election of members of the House of Representatives following the Justice's appointment and again after every ten years following the Justice's appointment.

The lower courts are established by law. They include eight high courts (*Koto saibansho*), 50 district courts (*Chiho saibansho*), 438 summary courts (*Kan'i saibansho*), and numerous family courts (*Katei saibansho*). High courts hear appeals from district court, family court, and summary court decisions. District courts are the courts of first instance for most criminal and civil cases. Family courts are the courts of first instance for cases involving domestic relations, including inheritance and juvenile delinquency. Summary courts are the courts of first instance for minor criminal and civil cases. The courts have the authority to determine the constitutionality of any official law, order, regulation, or act.

Internet Resources:

House of Representatives:	http://www.shugiin.go.jp
House of Councilors:	http://www.sangiin.go.jp
National Diet Library:	http://www.ndl.go.jp
Prime Minister of Japan / Cabinet:	http://www.kantei.go.jp
Cabinet Legislation Bureau:	http://www.clb.go.jp
Ministry of Justice:	http://www.moj.go.jp
Supreme Court:	http://www.courts.go.jp
Japanese Government's Database for Japanese Statutes and Decrees (Japanese):	http://law.e-gov.go.jp/cgi-bin/ idxsearch.cgi
Japanese Government's English Translation of Laws (unofficial translation):	http://www.cas.go.jp/jp/seisaku/ hourei/data2

II. CITATION GUIDE

In Japan, there is no uniform national citation manual. A number of editors of legal periodicals and journals advocate a citation practice provided in the book *Horitsu bunken to no shutten no hyoji hoho* by Horitsu Henshusha Konwakai, though it is not followed by all authors. The following represents a common practice for Japanese citations using Roman lettering.

0.1 Citing Dates in Japan

Japanese citations often refer to the name of the Emperor and year of the Emperor's reign rather than the Gregorian calendar year. Recent names of Emperors are Meiji 1-45 (1868-1912), Taisho 1-15 (1912-1926), Showa 1-64 (1926-1989), and Heisei 1- (1989-).

1.0 Constitution

Cite the Constitution (*Nihonkoku Kenpo* (1946)) by abbreviated title ("Kenpo"), date, and article and paragraph referenced:

Kenpo, Nov. 3, 1946, art. 9, para. 2.

The previous Constitution (*Dai Nippon Teikoku Kenpo* (1889)) is abbreviated "Meiji Kenpo."

2.0 Legislation

2.1 Statutes, Laws, and Decrees

Cite statutes (*horitsu*) and decrees by title, translation (in square brackets), followed by "Law No. ___ of [date]," year, article and paragraph referenced, and amendment information. Long titles are often abbreviated:

Chiho jichiho [Local Autonomy Law] Law No. 67 of Apr. 17, 1947, art. 4, para. 1 no. 3, as last amended by Law No. 135 of Dec. 28, 2007.

Joshei rodo kijun kisoku [Rules on Women's Labor Standards] Ordinance of the Ministry of Labor No. 3 of Jan. 27, 1986, art. 3, para. 2, as last amended by Ordinance No. 183 of Oct. 11, 2006.

Decrees subordinating *horitsu* include rules of Houses of the Diet (*giin kisoku*), court rules (*saibansho kisoku*), cabinet orders (*seirei*), orders of the Prime Minister's Office (*naikaku furei*), ministry ordinances (*shorei*), instructions (*kunrei*), notifications (*kokuji*), and circulars (*tsutatsu*). Statutes and decrees are published in the daily official gazette, *Kanpo*. With very limited exceptions, the Japanese government does not provide official English translations of statutes and decrees.

2.2 Codes

Japanese law does not distinguish codes from statutes. For example, both *Chiho jichiho* (Local Autonomy Law) cited above and *Minpo* (Civil Code) have the same legal status, their titles notwithstanding. However, generally speaking, the term "code" is often reserved for laws having a more fundamental nature. Cite codes in the same way as statutes:

Minpo [Civil Code], Law No. 9 of June 21, 1899, art. 1, para. 1, as last amended by Law No. 78 of June 21, 2006.

Keiho [Penal Code], Law No. 45 of Apr. 24, 1907, art 197, para. 2, as last amended by Law No. 54 of May 23, 2007.

Codes may be also cited by abbreviated title, and article and paragraph referenced:

Minpo, art. 398, para. 1, no. 5.

Keiho, art. 211, para. 2.

The abbreviations of major Codes are:

Civil Code: (Minpo)
Commercial Code: (Shoho)
Penal Code: (Keiho)
Code of Civil Procedure: *Minji soshoho* (Minsoho)
Code of Criminal Procedure: *Keiji soshoho* (Keisoho)

2.3 Treaties and Conventions

Cite treaties and conventions as described in Section 1.0 of Part II, on Treaties and Conventions, filling in the source information with a Japanese treaty series (e.g., "Nikokukan Joyakushu") by title, first page, and page referenced:

[Treaty information], Nikokukan Joyakushu, 100, 110, [date of entry, etc.].

Official Treaty sources include *Nikokukan Joyakushu* and *Tasukokukan Joyakushu*. Treaties may also be cited to the *Horei zensho* or *Kanpo*.

3.0 Jurisprudence

Cite cases by court, date, volume, title of the reporter, and page referenced:

Supreme Court, June 30, 1978, 32 Keishu 670, 674-675.

The names of parties are rarely cited in Japanese documents. When they are cited, they precede the court's name.

3.1 Reports

The official reporters of courts (and their abbreviations in parentheses) are:

- Supreme Court reporters:
  - Report of Civil Cases: *Saiko saibansho minji hanreishu* (Minshu)
  - Report of Criminal Cases: *Saiko saibansho keiji hanreishu* (Keishu)

- Lower court reporters:
  - Report of Civil Cases: *Kakyu saibansho minji hanreishu* ("Kaminshu" or "Kamin")
  - Report of Criminal Cases: *Kakyu saibansho keiji hanreishu* ("Kakeishu" or "Kakei")

- Major topical reporters:

  · Report of Administrative Cases: *Gyosei jiken saiban reishu* (Gyoshu)
  · Report of Civil and Administrative Cases Related to Intellectual Property Issues: *Chiteki zaisanken kankei minji gyosei saiban reishu* (Chiteki saishu)
  · Report of Labor Cases: *Rodo kankei minji saiban reishu* ("Rominshu" or "Romin")

- Fair Trade Commission (*Kosei Torihiki Iinkai*) reporters (for decisions (*shinketsu*) and orders (*meirei*)):

  · *Kosei Torihiki Iinkai shinketsushu* (Shinketsushu)
  · *Kosei Torihiki Iinkai haijo meireishu* ("Haijo meireishu" or "Haimeishu")

There are two major unofficial periodicals commonly used by authors and practitioners, *Hanrei Jiho* and *Hanrei Taimuzu*. Cite each by volume, title, pages referenced, court, and date:

1376 Hanrei jiho 80-88 (Tokyo District Court, May 1, 1991).
1140 Hanrei taimuzu 1-10 (Supreme Court, Oct. 16, 2003).

Note: *Hanrei jiho* is frequently abbreviated as *Hanji*, and *Hanrei taimuzu* as *Hanta*.

III. SELECTED REFERENCES

NOBUYOSHI ASHIBE, KENPO [THE CONSTITUTION] (2d ed., Iwanami Shoten 1999).

SHIGEMITSU DANDO, HOGAKU NO KISO [THE BASICS OF JURISPRUDENCE] (Yuhikaku 1996).

MASATO ICHIKAWA ET AL., GENDAI NO SAIBAN [MODERN TRIALS] (Yuhikaku 1998).

MASAMI ITO, KENPO NYUMON [AN INTRODUCTION TO THE CONSTITUTION] (4th ed., Yuhikaku 1998).

THE JAPANESE LEGAL SYSTEM: INTRODUCTORY CASES AND MATERIALS (Hideo Tanaka ed., University of Tokyo Press 1976 (English)).

HAJIME KANEKO & MORIO TAKESHITA, SAIBANHO [COURT LAW] (3d ed., Yuhikaku 1994).

KOJI SATO, KENPO [THE CONSTITUTION] (3d ed., Seirin Shoin 1995).

M A L A Y S I A

Federation of Malaysia

COUNTRY PROFILE (COMMON LAW)

The Federation of Malaysia was established on August 31, 1957. The name "Malaysia" was adopted on September 16, 1963. Malaysia is a parliamentary democracy with a constitutional monarch. It is composed of 13 states and three federal territories. The official language of Malaysia is Bahasa Melayu. Malaysia's legal system is based on common law tradition.

The Constitution is Malaysia's foundational law. It separates governmental authority between the legislative, executive, and judicial branches. Executive power is vested in the Paramount Ruler (*Yang di-Pertuan Agong*), who is the head of state, and is exercised by the Cabinet of Ministers headed by the Prime Minister.

The legislative power is vested in a bicameral Parliament (*Parlimen*) composed of the 69-member Senate (*Dewan Negara*), of which 43 members are appointed by the Paramount Ruler and 26 by the state legislatures, and the House of Representatives (*Dewan Rakyat*), whose 193 members are directly elected by popular vote weighted toward the rural Malay population to five-year terms. Parliament enacts legislation and may delegate authority to subsidiary persons or bodies.

Judicial power is vested in the courts. The Federal Court is the highest court. Federal Court Judges are appointed by the Paramount Ruler on the advice of the Prime Minister. The court system below the Federal Court is organized in two branches. The highest court in the first branch is the High Court of Malaya, under which are the Sessions Court, Magistrates Court, and Penghulu's Court. The highest court in the second branch is the High Court of Borneo, under which are the native courts and Magistrates courts. In addition, Islamic law is an important source of Malaysian law, but it is applicable to Muslims only and is administered by a separate system of courts.

Internet Resources:

Parliament:	http://www.parlimen.gov.my
Judiciary:	http://www.kehakiman.gov.my
Prime Minister's Office:	http://www.jpm.my
Civil Service:	http://mcsl.mampu.gov.my
The Attorney General's Chambers:	http://www.ag.gov.my
The Federal Court Library:	http://www.mahkamah.gov.my

II. CITATION GUIDE

1.0 Constitution

Cite the Constitution by "Const." or "Federal Constitution," followed by "Art." and article referenced:

Federal Constitution, Art. 32(3).

2.0 Legislation

Cite legislation by title and year, followed by "s." or "ss." and section(s) referenced:

Companies Act 1989, ss.395-407.

3.0 Jurisprudence

Cite cases by name of the parties (italicized and separated by "v."), year (in square brackets), and reporter in which the case is published by volume, abbreviated title, and first page of the case:

Public Prosecutor v. Anthony Wee Boon Chye and Anor [1965] 1 M.L.J. 189.

3.1 Reports

Major reports include:

Malayan Law Journal: (M.L.J.)
Malayan Cases
Malayan Law Reports
Law Reports of the Malayan Union

III. SELECTED REFERENCES

Wu Min Aun, Malaysian Legal System (2d ed., Heinemann Educational Books (Asia) Ltd. 1978).

RH Hickling, Malaysian Law (Professional (law) Books Publishers 1987).

RH Hickling et al., The Constitution of Malaysia: Its development: 1957-1977 (Tun Mohamed Suffian et al. eds., Oxford University Press 1978).

Tun Haji Mohd et al., The Constitution of Malaysia: Further Perspectives and Developments: Essays in Honour of Tun Mohamed Suffian 1957-1977 (F.A. Trindade & H.P. Lee eds., Oxford University Press 1986).

M E X I C O

Estados Unidos Mexicanos (United Mexican States)

I. COUNTRY PROFILE (CIVIL LAW)

Mexico is a democratic, federal republic, composed of 31 states and the Federal District, which comprises some of the metropolitan area known as Mexico City. The official language is Spanish. Mexico's legal system is based on the civil law tradition.

The Political Constitution of the United Mexican States (*Constitución Política de los Estados Unidos Mexicanos*) was promulgated on February 5, 1917. It provides for separation of powers and guarantees personal freedoms and civil liberties. Governmental powers both at the federal and at the state level are divided between executive, legislative, and judicial branches.

Legislative power is vested in the bicameral Congress of the Union (*Congreso de la Unión, Congreso Federal* or simply *Congreso*), which is composed of the Chamber of Deputies (*Cámara de Diputados*) and the Senate (*Senado*, often cited *Senado de la República*). The Chamber of Deputies has 500 members who are elected by the people to three-year terms. Three hundred members are elected by plurality in single-member districts, and the remaining 200 members are selected from political party lists on the basis of proportional representation according to each party's share of the national vote. The Chamber of Deputies has exclusive authority to approve the federal budget and review the annual public account. The Senate has 128 members, elected to six-year terms. Sixty-four members are elected by relative majority vote (i.e., candidates who win the most votes in their respective districts), 32 seats are assigned by the first minority (i.e., political party that finished second in vote preferences) and 32 members are assigned on the basis of proportional representation. The Senate has exclusive authority to ratify international treaties signed by the President, declare the dissolution of local powers, and confirm Ministers of the Supreme Court of Justice (*Suprema Corte de Justicia*).

All members of the Congress have an alternate, and incumbents may not be reelected immediately following their term. The two chambers share authority to pass constitutional amendments (together with local legislatures), enact federal legislation, initiate and prosecute impeachment proceedings, and exercise concurrent control of the federal public administration.

Executive power is vested in the President (*Presidente de los Estados Unidos Mexicanos*). The President is directly elected by the people and can serve only one six-year term. The President is empowered to freely select his Cabinet and, with the consent of the Senate, to select the Attorney General, diplomats, ambassadors, and high-ranking military officers. He also presents a list of candidates to the Senate for positions on the Supreme Court of Justice. The President is granted a quasi-legislative prerogative or regulatory power (*Facultad Reglamentaria*) that allows him to enact regulations (*Reglamentos*) for the purpose of implementing or enforcing federal law.

The Federal Public Administration includes the Departments of State (*Secretarias de Estado*), which are under the direct supervision of the Executive; government-owned or government-controlled companies (*Administración Paraestatal*); and certain Autonomous Bodies (institutions that are not under the direct control of the Executive).

Judicial power is vested in the courts. The Supreme Court of Justice is the highest court. Its 11 members serve 15-year terms. The Supreme Court hears cases in panels specialized by subject matter (*Salas*) or by sitting *en banc*. The Supreme Court hears only cases that involve constitutional interpretation or that are of special interest to the nation.

Under the Supreme Court are the Collegiate Circuit Courts, the Unitary Circuit Courts, and the District Courts. The Collegiate Circuit Courts are composed of three Magistrates, the Unitary Circuit Courts of one Magistrate. The District Courts are the courts of first instance in the federal judiciary. The Council of the Federal Judicature appoints all federal judges to six-year terms.

The Federal Electoral Court decides disputes arising out of federal elections. It is divided into a High Division and several Regional Divisions. Seven Electoral Magistrates, who serve ten-year terms, compose the High Division; three Electoral Magistrates, who serve eight-year terms, compose each of the Regional Divisions. Electoral Magistrates are appointed by the Senate, which selects them based upon the recommendations of the Supreme Court of Justice.

The Council of the Federal Judicature is composed of seven members: the President of the Supreme Court of Justice, who serves as president of the Council; one Magistrate from the Collegiate Circuit Courts; one Magistrate from the Unitary Circuit Courts; one judge from the District Courts; two members appointed by the Senate; and one member appointed by the President. The Council administers federal court resources and appoints Magistrates to the Collegiate and Unitary Circuit Courts and judges to the District Courts. It also supervises the quality and improvement of judicial work through a program of academic and practical specialization.

Each state is served by two levels of government: state and municipal. At the state level, authority is divided between the legislative, executive, and judicial branches. The state legislatures are composed of only one chamber, the Chamber of Deputies of the Congress of the State of <name of the state> (*Cámara de Diputados del Congreso del Estado de* <name of the state>, sometimes *Cámara de Diputados* or *Congreso del Estado*, depending on the context). There are State Superior Courts as well as trial-level civil, criminal, commercial, and other specialized courts. Municipal government deals primarily with local administrative issues.

Internet Resources:

Congress of the Union:	http://www.congreso.gob.mx
Chamber of Deputies:	http://www.camaradediputados. gob.mx
Senate:	http://www.senado.gob.mx
Presidency of the Republic:	http://www.presidencia.gob.mx
Supreme Court of Justice of the Nation:	http://www.scjn.gob.mx
Council of the Federal Judicature:	http://www.cjf.gob.mx

II.   CITATION GUIDE

There is no comprehensive uniform national or local citation manual in Mexico or its states. Nevertheless, there are certain official rules and some generally accepted citation practices.

The most important of such official rules at the federal level are contained in articles 271 and 272 of the Federal Code of Civil Procedure (*Código Federal de Procedimientos Civiles*), and articles 15 and 17 of the Federal Code of Criminal Procedure (*Código Federal de Procedimientos Penales*), though these rules are relaxed in administrative or day-to-day usage:

• Prohibition against the use of abbreviations in judicial records, orders, resolutions, briefs, bills, and all kinds of court proceedings (however, the use of shorter phraseology is allowed when the reference is clear from the context; only abbreviations are prohibited);

• All such documents must be produced in Spanish or be accompanied by official translation; and

• All dates and amounts must be in words. (However, in practice both words and numbers are used.)

Each of the states and the Federal District have similar rules embodied in their local laws.

1.0 Constitution

Cite the Constitution by "Artículo" followed by article number, and any of the following: *"Constitución Política de los Estados Unidos Mexicanos,"*

125

"Constitución," "Constitución Federal," "Carta Magna," "Carta Fundamental," or *"Ley Suprema"*:

Artículo 22 Constitución.

Artículo 22 de la Carta Magna.

2.0 Legislation

2.1 Statutes, Codes, Laws, and Regulations

Cite statutes, codes, laws, and regulations by "Artículo" followed by article number, and the words "de la" or "del" before the official title. Date of publication is optional and is often included in a footnote.

Artículo 80 de la Ley General de Sociedades Mercantiles.

Artículo 14 del Código Civil Federal.

Cite statutes, codes, laws, and regulations no longer in force by official title and indication of subsequent legislative history (abrogated, modified, derogated, etc.):

Ley Federal de la Reforma Agraria, derogada por la Ley Agraria.

Statutes, codes, laws, and regulations can also be cited to include the year when they became effective law. Cite by official title, "vigente desde" (meaning "effective since"), and the applicable year:

Ley General de Asentamientos Humanos, vigente desde 1976.

Names of Codes and Statutes can be abbreviated. However, it is not recommended to do so. Some of the most common abbreviations are:

Código Civil Federal (C.C.F.)
Código Federal de Procedimientos Civiles (C.F.P.C.)
Código Penal Federal (C.P.F.)
Código Federal de Procedimientos Penales (C.F.P.P.)
Ley General de Títulos y Operaciones de Crédito (L.G.T.O.C.)
Ley General de Sociedades Mercantiles (L.G.S.M.)
Ley de Concursos Mercantiles (L.C.M.)
Código Fiscal de la Federación (C.F.F.)
Ley del Impuesto Sobre la Renta (L.I.S.R.)
Ley Federal del Trabajo (L.F.T.)
Ley de Inversión Extranjera (L.I.E.)
Ley del Mercado de Valores (L.M.V.)

2.2 Decrees

Cite decrees of Congress or the President by type, date, and official title or main subject:

> Decreto de fecha 29 de abril de 1996 por el que se deroga el artículo 115 bis del Código Fiscal de la Federación.

3.0 Jurisprudence

Cite local cases by type of process or action, docket number (for cases after the year 2000 [number/year(0000)]; for prior cases, [number/year(00)]), tribunal, jurisdiction (in parentheses), and name of the main parties (separated by "vs."):

> Juicio Mercantil Ordinario, Expediente 1896/99, Juzgado Segundo Mercantil (Primer Partido Judicial del Estado de Jalisco), Bancomer S.A. vs. Karl Steins.

Cite federal cases by type of process (e.g., "Amparo directo" or "Amparo indirecto"), docket number (for cases after the year 2000 [number/year(0000)]; for prior cases, [number/year(00)]), name of the petitioner; and tribunal and jurisdiction:

> Amparo directo 91/99, Jorge Cassals Romero, Segundo Tribunal Colegiado en Materia Administrativa del Tercer Circuito.

The abbreviations of *Amparos* are:

Amparo Directo (A.D.)
Amparo en Revisión (A.R.)
Amparo Indirecto (A.I.)

3.1 Legal Interpretations

Cite summaries of decisions by the Supreme Court of Justice and the Collegiate Circuit Courts (*tesis de jurisprudencia*) by title or heading (*Rubro*) (in capital letters), legal abstract of the decision (*tesis*), period (*Época*), level of court (*Instancia*), source (*Fuente*), volume and date (*Tomo o Parte y fecha*), legal abstract number (*Tesis*), first page of the case (*Página*), and precedents (*Precedentes*).

> TRATADOS INTERNACIONALES. SE UBICAN JERARQUICAMENTE POR ENCIMA DE LAS LEYES FEDERALES Y EN UN SEGUNDO PLANO RESPECTO DE LA CONSTITUCION FEDERAL. Tesis. Novena Época. Instancia: Pleno. Fuente: Semanario Judicial de la Federación y su Gaceta. Tomo: X, noviembre de 1996. Tesis: P. LXXVII/99. Página: 46. Precedentes [Precedents].

3.2 Official Reports

Cite only official reporters, the names of which must not be abbreviated. Cases are divided by period (*Época*), and the reporters differ depending on the *Época* that is cited:

Fifth (*Quinta*) to Seventh (*Séptima*) *Época*: Semanario Judicial de la Federación

Eighth (*Octava*) *Época*: Semanario Judicial de la Federación; Gaceta del Semanario Judicial de la Federación

Ninth (*Novena*) *Época*: Semanario Judicial de la Federación y su Gaceta

Note: State courts do not use reports of decisions, since they do not elaborate *jurisprudencia* in the same sense as the federal high courts do.

III.   **SELECTED REFERENCES**

FRANCISCO AVALOS, THE MEXICAN LEGAL SYSTEM (Greenwood Press 1992).

JAMES E. HERGER, AN INTRODUCTION TO THE MEXICAN LEGAL SYSTEM (W.S. Hein 1978).

GUILLERMO FLORES MARGADANT S., AN INTRODUCTION TO THE HISTORY OF MEXICAN LAW (Oceana Publications 1981).

ALBERTO MAYAGOITIA G., GUIDE TO MEXICAN LAW (University of New Mexico Press 1977).

MEXICAN LAW: A TREATISE FOR LEGAL PRACTITIONERS AND INTERNATIONAL INVESTORS (West Group 1998).

EARL WEISBAUM, MEXICO: A LEGAL AND BIBLIOGRAPHIC GUIDE (Law Library University of Houston ed., 1990).

M O R O C C O

Al-Mamlakah al Maghribiyah (Kingdom of Morocco)

I. COUNTRY PROFILE (CIVIL LAW)

Morocco is a constitutional monarchy with an elected bicameral Parliament. Morocco's official language is Arabic. The country is divided into 16 regions, which are further divided into 65 provinces and prefectures. The provinces and prefectures are in turn subdivided into 1,544 urban and rural communes. Morocco's legal system is a mixture of the Islamic and civil law traditions.

The Constitution, adopted by referendum on September 13, 1996, guarantees certain basic freedoms, procedural rights, and property rights. It also provides for the system of governance.

The King, or "Commander of the Faithful" (*Amil Al-Muminin*), is the head of state, the supreme Muslim religious authority in the country, and commander in chief of the armed forces. The King appoints the Prime Minister and, based on the Prime Minister's recommendations, appoints and dismisses Cabinet Ministers. The King presides over Cabinet meetings and may dismiss the Government. In times of crisis, the King may declare a state of emergency and take all necessary measures to defend the country and to restore the normal functioning of constitutional institutions, except that he cannot dissolve the Parliament without first consulting the presidents of the Houses of Parliament.

Executive and administrative power is vested in the Government, which is composed of the Prime Minister and Cabinet Ministers. It is accountable to both the King and Parliament. The Government ensures that the laws are executed and oversees the activities of the ministries and other administrative bodies. In addition, the Prime Minister may introduce bills in Parliament.

Legislative power is vested in Parliament, which consists of the House of Representatives and the House of Counselors. The 325 members of the House of Representatives are directly elected by the people to five-year terms. The 270 members of the House of Counselors serve nine-year terms; one-third of the members are elected every three years. One hundred sixty-two members are elected by the local councils, and the remaining 108 members are selected by representatives of business associations and trade unions. All legislation is enacted by Parliament. Members of both Houses may initiate legislation. Parliament may also vote to censure the Government, which forces its resignation.

Judicial power is vested in the courts. The Constitutional Council is composed of twelve members, each of whom serves a single nine-year term. Six members are appointed by the King, three by the President of the House of Representatives, and three by the President of the House of Counselors. The Council determines the fairness of elections of members of Parliament and referenda. It also reviews the constitutionality of organic laws (laws pertaining to fundamental laws of governance) and of the rules of procedure of the two houses of Parliament, both of which are subject to mandatory review before they are promulgated. The Council also rules on the constitutionality of laws prior to promulgation. Only the King, the Prime Minister, the President of the House of Representatives, the President of the House of Counselors, or one-third of the members of Parliament may request such review. Decisions of the Council are final, and laws cannot be reviewed after they are promulgated.

The Supreme Court is the highest court in Morocco. It supervises a legal system consisting of 21 Courts of Appeal, 68 Courts of First Instance, 837 Communal and District Courts, eight Trade Courts, and seven Administrative Tribunals. The Supreme Court is the final court of appeal from judgments of all lower courts. The Courts of Appeal try criminal cases and hear appeals from lower courts. Cases involving small sums of money are heard by the Communal and District Courts, while more important civil cases are heard by the Courts of First Instance. The Trade Courts handle certain commercial disputes. Finally, the Administrative Tribunals rule on disputes relating to the powers of the administration, administrative contracts, and claims for compensation for wrongs done by public entities. They are also empowered to ascertain the consistency of administrative acts with legal provisions.

The Qur'an is still a source of law. It is applied by the *Quadis* (Muslim judges who interpret and administer the religious law of Islam) and is limited to the family law issues of Muslims. Likewise, rabbinical law applies to issues of family law for Jews.

Internet Resources:

Ministry of Culture and Communication:	http://www.mincom.gov.ma/english/e_page.html
House of Representatives:	http://www.majliss-annouwab.ma/
Prime Minister's Office:	http://www.pm.gov.ma/fr/index.html
Ministry of Justice:	http://www.justice.gov.ma/

II. CITATION GUIDE

There is no uniform national citation manual in Morocco. There are some accepted practices, but not all authors follow them.

1.0 Constitution

Cite the Constitution (*Dustur al-Mamlakah al-Maghribiyah*) by abbreviated title ("Mor Const"), followed by "Art." and article number:

Mor Const, Art. 3.

2.0 Legislation

2.1 Laws and Decrees

Cite laws and decrees by title or abbreviated title, number, and date. Citations may be followed by the date and number of the issue of the Official Gazette of Morocco (*al-Jaridah al Rasmiyah al-Maghribiyah*, abbreviated Mor OG) in which the law or decree is published:

Law no. 608.76.1 of October 1976 amending the law of Military Justice (*Qanun al-Adl al-Askari*). *In* Mor OG of January 5, 1977, no. 3349, p.3.

2.2 Codes

Cite codes by title or abbreviated title, followed by "art." and article number. Citations may be followed by the date and number of the issue of the Official Gazette in which the code is published:

Criminal Code of Morocco (*al-Majmuah al-Jinaiyah al-Magribiyah*), art. 21. *In* Mor OG of June 5, 1963, no. 2640 bis, p. 11.

Note: the Criminal Code of Morocco (*al-Majmuah al-Jinaiyah al-Magribiyah*) is abbreviated "Mor CrimC."

3.0 Jurisprudence

Cite cases by court, date, name of the parties (italicized and separated by "v."), and number. For cases other than those decided by the Supreme Court, include a reference to the law review in which the case is published:

Supreme Court Decision, March 19, 1982, *ONCF* v. *Maghribi Mohamed* in *Supreme Court Reports*, no. 31, March 1983, p. 145.

Rabat Court of Appeal, Dec. 14, 1962 in *Revue marocaine de droit, 1965*, p. 74.

Most Moroccan cases are not reported in any official system of case reporting and remain unpublished.

III. Selected References

DRISS BASRI ET AL., TRENTE ANNEES DE VIE CONSTITUTIONNELLE AU MAROC [THIRTY YEARS OF CONSTITUTIONAL LIFE OF MOROCCO] (Lib. générale de droit et de jurisprudence, Paris 1993).

ABDELLAH BOUDAHRAIN, ELÉMENTS DE DROIT PUBLIC MAROCAIN [ELEMENTS OF MOROCCAN PUBLIC LAW] (L'Harmattan, Paris 2000).

BERNARD CUBERTAFON, LA VIE POLITIQUE AU MAROC [POLITICAL LIFE OF MOROCCO] (L'Harmattan, Paris 2001).

JEAN-LOUIS MIEGE, LE MAROC [MOROCCO] (PUF, Paris 2001).

MOHAMED TOZY, MONARCHIE ET ISLAM POLITIQUE AU MAROC [MONARCHY AND POLITICAL ISLAM OF MOROCCO] (Presses de Sciences Po, Paris 1999).

JOSEPH N. WEATHERBY, THE MIDDLE EAST AND NORTH AFRICA: A POLITICAL PRIMER (2001).

THE NETHERLANDS

Koninkrijk der Nederlanden
(Kingdom of the Netherlands)

I. COUNTRY PROFILE (CIVIL LAW)

The Kingdom of the Netherlands is a constitutional monarchy that consists of 12 provinces. It also includes the Netherlands Antilles and Aruba. The Netherlands Antilles and Aruba have a separate legal system that is nevertheless still based on the Dutch system. The capital of the Netherlands is Amsterdam, but the political capital is The Hague. The country's official languages are Dutch and Frysian. The Netherlands' legal system is based on the civil law tradition. The Netherlands is a Member State of the European Union.

Executive power is vested in the Government. The Government is nominally headed by the Monarch, whose duties are largely ceremonial. Executive power is exercised primarily by the executive cabinet, the Prime Minister, and the Council of Ministers. The Monarch's functions include reading the *Troonrede*, a presentation of the most important governmental plans for the coming year, on the third Tuesday of September. During elections, the Monarch appoints the person who is in charge of the formation of a new cabinet. The cabinet consists of 14 ministers, headed by the Prime Minister, who are selected from the party or parties who hold a majority of the seats in Parliament.

The Council of State (*De Raad van State*), composed of the Monarch, the heir apparent, and the Councilor, advises the Prime Minister regarding legislation, signature and ratification of international treaties, and other matters that should, by law, be heard by the Council of State before the Government can act. Furthermore, the Council can give unsolicited advice to the Government.

Legislative power is vested in a bicameral legislature. Within the legislature, the First Chamber (*Eerste Kamer*) has 75 members who are elected by members of the Provincial governors (*Provinciale Staten*). Its tasks include rejecting or accepting legislation (it cannot propose legislation) and controlling the cabinet. The 150 members of the Second Chamber (*Tweede Kamer*) are directly elected by the people. The Second Chamber controls the cabinet and has the right to change, approve, or reject legislation proposed by the Government.

Judicial power is vested in the courts. Dutch courts usually have three different chambers: civil law, criminal law, and administrative law chambers. There are four levels of courts. The lowest level is made up of the 62 subdistrict sector

courts (*Kantongerechten*), each administered by one judge, which are distributed over the whole country and serve as courts of first instance in labor and
rent disputes, and claims involving small amounts of money. The second-level
courts, serving as courts of first instance in other matters such as administrative
law, are the District Courts (*Rechtbanken*), of which there are 19. Each consists
of several chambers composed of three judges, one of whom is the presiding
judge. The third-level courts are the five Courts of Appeal (*Gerechtshoven*),
which serve as general courts of appeal and courts of first instance for tax
law. The Courts of Appeal also consist of several chambers, again composed
of three judges, including a presiding one. Some of these courts have divisions
that handle cases in particular subject areas, such as enterprise or military
issues.

The highest court is the Supreme Court of the Netherlands (*Hoge Raad*),
which deals with matters of criminal law, tax law, and private law. The Supreme
Court is also divided into three chambers, composed of three or five judges
(except in cases against government officials or in cases of transgressions by
MPs, ministers, constitutional committees, and provincial governors, in which
there are ten judges). The administrative law system consists of several supreme
courts: the *Afdeling bestuursrechtspraak*, which is part of the *Raad van State* and
has jurisdiction primarily over planning law and environmental law; the *Centrale
Raad van Beroep*, which deals primarily with matters related to social security and
civil servants; and the *College van beroep voor het bedrijfsleven*, which deals with
trade and economic administrative law matters.

The most important form of local government is the municipalities (*gemeen-
ten*). There are approximately 670 municipalities, which are run by a directly
elected council that varies in size from seven to forty-five members, depending
on population.

Internet Resources:

Access to all government sites: http://www.overheid.nl
Parliament: http://www.parlement.nl
First Chamber: http://www.eerstekamer.nl
Second Chamber: http://www.tweede-kamer.nl
Council of State: http://www.raadvanstate.nl
Judicial system: http://www.rechtspraak.nl

II. CITATION GUIDE

In the Netherlands there are no official legal citation rules. The *Leidraad voor
juridische auteurs* (available online at http://www.kluwer.nl/images/multimedia/

pdf/leidraad2004.pdf) is often used by legal scholars and is considered to be an important guideline for legal citations, although it is not complete.

1.0 Constitution

For a number of reasons, the Dutch Constitution (officially entitled *Grondwet voor het Koninkrijk der Nederlanden van 24 augustus 1815, Stb. 45, zoals deze wet laatstelijk laatstelijk is gewijzigd bij de Wet van 25 februari 1999, Stb. 133, 134 en 135*) does not play an important role in lawmaking in the Netherlands. Cite, when necessary, to the shortened name (*De Grondwet*), or the abbreviation (Gw):

Art.1 Gw

2.0 Legislation

2.1 Statutes

Statutes are published in the official law gazette, the *Staatsblad* (abbreviated *Stb.*). Cite statutes by title, "*Stb.*" (italicized), and year and number of the relevant *Staatsblad*:

Wet van 28 maart 1996, *Stb.* 1996, 320.

Wet op de Telecommunicatievoorzieningen, *Stb.* 1988, 520.

2.2 Codes

Cite codes by "Art." followed by article number and abbreviated title:

Art. 6:162 BW.

The abbreviations of major Codes are:

Burgerlijk Wetboek (BW)
Wetboek van Burgerlijke Rechtsvordering (Rv.)
Algemene Wet Bestuursrecht (Awb)
Wetboek van Strafrecht (Sr.)
Wetboek van Strafvordering (Sv.)

2.3 Decrees

Ministerial decrees and regulations are published in the *Staatscourant* (abbreviated *Stcrt.*), the official newspaper of the state. Cite decrees and regulations by title, "*Stcrt.*" (italicized), followed by year and number of the relevant *Staatscourant*, "p.", and page referenced:

Besluit van de Minister-President van 31 maart 1996, *Stcrt.* 1996, 18, p. 7.

135

2.4 Treaties and Conventions

Treaties and conventions are published in the official treaty gazette, the *Tractatenblad* (abbreviated *Trb.*). Cite treaties and conventions by title, place, and date of establishment, "*Trb.*" (italicized), followed by year and number of the relevant *Tractatenblad*:

> Verdrag inzake verhaal in het buitenland van uitkeringen tot onderhoud, New York 20 juni 1956, *Trb.* 1957, 121.

3.0 Jurisprudence

While there is no mandatory citation form for cases, cases are typically cited by court or source (abbreviated), location of the court (if necessary to distinguish), date, title of the reporter in which the case is published (abbreviated and italicized), year, and sequence number or page and paragraph referenced:

> Hof Amsterdam 7 december 1995, *NJ* 1996, 12.
>
> Pres. Rb. 's-Hertogenbosch 16 juli 1982, *NJCM-Bulletin* 1982, p. 334.

If the decision has not been published, provide the court's docket number:

> Hof Amsterdam 8 december 1995, rolnr. 95/345.

If possible, cite other relevant information such as the location of the holding or the name of the Attorney-General:

> HR 23 september 1994, *NJ* 1996, r.o. 35 (concl. A-G Hartkamp).

3.1 Courts

Ordinary Jurisdiction Courts include:

High Court: *Hoge Raad* (HR)
Appeals Court: *Gerechtshof* (Hof <region>)
First Instance Court: *Arrondissementsrechtbank* (Rb. <region>)
Court of First Instance for minor cases: *Kantongerecht* (Ktg. <region>)
Military Court of Appeals: *Hoog Militair Gerechtshof* (HMG <region>)
Court martial: *Krijgsraad* (Kr.)

Special Jurisdiction Courts include:

High Administrative Court: *Afdeling Rechtspraak van de Raad van State* (Adf. Rechtspr.)
Special Court of Appeals: *Centrale Raad van Beroep* (CRvB)
Social Security Court: *Raad van Beroep (Sociale Verzekering)* (RvB)
Civil Service Court: *Ambtenarengerecht* (Ambt.)

Public Trade Appeals Court: *College van Beroep voor het Bedrijfsleven* (CBB)
Tax Court: *Tariefcommisie* (Tar. Comm.)

3.2 Reports

The most common jurisprudential reporters (and abbreviations) are:

The main publisher of Supreme Court and other relevant lower court cases: *Nederlandse Jurisprudentie* (*NJ*)

Decisions by administrative agencies: *Administratiefrechtelijke Beslissingen* (*AB*)

Summary judgment cases: *Kort Geding* (*KG*) (succeeded by *NJ Feitenrechtspraak*)

Tax court decisions: *Beslissingen in Belastingzake, Nederlandse Belastingrechtspraak* (*BNB*)

National number assigned to each decision: *Landelijk Jurisprudentie Nummer* (*LJN*) on http://www.rechtspraak.nl

Note: Jurisprudential reporters (and their abbreviations) are always italicized in citations.

N E W   Z E A L A N D

I.   COUNTRY PROFILE (COMMON LAW)

New Zealand is a constitutional monarchy within the Commonwealth, nominally subject to the British Sovereign, who appoints a Governor General to represent her locally. The country's basic form of government is parliamentary democracy. Though not a federal system, the country consists of some 16 Administrative Divisions providing local government services. New Zealand's legal system is based on the common law tradition. The official languages are English and Māori.

Although the Constitution nominally divides power among executive, legislative, and judicial branches of government, the branches are not entirely separate. New Zealand has a unicameral Parliament made up of a House of Representatives with 120 members elected to three-year terms. Sixty-nine members are directly elected from single-member constituencies, with the remainder selected from party lists based on the principle of proportional representation. The Sovereign is also formally part of Parliament.

As head of state, the Governor General officially has the power to summon, dissolve, or suspend Parliament and to name the Prime Minister, along with other Ministers and important office holders. The Governor General nominally presides over the Executive Council (Cabinet). All Cabinet Ministers must be members of Parliament. The executive branch has the power to make treaties, though most are presented to the House of Representatives for review. Most legislation originates in the Cabinet before being submitted for approval by Parliament and assent by the Governor General. Sovereign assent is required before a bill may become law. Parliament may also delegate some rulemaking authority to the executive. Such regulations are reviewed by a Parliamentary committee and published in a gazette prior to taking effect.

New Zealand's Constitution derives from several sources, including not only written statutes and jurisprudence but also the common law discretionary power of the Sovereign. Its principal formal statement is contained in the Constitution Act of 1986, which outlines the basic structure of government and formally abrogates the British Parliament's power to legislate to New Zealand. Several other New Zealand statutes are important components of the Constitution, including the State Sector Act of 1988, the Electoral Act of 1993, the Judicature Act of 1908, and the New Zealand Bill of Rights Act of 1990. The Constitution also incorporates relevant statutes from the United Kingdom, such as the Magna Carta, Bill of Rights of 1688, Act of Settlement of 1700, and Habeas Corpus Acts.

The Treaty of Waitangi, which transferred sovereignty to the British Queen in 1840, gained importance after the establishment of the Waitangi Tribunal in 1975 and is increasingly considered a constitutional document. Written in both English and Māori, it acts to limit majority decision-making in order to protect the interests of the indigenous Māori population.

Most government acts are reviewable by New Zealand's independent judiciary. In addition to specialist courts and tribunals dealing with family law, youth, employment, environment, Māori lands, and so forth, New Zealand has several courts of general jurisdiction. Minor criminal offenses, and civil claims under $200,000, may be heard in the 66 district courts. Original jurisdiction over serious crimes and larger civil claims rests with the High Court, which may also hear appeals of some decisions by the district courts and some specialist tribunals. The Court of Appeal has appellate jurisdiction over all matters originating in the High Court as well as some criminal matters from the district courts and some employment appeals. The Court of Appeal may by leave hear matters previously appealed to the High Court from the district court if they are of sufficient significance.

The Supreme Court Act of 2003 created a Supreme Court of New Zealand to replace the Judicial Committee of the Privy Council, which sat in England. This Court was established on January 1, 2004, and began hearing cases on July 1, 2004. The Privy Council retains interim jurisdiction over some cases (generally those cases appealed to the Council prior to January 1, 2004). The Supreme Court may hear appeals by leave in criminal or civil cases from the Court of Appeal and, in exceptional circumstances, from lower courts. Its decisions will bind the Crown.

The Waitangi Tribunal, established in 1975 as a forum for Māori claims against the Crown, is more a permanent commission of inquiry than a true court. Although it generally has the power only to make nonbinding recommendations to parties or the Crown on how a claim should be settled, the Tribunal is said to have exclusive authority to interpret the Treaty of Waitangi.

Internet Resources:

The Government:	http://www.govt.nz
Parliament:	http://www.parliament.govt.nz
Ministers of the Crown:	http://www.cabinet.govt.nz
Law Commission of New Zealand:	http://www.lawcom.govt.nz
New Zealand Government On-line:	http://www.nzgo.govt.nz
New Zealand Local Government On-line:	http://www.localgovt.co.nz
New Zealand Parliamentary Counsel Office:	http://www.pco.parliament.govt.nz
Ministry of Justice:	http://www.justice.govt.nz

II. CITATION GUIDE

There is no official guide to legal citations in New Zealand. The following therefore only reflects some accepted practices and suggestions.

1.0 Constitution

New Zealand does not have a formal written constitution, though its constitutional framework is derived from historical and recent legislation, the Treaty of Waitangi, Conventions, and Letters Patent of the Governor-General (available at http://www.adls.org.nz/lawnz/sourcenz.html).

2.0 Legislation

2.1 Statutes, Acts, and Laws

Cite acts by short title or, if the act does not have a short title, full title (italicized), year, jurisdiction (if necessary) (in parentheses), and subdivision referenced:

Contractual Remedies Act 1979, s 9(1).

2.2 Bills

Cite bills in the same way as acts but do not italicize the title:

Forests Amendment Bill 1992.

2.3 Treaties and Conventions

Cite treaties and conventions, as described in Section 1.0 of Part II, on Treaties and Conventions, filling in the source information with the New Zealand treaty series by year, abbreviated title ("N.Z.T.S."), and treaty number:

[Treaty information], 1950 N.Z.T.S. No. 1, [date of entry, etc.]

3.0 Jurisprudence

Cite cases by name of the parties (first plaintiff and defendant only, separated by "v") (italicized), year, volume, title of the reporter in which the case is published (often abbreviated), first page of the case, and page referenced.

Where appropriate, the author(s) of the judgment may be identified in parentheses after the page number. Cite the year in square brackets instead of parentheses if the case appears in a report in which volumes are organized by year.

141

When available, citations should be made to the *New Zealand Law Reports* (NZLR):

Estate Realities Ltd v Wignall [1992] 2 NZLR 615, 631 (Tipping J).

3.1 Māori Land Court and Māori Appellate Court

Cite decisions as above, using minute book references:

Re Wharekawa East 4A and K Waaka (1983) 207 Rotorua MB 212.

The abbreviations of minute books are:

Minute Book (MB)
Appellate Court Minute Book (ACMB)
Chief Judge's Minute Book (CJMB)

3.2 Waitangi Tribunal

Cite reports of the Waitangi Tribunal in the same way as books:

Waitangi Tribunal, *The Taranaki Report — Kaupapa Tuatahi* (1996).

III. | **SELECTED REFERENCES**

AUSTRALIAN GUIDE TO LEGAL CITATION (Melbourne University Law Review Association Inc. ed., 1998).

COLIN FONG & ALAN EDWARDS, AUSTRALIAN AND NEW ZEALAND LEGAL ABBREVIATIONS (2d ed. 1995).

RAYMOND D. MULHOLLAND, INTRODUCTION TO THE NEW ZEALAND LEGAL SYSTEM (Butterworths 1979).

N I G E R I A

Federal Republic of Nigeria

I. COUNTRY PROFILE (COMMON LAW)

Nigeria is a federal republic composed of 36 states and the Federal Capital Territory. Nigeria became an independent nation on October 1, 1960. Its official language is English. Nigeria's legal system is based on the common law tradition. The current Constitution entered into force on May 29, 1999.

Executive power is vested in the President, who is directly elected by the people. Legislative power is vested in the National Assembly, which consists of a Senate and a House of Representatives. Members of both houses are directly elected by the people to four-year terms. Under the Constitution, the National Assembly has the power to make laws "for the peace, order and good government of the Federation." Any law made by the National Assembly is referred to as an "Act" or an "Act of the National Assembly." Each state within the Nigerian Federation has a House of Assembly, which has the power to make laws for the state. Legislation passed by state assemblies is known as a "Law." The Constitution provides that laws enacted by the National Assembly prevail over inconsistent state laws.

Judicial power is vested in the courts. In addition to common law, the courts may also apply local customary law, particularly in disputes concerning matrimonial issues, family disputes, inheritance, and personal relations. The Supreme Court of Nigeria has original jurisdiction over matters of constitutional interpretation and disputes between the Federation and a state or between states. The Supreme Court also has original jurisdiction over any other matter that may be brought before it pursuant to an Act of the National Assembly. The Supreme Court is the court of final appeal for decisions of the Federal Court of Appeal on questions of law relating to any civil or criminal matter. The Court of Appeal has appellate jurisdiction over decisions of the Federal High Court and State High Courts regarding both civil and criminal matters. It also has appellate jurisdiction over decisions of specialized courts, namely, the Sharia Court of Appeal (with respect to any question of Islamic personal law) and the Customary Court of Appeal (on questions of customary civil law).

The Federal High Court has jurisdiction over civil and criminal matters at the federal level. The capital city, Abuja, also has its own High Court of the Federal Capital Territory, a Sharia Court of Appeal of the Federal Capital Territory, and a Customary Court of Appeal of the Federal Capital Territory.

Each state has a Magistrate Court, which is the court of first instance for certain categories of criminal and civil cases. Each state also has a High Court, which has unlimited civil and criminal jurisdiction and which hears appeals from lower courts. Some states have also followed the model of the Federal system by having their own specialized courts, such as the state Sharia Court of Appeal and the state Customary Court.

In the Northern Region of Nigeria, Magistrate Courts have only criminal jurisdiction. Civil jurisdiction is vested in district High Courts. There are also separate Native Courts, which apply customary or Islamic law. Appeals from decisions of the Native Courts are heard by the native appeals division of the state's High Court. Northern states also have a Sharia Court of Appeal, which hears appeals from lower courts in matters of Muslim personal law. Decisions of the Sharia Court of Appeal are final, except in cases where a constitutional question brings the case before the Federal Supreme Court.

Internet Resources:

Government of Nigeria:	http://www.nigeria.gov.ng
International Centre for Nigerian Law:	http://www.nigeria-law.org

II. CITATION GUIDE

There is no uniform code of citation in Nigeria. However, there is a widely recognized system of citation based upon the United Kingdom's system of citation. Although citations are generally recognizable, there is some variance in citation style, even among Supreme Court opinions.

1.0 Constitution

There have been a series of Constitutions adopted over the years in Nigeria; therefore, it is customary to refer to the specific Constitution in mind. Cite Constitutions by title, year, chapter number (optional, in square brackets), and section number:

Constitution of the Federal Republic of Nigeria, 1979, [cap.63] S.258(1).

2.0 Legislation and Other Non-Judicial Sources of Law

2.1 Act of National Assembly

Cite acts by title, year, part, chapter, section, and subsection and subparagraph (in parentheses):

Land Use Act 1978 S.25(1)(a).

2.2 Law of State House Assembly

Cite laws by title, number, year, and name of the state (in parentheses):

Bush Burning Prohibition Law No. 5 of 1997 (Ogun State).

2.3 Decrees

Cite decrees by some or all of the following: title, decree number, year, section, and subsection and subparagraph (in parentheses):

Robbery and Firearms (Special Provisions) Decree, 1970 S.2(1)(a).

Alternatively, cite decrees by title, decree number, and year:

Constitution (Suspension and Modification) (Amendment) Decree No. 17 of 1985.

Or cite by number and year:

Decree No.28 of 1970.

2.4 Edicts

Cite edicts by number and year. Optionally, include title and state concerned (in parentheses):

Edict No. 5 of 1997.

3.0 Jurisprudence

3.1 Reported Cases

Cite reported cases by name of the parties (underlined and separated by "v."), year (in parentheses), and reporter in which the case is published by volume, abbreviated title, part number (if available, in parentheses), and page referenced:

Bolaji v. Bamgbose (1986) 4 N.W.L.R (Pt. 37) 632.

3.2 Unreported Cases

Cite unreported cases by name of the parties (underlined and separated by "v."), "(unreported)", case number (if available), date, and, optionally, name of court, and division (in parentheses):

The State v. Ado (unreported) delivered on 9th day of April 1999, Lagos State High Court (Civil Division).

Alternatively, cite unreported cases as follows:

Akinloye v. Oyejide (unreported) Suit No HC/9A/81 of 17 July 1982.

3.3 Reports

There is no longer an official law reporter in Nigeria. Reporting of cases in Nigeria is predominantly carried out by individuals or individual organizations, and the citation format depends on the Law Report being cited. The most popular law report is the Nigerian Weekly Law Reports (N.W.L.R), which is published by Nigerian Law Publications. Most of the reported decisions are those of the Supreme Court and the Court of Appeal.

N O R W A Y

Kongeriket Norge (The Kingdom of Norway)

I. COUNTRY PROFILE (CIVIL LAW)

Norway is a constitutional monarchy with a modified unicameral parliament. It is divided into 19 counties (*fylker*), each of which is composed of smaller municipalities (with their own political organs and administrative powers). Norway's two official written languages are Bokmål and Nynorsk. Its legal system is a mixture of customary law and the civil and common law traditions.

Executive power is vested in the Government. The King is the head of state, although this role is primarily ceremonial. Executive power is almost always exercised by the Council of Ministers in the name of the King (the King's Council). The King's Council consists of the Prime Minister and other Ministers (collectively, the Government). The Prime Minister, who heads the Government, is selected by the party or parties that hold a majority of seats in the Parliament (*Storting*). Parliament may remove the Government by a vote of no-confidence.

Legislative power is vested in Parliament. The 165 members of Parliament are elected from the counties to four-year terms according to a complex system of proportional representation. After elections, the Storting divides into two chambers, the *Odelsting* and the *Lagting*, which meet separately or jointly depending on the legislative issue under consideration.

Judicial power is vested in the courts. The courts are administered by the Ministry of Justice, which is responsible for budget, personnel, organizational development, and other purely administrative matters. Courts include the regular courts and the High Court of the Realm, which hears impeachment cases. The regular courts include the Supreme Court, which is composed of 17 judges and a President; Courts of Appeal; City and County Courts; the Labor Court; and conciliation councils, which are composed of laypersons and function both as a mediation body and a court. In addition to the regular courts, there are several specialized tribunals, including the Severance Tribunal, which hears cases involving, *inter alia*, agricultural land area and boundary disputes; the Industrial Tribunal, which hears labor disputes relating to wage agreements; and the Social Security Tribunal, which is a quasi-judicial administrative body that hears appeals from decisions rendered pursuant to the National Insurance Act. Judges of the regular courts are appointed by the King's Council after nomination by the Ministry of Justice.

All regular courts have jurisdiction over both civil and criminal cases. The courts may set aside laws enacted by Parliament if they conflict with the Constitution and may also rule on the validity of decisions made by state and municipal authorities.

Internet Resources:

Norwegian Government: http://www.odin.dep.no
Norwegian Law: http://www.lovdata.no

II.   CITATION GUIDE

1.0 Constitution

Cite the Constitution (*Grunnloven*) by abbreviated title ("Grl."), and subdivision referenced:

Grl § 105.

2.0 Legislation

2.1.1 Statutes, Decrees, and Regulations

Cite statutes and decrees by title (often abbreviated), date [day month year], number, and subdivision referenced:

Lov om fri rettshjelp 13 juni 1980 nr. 35 §§4-5.

From 1969 onward the laws are numbered consecutively within each calendar year. Thus, citations to laws and decrees enacted after 1969 may omit the date, although retaining the date is considered better form.

Cite administrative regulations enacted pursuant to statutes in the same form as statutes:

Forskrift om Bouvet — øya 19 sept. 1930 nr. 3663.

2.1.2 Royal Decrees

Some regulations are enacted through Royal Decrees (*kongelig resoulusjon*), which are governmental acts taken pursuant to a decision by the King's Council. Cite Royal Decrees by abbreviated title ("Kgl. Res."), date [day month year], and number:

Kgl. Res. 23 des. 1994 nr. 1129.

2.2 Gazette

Laws and administrative regulations are published in the official gazette (*Norsk Lovtidend*). There is generally no need to reference the date or page when citing to the official gazette.

3.0 Jurisprudence

Cite reported cases by abbreviated title of the reporter, year, and page referenced. Include name of the court (in parentheses) when citing an Appeals Court or Lower Court decision:

Rt. 1975 s. 220.

RG 2003 s. 858 (Bergen Tingrett).

3.1 Reporters

The most common reporters and their abbreviations are:

Supreme Court decisions: *Norsk Rettstidende* (Rt.)
Selected Appeals Court decisions and lower court decisions: *Rettens Gang* (RG)

3.2 Unreported Decisions

Cite unreported cases by case number and date [day, month, year].

P A K I S T A N

Islam-i Jamhuriya-e Pakistan
(The Islamic Republic of Pakistan)

I. COUNTRY PROFILE (COMMON LAW)

Pakistan is a constitutionally based parliamentary democracy that became independent in 1947. Pakistan's official language is Urdu.

The Constitution of 1973, amended substantially in 1985, was suspended in October 1999. It was restored on December 31, 2002. The Constitution outlines Pakistan's governmental structure.

The Pakistani Constitution provides that the President is the head of state and the Prime Minister is the head of Government. Both must be Muslims. The President, who must be a member of the National Assembly, is elected to a five-year term by an electoral college consisting of members of both houses of Parliament and members of the Provincial Assemblies. The Prime Minister is selected by the National Assembly and serves a four-year term.

The bicameral Parliament (*Majlis-e-Shoora*) consists of the Senate, whose 100 members are indirectly elected by the Provincial Assemblies to six-year terms, and the National Assembly. Sixty of the 342 members of the National Assembly must be women, and ten must be minorities. All members are directly elected by the people to five-year terms.

The judicial system is composed of a Supreme Court, Provincial High Courts, and Federal Islamic (or Sharia) Court. The Supreme Court is Pakistan's highest court. The President appoints the Chief Justice, and together they determine the other judicial appointments. The Supreme Court may, upon the filing of a proper petition, determine whether a law or provision is repugnant to Islam based on the teachings of the Holy Qur'an and the Sunnah of the Prophet Muhammad. Each province has a High Court, the justices of which are appointed by the President after conferring with the Chief Justice of the Supreme Court and the Provincial Chief Justice.

Despite the country's common law roots, both pre- and post-independence legislation has been codified and compiled in the Pakistan Code. Under the Constitution, the government of Pakistan is obligated to bring all laws into conformity with Islam. To achieve this objective, many statutes based on Islamic injunctions have been enacted.

Each province is headed by a Governor and Provincial Cabinet, all of whom are appointed by the President. The Northern Areas and Federally Administered Tribal Areas are administered by the federal government but enjoy considerable autonomy.

151

Internet Resources:

Government of Pakistan: http://www.pakistan.gov.pk/

II.   CITATION GUIDE

There is no uniform code of citation in Pakistan. What follows represents a common form for citations in English.

1.0 Constitution

Cite the Constitution by abbreviated title ("Const.") (in small caps), article, and section. When the Constitution cited is no longer in force, place the year in parentheses:

CONST. art. X, sec. 4.

CONST. (1973), art. III, sec. 1.

2.0 Legislation

2.1.1 Federal Statutes

Cite federal statutes by article or section referenced, title, and number and year (in parentheses):

S.11, Federal Minister and Ministers of State (Salaries and Allowances and Privileges) Act (LXII of 1975).

2.1.2 Provincial Statutes

Cite provincial statutes by article or section referenced, title, and year:

S.21, Punjab Civil Servants Act, 1974.

2.1.3 Presidential Orders

Cite presidential orders by title (optional), "Pres. Order No." or "P.O. No.", order number, year, and article or section referenced:

Revival of the Constitution of 1973 order, 1985: P.O. No. 14 of 1985, Art.2 and Sch. item 1.

2.1.4 Executive Orders (February 23, 1986 to July 26, 1987)

Cite executive orders by title (optional), "Exec. Order No." or "E.O. No.", order number, year (in parentheses), and the reporter in which the order is published (usually the Official Gazette, abbreviated "O.G.") by volume, abbreviated title, page, date [month year (in parentheses)], and article or section referenced:

Exec. Order No. 200 (1986), 4 O.G. 132 (May 1986), art. 2.

2.2 Codes

Some statutes are commonly cited as codes and need not include the type of session law that created the code. Cite codes by name, number and year (in parentheses), and section:

Civil Procedure Code (V of 1908), S.115.

3.0 Jurisprudence

Cite cases by name of the parties (separated by "v."), year (in parentheses), name of the court, first page of the case, and page referenced.

Zulfiqar Ali Bhutto v. State, 1979 Supreme Court 53.

Alternatively, and more commonly, cite cases by name of the parties (separated by "v."), and reporter in which the case is published by year, abbreviated title, first page of the case, and page referenced:

Zulfiqar Ali Bhutto v. State, 1979 SCMR 427.

Gov't of West Pakistan v. Begum Agha Shorash Kashmiri, PLD 1969 SC 14, 17.

3.1 Reporters

Cases in Supreme Court and High Court reporters may be cited by abbreviated title of the reporter, year of the judgment, abbreviated name of the court, first page of the case, and page referenced:

PLD 1950 Lah. 253, 254.

PLD 1993 Kar. 413.

Supreme Court official reporters (and abbreviated titles) are:

Pakistan Law Digest (PLD)
Pakistan Law Journal (PLJ)
Supreme Court Monthly Review (SCMR)

High Court official reporters (and abbreviated titles) are:

Pakistan Law Digests (PLD)
Pakistan Law Journal (PLJ)

3.1.1 Special Legislation Reporters

Other special courts and tribunals created by special legislation have their own reporters in which decisions are published.

Cite cases published in these reporters by name of the parties (separated by "v."), and reporter in which the case is published by year, abbreviated title, and page number:

> Khawaja Textile Mills Ltd. v. Deputy Commissioner Income Tax Mirpur circle, Mirpur and Others, 1998 PTD 245.

THE PHILIPPINES

Republika ng Pilipinas **(Republic of the Philippines)**

I. COUNTRY PROFILE (CIVIL AND COMMON LAW)

The Philippines is a republic composed of 81 provinces. The provinces contain 136 chartered cities, which are further subdivided into component districts called *barangays*. The Philippines became an independent nation on July 4, 1946. Its official languages are Filipino and English. The Philippine legal system incorporates both the civil and common law traditions.

The Philippine Constitution became effective on February 11, 1987. The Constitution establishes the form of government and protects certain individual rights.

Executive power is vested in the President, who is both head of state and head of the Government. The President is directly elected by the people to a nonrenewable, six-year term. In addition to the President, the Government includes various Cabinet Ministers, who are appointed by the President with the consent of the Commission of Appointments.

Legislative power is vested in the bicameral Congress (*Kongreso*), consisting of the Senate (*Senado*) and the House of Representatives (*Kapulungan Ng Mga Kinatawan*). The 24 members of the Senate are directly elected by the people to six-year terms. Half of the members stand for election every three years. The House of Representatives is limited by the Constitution to 250 members, although it may be smaller. The majority of members of the House of Representatives—240 members as of 2008—are elected by the people from single-member districts. A number of members—21 as of 2008—represent sectoral parties and are elected at large.

Judicial power is vested in the courts, which consist of the Supreme Court and such other courts as may be created by law. The Supreme Court itself is composed of 14 Associate Justices and a Chief Justice. All Justices are appointed by the President on the recommendation of the Judicial and Bar Council, and serve until the age of 70. The Supreme Court is vested with both appellate and original jurisdiction, depending on the type of case. The Court automatically reviews criminal cases where the accused is sentenced to death. The Court sits not only *en banc* but also in divisions of seven, five, or three members. Certain cases, however, must be heard by the Court *en banc*.

Lower courts, over which the Supreme Court exercises administrative supervision, are structured as follows: Municipal and Metropolitan Trial Courts, which are trial courts of limited jurisdiction; Regional Trial Courts, which are trial courts of general jurisdiction and which exercise appellate jurisdiction over decisions of the Municipal and Metropolitan Trial Courts; and the Court of Appeals, which has appellate jurisdiction over decisions of the Regional Trial Courts. Both Municipal and Regional Trial Courts exercise jurisdiction over civil and criminal cases and are considered courts of law and equity. Special courts of limited jurisdiction include the Court of Tax Appeals, which decides tax assessments and protests and whose decisions may be appealed to the Court of Appeals, and the *Sandiganbayan*, a special criminal tribunal which hears cases filed against government officials. Finally, several administrative bodies exercise limited quasi-judicial powers. Their decisions may be appealed to the Court of Appeals.

Internet Resources:

House of Representatives:	http://www.congress.gov.ph
Office of the President:	http://www.erap.com
Office of the Press Secretary:	http://www.opsphil.com

II.   CITATION GUIDE

General citation practice in the Philippines is provided in the *Philippine Manual of Legal Citation,* cited in the Selected References below.

1.0 Constitution

Cite the Constitution by abbreviated title ("Const.") (in small caps), article, section, and paragraph. When the Constitution being cited is no longer in force, place the year in parentheses:

CONST. (1973), art. III, sec. 1.

CONST. art. VII, sec. 12.

2.0 Legislation

2.1 Session Laws

Cite laws by type, number, year (in parentheses), and, for Executive Orders only, reporter in which the order is published (usually the Official Gazette, abbreviated

"O.G.") by volume, abbreviated title, first page of the law, date (in parentheses), and article or section referenced:

Rep. Act No. 6957 (1993), sec. 1.

Exec. Order No. 200 (1986), 15 O.G. 311 (May 1986), art. 2.

2.2 Types of Law

Types of law include:

Public Laws (1900-1934): "Act No."
Commonwealth Acts (1935-1945): "Com. Act"
Presidential Decrees (9.21.1972-2.20.1986): "Pres. Decree"
Batas Pambansa (1978-1986): "Batas Pambansa Blg."
Executive Orders (2.23.1986-7.26.1987): "Exec. Order"
Republic Acts (1946-1972; 7.27.1987 to present): "Rep. Act"

2.3 Codes

Cite codes by common title (in small capitals) and article referenced. Some statutes are commonly cited as codes (in small capitals) and need not include the type of session law that created the code:

CIVIL CODE, art. 1234.

REV. PENAL CODE, art. 48.

3.0 Jurisprudence

Cite cases by name of the parties (if an individual, family name is sufficient; separated by "v."), and reporter in which the case is published by volume, abbreviated title, and first page of the case and page referenced, followed by year of decision (in parentheses):

Ariaga v. Javellana, 92 Phil. 330, 332 (1952).

3.1 Reports

The abbreviations of major reporters are:

• Supreme Court:

  · Philippine Reports (Phil.)
  · General Register of advance decisions (G.R.)
  · Supreme Court Reports Annotated (SCRA)

- Court of Appeals:

  - Appellate Court Reports (C.A. Rep.)
  - Court of Appeals Reports, Second Series (C.A. Rep. 2d)
  - Court of Appeals General Register (C.A.-G.R.)

- Both Courts:

  - Official Gazette (O.G.)

3.2.1 Supreme Court

Cite Supreme Court cases published in the Official Gazette by name of the parties, followed by "G.R. No." and General Register number, date of decision, and the Official Gazette by volume, abbreviated title, first page of the case, and month and year of publication (in parentheses). Cases published neither in the Official Gazette nor in another reporter may be cited by General Register number alone:

> Espiritu v. Rivera, G.R. No. 17092, September 30, 1963, 62 O.G. 7226 (Oct. 1966).

> Estepa v. Diansay, G.R. No. 14733, September 30, 1960.

3.2.2 Court of Appeals

Cite Court of Appeals cases published in the Official Gazette by name of the parties, docket number, date of decision, and the Official Gazette by volume, abbreviated title, first page of the case, and month and year of publication in parentheses:

> Manila Electric Co. v. Allarde, C.A.-SP No. 11850 (May 15, 1987), 86 O.G. 3447 (May 1990).

> Caliboso v. Bueno, C.A.-G.R. No. 20401-R (April 8, 1960).

3.3 Other Courts

3.3.1 *Sandiganbayan*

Cite *Sandiganbayan* cases by name of the parties, case type, case number, date of decision, and the reporter in which the case is published ("Sandiganbayan Rep.") by volume, abbreviated title, first page of the case, and year of publication (in parentheses):

> People v. Sabarre, Sandiganbayan Crim. Case No. 001, December 12, 1979, 1 Sandiganbayan Rep. 305 (1979).

3.3.2 Court of Tax Appeals

Cite Court of Tax Appeals cases by name of the parties, "CTA Case No.", case number, and date of decision:

Abad v. Commissioner of Internal Revenue, CTA Case No. 717, June 4, 1963.

3.3.3 Regional Courts

Cite Regional Court cases by name of the parties, abbreviated name of the court, location and branch number in parentheses, type of case, case number, and date of the decision:

People v. Johnson, RTC (San Jose, Occidental Mindoro, Br. 45) Crim. Case R-1681, August 6, 1984.

Shell Distribution Co., Inc. v. Balmaceda, MTC (Manila, Br. X) Civil Case No. 59563, July 20, 1982.

The abbreviations of Regional Courts are:

Regional Trial Courts (RTC)
Metropolitan Trial Courts (MeTC)
Municipal Trial Courts (MTC)

III.   SELECTED REFERENCES

JOAQUIN G. BERNAS, S.J., THE CONSTITUTION OF THE REPUBLIC OF THE PHILIPPINES: A COMMENTARY (2d ed. 1996).

IRENE R. CORTES, MERLIN M. MAGALLONA, & MYRNA S. FELICIANO, PHILIPPINE MANUAL OF LEGAL CITATION (4th ed. 1995).

LUIS B. REYES, THE REVISED PENAL CODE (14th ed. 1998) (2 volumes).

ARTURO M. TOLENTINO, COMMENTARIES AND JURISPRUDENCE ON THE CIVIL CODE OF THE PHILIPPINES (8th ed. 1997) (5 volumes).

P O L A N D

Rzeczpospolita Polska (Republic of Poland)

I. COUNTRY PROFILE (CIVIL LAW)

Poland is a unitary state composed of 16 voivodships, or provinces (*województwa*). The provinces are further divided into counties (*powiaty*) and then into communes (*gminy*). Poland declared independence from Prussian, Russian, and Austrian occupancy after World War I on November 11, 1918. However, it lost its independence in World War II and later became a socialist republic in the Eastern Bloc. The Communist rule was overthrown in 1989, and Poland became what is constitutionally known as the "Third Polish Republic." Poland's official language is Polish. Its legal system is based on the civil law tradition. Poland became a Member State of the European Union in 2004.

The Polish Constitution, which became effective on October 17, 1997, establishes the form of government. Executive power is vested in the President, who is the head of state, and the Council of Ministers, which is headed by the Prime Minister and is responsible to the Lower House of the Polish Parliament. The President is directly elected by the people to a five-year term. The Prime Minister is appointed by the President and confirmed by the Lower House. Other members of the Council of Ministers are proposed by the Prime Minister, appointed by the President, and approved by the Lower House.

Legislative power is vested in a bicameral Parliament, which consists of a Lower House (*Sejm Rzeczypospolitej Polskieje* or *Sejm*) and an Upper House (*Senat Rzeczypospolitej Polskieje* or *Senat*). The 460 members of the Lower House are elected by a complex system of proportional representation to four-year terms. The 100 members of the Upper House are directly elected by the people on a provincial basis, with the exception of two members who represent ethnic minority parties. On rare occasions when the two houses meet jointly, the term National Assembly (*Zgromadzenie Narodowe*) is used.

Judicial power is vested in the courts, which include the Constitutional Tribunal (*Trybunal Konstytucyjny*), Supreme Court (*Sąd Najwyższy*), and other common and special courts. The Constitutional Tribunal adjudicates cases that deal with political and criminal infringements of the Constitution or other laws by high-ranking state officials. The 15 judges of the Constitutional Tribunal are appointed by the Lower House to nine-year terms. They are all fully independent. The Supreme Court supervises adjudication in lower general and military courts, and is Poland's highest court of appeal. Judges of the Supreme

Court are appointed by the President based on recommendations by the National Council of the Judiciary to indefinite terms.

Common courts include Courts of Appeal, Regional Courts, District Courts, and Administrative Courts. The District Courts are courts of first instance for a wide variety of cases, including criminal, civil, commercial, labor, family, land, and mortgage matters. Each District Court has jurisdiction over several counties. The Regional Courts are established in all the major cities and have jurisdiction over appeals of District Court decisions. They also serve as courts of first instance for specific cases as defined by law. These cases usually involve serious crimes or high claim value and tend to be more complicated. The Regional Courts also include Commercial Courts, which specifically hear commercial cases. The Courts of Appeal hear appeals of decisions of the Regional Courts. There are 11 Courts of Appeal in total. Finally, Administrative Courts have jurisdiction to review cases between private citizens or corporations and administrative bodies. The Supreme Administrative Court is the court of last resort against decisions of lower Voivodship Administrative Courts.

Internet Resources:

Official Site:	http://www.poland.pl
Polish Parliament:	http://www.sejm.gov.pl
Biblioteka Kodeksó (Codes):	http://www.kul.lubin.pl/~fajgiel/
	kodx.htm
ABC (legislation since 1996, free):	http://www.abc.com.pl/serwis/
LexPolonica (leg. database):	http://www.lexpolonica.pl
Polskie Prawo (leg. database):	http://www.pp.pl

II. CITATION GUIDE

There is no uniform code of citation in Poland. The following represents common citation practices.

1.0 Constitution

Cite the Constitution formally by title and the Official Gazette (*Dziennik Ustaw*) in which it is published by abbreviated title (Dz. U.), year, number (nr #), and item (poz. #), followed by article and chapter (*Rozdział*) referenced:

Tekst Konstytucji Rzeczypospolitej Polskiej ogłoszono w Dz.U. 1997, nr 78 poz. 483, Art. 163, Rozdział VII.

Cite the Constitution informally by article and chapter (*Rozdział*) referenced, and abbreviated title:

Art. 163, Rozdział VII, Konstytucja Rzeczypospolitej Polskiej.

2.0 Legislation

2.1 Statutes, Laws, and Decrees

Cite statutes, laws, and decrees (collectively, legislation (*Prawo Budowlane*)) formally by title, and reporter in which it is published (preferably the Official Gazette, *Dziennik Ustaw*, abbreviated "Dz. U", cited in this context "r. Dz. U") by year, abbreviated title, number (nr), and item (poz.) and article referenced (enclosing everything after the title of the law in parentheses):

Prawo Prywatne Międzynarodowe (1965 r. DZ. U. nr 46, poz. 290 art. 27).

Cite statutes, laws, and decrees informally by title of the reporter in which it is published, number (nr.), and item (poz.) referenced. Alternatively, cite statutes, laws, and decrees by article referenced, reporter in which it is published by abbreviated title and number, and item (poz.) referenced:

Dziennik Ustaw nr. 129, poz 1439.

Art. 1, DZ. U. nr 129, poz. 1439.

2.2 Codes

Cite codes (*Kodek*) by article referenced and abbreviated title of the code:

Art. 200 k.k.

Alternatively, include reporter in which the code is published (preferably the Official Gazette) by year, abbreviated title, number (nr), and item (poz.) (in parentheses):

Art. 200 k.k. (1997 r. Dz. U. nr 88, poz. 553).

The abbreviations of major codes are:

Civil Code: *Kodeks cywilny* (k.c.)
Code of Civil Procedure: *Kodeks postpowanie cywilne* (k.p.c.)
Criminal Code: *Kodeks karni* (k.k.)

3.0 Jurisprudence

Cite reported cases by reporter in which the case is published by title (often abbreviated), and case number and year of publication [number/year]:

Biuletyn 09/2001.

ZP 19/01.

Alternatively, include additional information, such as date of decision and name of the court:

IPZP 19/01 of September 3, 2001 of the Supreme Court.

ROMANIA

România

I.   COUNTRY PROFILE (CIVIL LAW)

Romania is a parliamentary republic composed of 41 counties (*judeţe*) and one municipality (*municipiu*). Romania's official language is Romanian. Its legal system is based on the civil law tradition.

The Romanian Constitution (*Constituţia României*), adopted in 1991 and most recently amended in 2003, establishes Romania's form of government. Executive power is vested in the President, who is the head of state. The President is elected directly by the people to a five-year term and may not serve more than two consecutive terms. The Prime Minister, who is the head of Government, is appointed by the President and confirmed by the Parliament. Members of the Council of Ministers are appointed by the Prime Minister to serve on the cabinet.

Legislative power is vested in the bicameral Parliament (*Parlamentul României*), which is composed of the Senate (*Senatul*) and the Chamber of Deputies (*Camera Deputaţilor*). Both the 137 members of the Senate and the 332 members of the Chamber of Deputies are elected by the people on the basis of proportional representation to four-year terms.

The judiciary consists of the High Court of Cassation (*Înalta Curte de Casaţie şi Justiţie*, formerly known as the Supreme Court), Courts of Appeal, Tribunals, and Lower Courts or Courts of First Instance. The courts are further divided by their areas of specialty. The High Court of Cassation exercises supreme judicial power and is in charge of unifying jurisprudence. Judges of the High Court of Cassation are appointed by the Prime Minister based on recommendations by the Superior Council of Magistrates. The terms of these judges last six years and may be consecutively renewed.

In addition, Romania has a Constitutional Court, which is the guarantor of the supremacy of the Constitution. The Constitutional Court is charged with *a priori* and *a posteriori* constitutional review of legislation, treaties, bylaws adopted by the Parliament, and governmental ordinances. It is additionally charged with validating elections and also supervises presidential elections, determines the procedures of referenda, and has jurisdiction over disputes between political parties. The Chamber of Deputies, the Senate, and the President each appoint three judges to the Constitutional Court. Each of those nine judges is appointed to a nonrenewable, nonconcurrent, nine-year term.

165

Internet Resources:

Government:	http://www.guv.ro
Foreign Office:	http://www.mae.ro
Ministry of Justice:	http://www.just.ro
Presidency:	http://www.presidency.ro
Parliament:	http://www.parlament.ro
Constitutional Court:	http://www.ccr.ro
High Court of Cassation:	http://www.scj.ro
The Official Gazette:	http://www.monitoruloficial.ro
The Chamber of Deputies:	http://www.cdep.ro

II.   CITATION GUIDE

There is no uniform code of citation in Romania. There are some accepted practices; however, they are not followed by all authors.

1.0 Constitution

Cite the Constitution (*Constituţia României*) by article referenced and abbreviated title ("Const. Ro."):

Art. 23, Const. Ro.

2.0 Legislation

2.1 Statutes, Laws, and Decrees

Cite statutes, laws, and decrees by type, number [number/year], title, and reporter in which it is published ("Monitorul Oficial") by "published in the Official Gazette no.", volume, page referenced, and date [day.month.year]:

Ordinance 137/2000 on the Prevention and Punishment of All Forms of Discrimination published in the Official Gazette no. 431/02.09.2000.

2.2 Codes

Cite codes by the article referenced and abbreviated title of code:

Art. 998, C. Civ.

The abbreviations of major codes are:

Civil Code: *Codul Civil* (C. Civ.)
Commercial Code: *Codul Comercial* (C. Com.)
Penal Code: *Codul Penal* (C. Pen.)
Code of Civil Procedure: *Codul de Procedură Civilă* (C. Proc. Civ.)
Code of Criminal Procedure: *Codul de Procedură Penală* (C. Proc. Pen.)

3.0 Jurisprudence

Cite cases by type of decision, name of the parties [separated by "c/"] (in quotation marks and parentheses), case number and year [number/year], name of the court, section (civil, criminal, administrative, etc.), followed by "DOSAR Nr.", file number and year [number/year], "Şedinţa publică de la," date, and page referenced:

> Decizia ("Ionescu c/ Năstase") 1/2003, CSJ Sect. civilă, DOSAR Nr. 3859 / 2001, Şedinţa publică de la 13 ianuarie 2003, p.12.

3.1 Reports

The official reporter for decisions of the Constitutional Court is the Official Gazette (*Monitorul Oficial al României*). Collections of decisions are published annually. Cite cases published in the Official Gazette by name of court, decision number, date of decision, the reporter by title, number, and date:

> Constitutional Court, Decision No. 107 of 1 November, 1995, published in Monitorul Oficial al României, No. 85 of 26 April, 1996.

For decisions of the various courts, authors and practitioners primarily use unofficial reports, published privately:

> Evidenţa legislaţiei României, 1990-1992, Constituţia României. Legile. Regulamentele Parlamentului. Ordonanţele. Tratatele internaţionale, Casa de Editură şi Presă "Şansa" — S.R.L., Bucureşti, 1994, p. 199

> Contencios electoral. Jurisprudenţă judiciară comentată. Alegeri prezidenţiale 1990, Editura Universităţii din Bucureşti, 1996, p. 179

III.   SELECTED REFERENCES

MIHAI CONSTANTINESCU, ION DELEANU, ANTONIE IORGOVAN, IOAN MURARU, FLORIN VASILESCU, & IOAN VIDA, CONSTITUŢIA ROMANIEI — COMENTATĂ ŞI ADNOTATĂ (Regia Autonomă Monitorul Oficial, Bucureşti 1992).

IOAN CONDOR, DREPT FINANCIAR ROMÂN. PARTEA I (Regia Autonomă Monitorul Oficial, Bucureşti 2002).

MIHAIL ELIESCU, CURS DE SUCCESIUNI (Editura Humanitas, Pro Jure, Bucureşti 1997).

H.B. JACOBINI, ROMANIAN PUBLIC LAW, EAST EUROPEAN MONOGRAPHS (Oct. 15, 1987).

R U S S I A

Rossiiskaya Federatsiya (Russian Federation)

I. COUNTRY PROFILE (CIVIL LAW)

Russia is a federation composed of 21 Republics (*respublika*), eight Territories (*krai*), 47 Regions (*oblast'*), two federal cities, one Autonomous Region (*avtonomnaya oblast'*), and ten Autonomous Circuits (*avtonomnii okrug*) — a total of 89 identifiable units that are commonly referred to as Subjects of the Russian Federation (*sub'ekti Rossiiskoi Federatsii*). The official language is Russian. Russia's legal system is based on civil law.

The Russian Constitution, which was adopted December 12, 1993, establishes the form of government. Executive power is vested in the President and the Government. The President, who is the head of state, is directly elected by the people to a four year term. The President coordinates the function and interaction of the state agencies, acts as the Chief of the Army, and appoints the Chairman of the Government (Prime Minister). The President may enact decrees without the consent of the legislature. The Prime Minister, who is the head of Government, is appointed by the President and must be confirmed by the lower house of the legislature. Other Ministers are appointed by the President at the Prime Minister's proposal. Collectively, the Premier and other Ministers form the Ministries of Government (or, simply, the Government).

Legislative power is vested in the bicameral Federal Assembly (*Federal'noe Sobranie*), but, as noted above, the power to enact decrees may also be exercised by the President. The Federal Assembly is composed of the Federation Council (*Soviet Federatsii*) and the State Duma (*Gosudarstvennaya Duma*). Two members of the 178-member Federation Council are appointed by the top executive and legislative officials of each Subject of the Russian Federation to four-year terms. Half of the 450 members of the State Duma are directly elected by the people on the basis of proportional representation of political parties, and the other half are directly elected by the people from single-member districts. All members of the State Duma serve four-year terms.

Judicial power is vested in the courts, which include the Constitutional Court (*Konstitutsionnii Sud Rossiiskoi Federatsii*), the Supreme Court (*Verhovnii Sud Rossiiskoi Federatsii*), and the Higher Commercial (or Supreme Arbitration) Court (*Visshii Arbitrazhnii Sud Rossiiskoi Federatsii*). Judges of all courts are appointed for life by the Federation Council on the basis of the President's recommendations. The Constitutional Court reviews, *inter alia*, the constitutionality of acts of legislative and executive branches and disputes regarding competence. Below the Constitutional Court the judicial system is bifurcated into courts of general jurisdiction, which deal with civil, criminal, and military matters, and commercial courts, which deal with all economic disputes.

The Supreme Court is the highest court of general jurisdiction. It hears cases involving civil, administrative, criminal, and military law. The Supreme Court has appellate jurisdiction over the decisions of the intermediate appellate courts. The intermediate appellate courts for civil and criminal matters are known as the Supreme Courts of the respective Subjects of the Russian Federation. These courts have appellate jurisdiction over the decisions of the District and City Courts, which are the courts of first instance. The Supreme Court and Supreme Courts of each Subject of the Russian Federation also act as courts of first instance for certain cases. There is also a system of Justices of the Peace (*mirovie sud'i*), which hears civil, administrative, and criminal cases of lesser importance.

As noted above, all economic disputes are litigated in commercial courts. The system of commercial courts is three-tiered. The highest court is the Higher Commercial Court. Ten Federal Circuit Commercial Courts have appellate jurisdiction over decisions of the 82 Commercial Courts, which hear disputes in the first instance. Presently, the system of commercial courts is in the process of transformation into a four-tier system with two levels of intermediate appellate courts.

Internet Resources:

President:	http://www.president.kremlin.ru
Government:	http://www.government.ru
Federal Authorities:	http://www.gov.ru
Ministry of Foreign Affairs:	http://www.mid.ru
Constitutional Court:	http://www.ksrf.ru
Supreme Court:	http://www.supcourt.ru
Official online version of legislation:	http://www.systema.ru

II.   CITATION GUIDE

There is no uniform code of citation in Russia. Citation styles vary greatly by reporter and publisher. The following represents a common citation form for transliterated citations.

1.0 Constitution

Cite the Constitution by article referenced ("St."), and title of the Constitution ("Konstitutsii Rossiiskoi Federatsii ot 12 dekabrya 1993" or "Konstitutsii RF"). Cite formally by including title and date of the Russian Gazette (*Rossiiskaya Gazeta*), in which the Constitution was first published:

> St. 3 Konstitutsii Rossiiskoi Federatsii ot 12 dekabrya 1993 goda // Rossiiskaya Gazeta, 25 dekabrya 1993.

Subsequently, cite by article referenced and abbreviated title:

> St. 3 Konstitutsii RF.

2.0 Legislation

2.1 Statutes, Laws, and Decrees

2.1.1 Laws

Cite laws by article referenced ("St."), type, date, number, title (in quotation marks), and the reporter in which the law is published by title, date, volume and page referenced:

> St. 4 Federalnii zakon ot 24 oktyabrya 1997 g. N 134-FZ "O prozhitochnom minimume" // Sobranie zakonodatel'stva Rossiiskoi Federatsii. 1997. N 43. st. 4904.

2.2 Codes

Cite codes (*kodeks*) by section [p. #], article [st. #], subsection referenced, and title of the code (which may be abbreviated):

> p. 2 st. 164 GK RF.
>
> ch. 4 st. 228 UK RF.

The abbreviations of the most significant of the 20 codes are:

Civil Code: *Grazhdanskii kodeks RF* (GK RF)
Code of Civil Procedure: *Grazhdanskii protsessual'nii kodeks RF* (GPK RF)
Criminal Code: *Ugolovnii kodeks RF* (UK RF)
Code of Criminal Procedure: *Ugolovno-processual'nii kodeks RF* (UPK RF)
Labor Code: *Trudovoi kodeks RF* (TK RF)
Code of Administrative Violations: *Kodeks ob administrativnikh pravonarusheniyah RF* (KoAP RF)
Family Code: *Semeinii kodeks RF* (SK RF)

2.2.1 Alternative Citation for Codes

Alternatively, cite codes in the same manner as regular federal laws:

St. 3 Trudovoi kodeks Rossiiskoi Federatsii ot 30 dekabrya 2001 g. N 197-FZ // Sobranie zakonodatel'stva Rossiiskoi Federatsii. 2002. N 1 (ch. 1).

2.3 Government and Presidential Acts

2.3.1 Government Acts

Cite government acts by type, issuing body, date, number, title (if any), and the reporter in which the act is published by title, date, volume and page referenced:

Razporyazhenie Pravitelstva Rossiiskoi Federatsii ot 6 fevralya 2004 g. N 145-r // Sobranie zakonodatel'stva Rossiiskoi Federatsii. 2004. N 6. st. 445.

There are two main types of government acts: Regulations (*postanovleniya*) and Resolutions (*rasporyazheniya*). The citation rule for government acts is also applicable for acts of ministries and departments of the executive branch.

2.3.2 Presidential Acts

Cite presidential acts by type, issuing body, date, number, title (if any), and reporter in which the act is published by title, date, volume and page referenced:

Ukaz Prezidenta Rossiiskoi Federatsii ot 31 yanvarya 2004 g. N 118 "Voprosi Federal'noi sluzhbi okhrani Rossiiskoi Federatsii" // Sobranie zakonodatel'stva Rossiiskoi Federatsii. 2004. N 6. st. 409.

There are two main types of presidential acts: Edicts (*ukaz*) and Resolutions (*rasporyazhenie*).

2.3.3 Amendments to and Revisions of Legislative and Executive Acts

Legislative and executive acts are revised, amended, and changed quite often. These changes need to be reflected in citation. It can be done in two ways:

(1) Cite by the above format and include a phrase such as "v red. ot 27 maya 2000 g." ["in redaction of May 27, 2000"]:

Federalnii zakon ot 24 oktyabrya 1997 g. N 134-FZ "O prozhitochnom minimume" (v red. ot 27 maya 2000 g.) // V dannom vide document opublikovan ne bil. Pervonachal'nii tekst dokumenta opublikovan v Sobranii zakonodatel'stva Rossiiskoi Federatsii. 1997. N 43. st. 4904.

The phrase "V dannom vide document opublikovan ne bil. Pervonachal'nii tekst dokumenta opublikovan v . . ." may be translated as "this document has not been officially published in this latest version. The initial text of the document was published in ..."

(2) Cite by the above format and include a phrase such as "s ism. i dop., vnesennimi Federal'nim zakonom ot 27 maya 2000 g. N 75-FZ" ["with changes and amendments brought by Federal law N 75-FZ of May 27, 2000"]:

> Federalnii zakon ot 24 oktyabrya 1997 g. N 134-FZ "O prozhitochnom minimume" (s ism. i dop., vnesennimi Federal'nim zakonom ot 27 maya 2000 g. N 75-FZ) // V dannom vide document opublikovan ne bil. Pervonachal'nii tekst dokumenta opublikovan v Sobranii zakonodatel'stva Rossiiskoi Federatsii. 1997. N 43. st. 4904.

2.4 Reports

Major current official reporters (and common abbreviations) include:

Rossiiskaya Gazeta (Ross. Gazeta)
Sobranie zakonodatel'stva Rossiiskoi Federatsii (SZ RF)
Biulletin normativnykh aktov federalnich organov ispolnitelnoi vlasti (Biull. Norm. Akt. RF)

Other reporters include:

Official Reporter of the Federal Legislative Body (*Federal'noe Sobranie*):
Parlamentskaya Gazeta

Reporter for Federal Laws Ratifying or Denouncing International Treaties:
Bulleten' Mezhdunarodnih Dogovorov

Commercial databases that provide access to electronic copies of legislative and executive acts, as well as judicial decisions of both federal and regional level, are Consultant Plus (http://www.consultant.ru), Garant (http://www.garant.ru), Kodeks (http://www.kodeks.ru).

3.0 Jurisprudence

3.1 Citing Judicial Acts

Cite cases by type of decision, name of the court, date of decision, number, title (if any, and if so, enclose in quotation marks), and reporter in which the case is published by title, date, volume and page referenced:

> Opredelenie Konstitutsionnogo Suda RF ot 5 noyabrya 1998 g. N 134-O "Po delu o tolkovanii stat'i 81 (chast' 3) i punkta 3 razdela vtorogo "Zaklyuchitel'nie

173

i perehodnie polozheniya" Konstitutsii Rossiiskoi Federatsii" // Sobranie zakonodatel'stva Rossiiskoi Federatsii. 1998. N 46. st. 5701.

There are three main types of judicial decisions:

Ruling: *opredelenie*
Decision: *reshenie*
Resolution: *postanovleniye*

3.2 Reports

There are various reporters used throughout Russia. The principal reporters include:

Bulletin of Constitutional Court of the Russian Federation: *Vestnik Konstitutsionnogo Suda Rossiiskoi Federatsii*
Bulletin of the Higher Commercial Court of the Russian Federation: *Vestnik Visshego Arbitrazhnogo Suda Rossiiskoi Federatsii*
Bulletin of the Supreme Court of the Russian Federation: *Bulleten' Verhovnogo Suda Rossiiskoi Federatsii*

III. SELECTED REFERENCES

W. BUTLER, RUSSIAN LAW (2d ed. 2003).

G. DANILENKO & W. BURNHAM, LAW AND LEGAL SYSTEM OF THE RUSSIAN FEDERATION (2000).

S A U D I   A R A B I A

Al-Mamlaka al-'Arabiya al-Saudiya
(Kingdom of Saudi Arabia)

I. COUNTRY PROFILE (ISLAMIC LAW)

Saudi Arabia is a monarchy composed of 13 provinces (*mintaqat*). Saudi Arabia's official language is Arabic. The Saudi Constitution is the Holy Qur'an. The nation is ruled according to Islamic law (*Sharia*). The Basic Law, which was introduced in 1992, establishes the form of government.

Executive power is vested in the King, who is chosen from and by members of the Al-Saud family. The King is the chief of state and head of Government, and also serves as the Prime Minister. The King rules by Royal Decrees, which are issued in conjunction with the Council of Ministers. The Crown Prince, who is appointed by the King and confirmed by a vote of the Allegiance Commission, is the Deputy Prime Minister and exercises executive power if the King becomes incapacitated. The Council of Ministers (also known as the Cabinet) consists of the Prime Minister (the King), the Deputy Prime Minister (the Crown Prince, who currently is also a Minister with portfolio), 21 other ministers with portfolio, and seven ministers of state. Members of the Council of Ministers are appointed by the King. The Council of Ministers formulates and supervises the implementation of governmental policy and also oversees the resolutions passed by the Consultative Council.

Legislative power is vested primarily in the King. There is, however, a Consultative Council (*Majlis Al-Shura*) that advises the King and the Council of Ministers on matters related to government programs and policies. The Council of Ministers, which includes many members of the Royal Family, and the 150 members of the Consultative Council are appointed by the King to four-year renewable terms and may be dismissed by the King at any time. In October 2003, the Council of Ministers announced its intention to introduce elections for half of the members of local and provincial assemblies and a third of the members of the national Consultative Council, incrementally over a period of four to five years. The Consultative Council may propose new legislation and amend existing laws without prior submission to the King, and any government action not approved by the Council is referred back to the King.

Judicial power is vested in the courts, including the Supreme Council of Justice, Expeditious Courts, *Sharia* Courts, and the Commission on Judicial Supervision. In addition to Islamic law, the courts consider the teachings and

175

deeds of the Prophet Muhammad (*Sunnah*), the consensus of religious scholars (*Ijma*), and legal analogy (*Qiyas*).

At the top of the legal system is the King, who acts as the final court of appeal and as a source of pardons. The Supreme Council of Justice is the next highest judicial authority. *Sharia* courts have jurisdiction to hear all civil and criminal cases. Commercial and business disputes are handled by a number of specialized, administrative bodies. They include the Board of Grievances, which has powers similar to a supreme administrative tribunal, and a number of commissions and committees, which hear cases relating to particular subject matters such as labor or commercial disputes. In addition, the Commission for the Settlement of Commercial Disputes hears cases involving disputes between companies. Decisions of the Commission may be appealed to a special appeals tribunal.

Each province is headed by an Emir (governor), who is appointed by the King, a deputy governor, and a provincial council. The provincial council is composed of the heads of the province's governmental departments and of at least ten prominent individuals in the community who are appointed to four-year, renewable terms. Emirs answer to the Ministry of the Interior.

Internet Resource:

Ministry of Information: http://www.saudinf.com/main/start.htm

II. CITATION GUIDE

There is no uniform code of citation in Saudi Arabia. The following represents English equivalents of common Arabic citation forms.

1.0 Constitution

Cite the Basic Law by title, year (in parentheses), and article referenced:

Basic Law of Government (1992), Art 1.

2.0 Legislation (Royal Decrees)

There are no codes promulgated by an assembly of general legislative jurisdiction. Legislation is generally in the form of royal decrees, with direction from (i) Organic Instructions of the kingdom of Hejaz of 1926; (ii) Statute of the Council of Deputies of 1932; and (iii) Constitution of the Council of Ministers of 1958.

Cite legislation by title, number, date (typically use the Hijira calendar, although the Gregorian calendar may be used), Gregorian calendar year (in parentheses, and only if the date is given according to the Hijira calendar), and subdivision referenced:

Royal Decree no.11, July 15, 1962, Niza al-Waqalat-al-Tijariyah [Commercial Representation Decree], art.1.

Royal Decree No. 7/13/8751, 17/9/1374H (1955).

Talimat Tameez Alahkam Alsharia [Directions for the Exercise of Appellate Review over Decisions of Shari'a Courts], § 13.

Council of Ministers Decision No.24836, 29/10/1386H (Feb. 9, 1967) (Riyadh File No. 122 "Sharia Jurisprudence," Institute of Public Administration).

Umm al-Qura Minister of Commerce Resolution No. 322/M, 25/4/1392H (1972).

III. SELECTED REFERENCES

W.M. Ballantyne, The Register of laws of the Arabian Gulf: A Register of the Laws of the States Members of the Gulf Cooperation Council (4th ed., Graham & Trotman 1989).

M. Khalid Masud, Brinkley Messick, & David S. Powers, eds., Islamic Legal Interpretation: Muftis and Their Fatwas (1996).

A. Al-Munifi, Islamic Constitutional Theory (1973) (Unpublished S.J.D. thesis, University of Virginia Law School).

Frank E. Vogel, Islamic Law and Legal System: Studies of Saudi Arabia (Brill 2000).

S I N G A P O R E

Singapura (Republic of Singapore)

I. COUNTRY PROFILE (COMMON LAW)

Since independence in 1965, Singapore's Constitution establishes the city-state as a republic with a parliamentary system of government. Political authority rests with the Prime Minister and the Cabinet. The Prime Minister is the leader of the political party having the majority of seats in Parliament. The unicameral Parliament currently consists of 84 members elected on the basis of universal adult suffrage. In the May 2006 general election, the governing People's Action Party (PAP) won 82 of the 84 seats and 66.6 percent of valid votes. During elections, a significant number of political constituencies tend to remain uncontested, and citizens in these constituencies do not actually participate in voting. The ruling party may pass legislation, amend existing legislation, and amend the Constitution with relative ease, as constitutional amendments require a two-thirds majority of votes in Parliament.

The President remains a mostly ceremonial head of state. Following constitutional amendments in 1991, the President was to be elected and was to act as a check on government budgetary affairs and financial reserves. However, subsequent legislative amendments curtailed the powers of the President. Restrictive criteria for candidacy also mean that only a very limited number of persons are eligible to run for office, as determined by the Presidential Elections Committee.

Article 93 of the Singapore Constitution vests judicial power in the Supreme Court, comprising the High Court and the Court of Appeal. The High Court exercises original criminal and civil jurisdiction in serious cases as well as appellate jurisdiction from the subordinate courts. Appeals from the High Court are heard by the Court of Appeal. The historical right of final appeal to the Privy Council in London was abolished effective April 1994. The Chief Justice, Judges of Appeal, and Judges of the High Court are appointed by the President if he, acting in his discretion, concurs with the advice of the Prime Minister. Non-tenured Judicial Commissioners, who exercise the powers of a High Court Judge, may also be appointed to the Supreme Court.

The Subordinate Courts comprise the District and Magistrate Courts, both of which exercise jurisdiction over civil and criminal matters, as well as specialized family, juvenile, and coroner's courts. The Senior District Judge, District Judges, and Magistrates in the Subordinate Courts are non-tenured legal officers employed by the Singapore Legal Service.

Internet Resources:

Government:	http://www.gov.sg
Parliament:	http://www.parliament.gov.sg
President:	http://www.istana.gov.sg
Prime Minister:	http://www.pmo.gov.sg
Judiciary, Supreme Court:	http://www.supcourt.gov.sg
The Cabinet:	http://www.cabinet.gov.sg
Judiciary, Subordinate Courts:	http://www.subcourts.gov.sg
Attorney-General's Chambers:	http://www.agc.gov.sg

II.   CITATION GUIDE

There is no official code of citation in Singapore. Nonetheless, the Style Guide issued by the Singapore Academy of Law is widely adhered to in law reports and academic legal publications in Singapore.

1.0 Constitution

Cite the Constitution by its full title, followed by article number:

Constitution of the Republic of Singapore (1999 Reprint) Art 93.

2.0 Legislation

2.1 Statutes for Which a Chapter Number Has Been Assigned

Cite statutes for which a chapter number has been assigned by title of statute, chapter number (Cap #) and edition in parentheses, followed by section number:

Internal Security Act (Cap 143, 1985 Rev Ed) s 8B(2).

Misuse of Drugs Act (Cap 185, 2001 Rev Ed) s 17.

Penal Code (Cap 224, 1998 Rev Ed) s 300(c).

2.2 Statutes for Which No Chapter Number Has Been Assigned

Cite statutes for which no chapter number has been assigned by title of statute, act number and year in parentheses, followed by section number:

Spam Control Act 2007 (Act 21 of 2007) s 5(1).

Casino Control Act 2006 (Act 10 of 2006) s 2(1).

2.3 Subsidiary Legislation

2.3.1 Legislation for Which a Chapter Number Has Been Assigned:

Cite legislation for which a chapter number has been assigned by title of statute, in parentheses chapter number (Cap), and the year of the current revised edition of the statute (optional), as well as order number (optional) and rule:

Maintenance of Religious Harmony Rules (Cap 167A).

Rules of Court (Cap 322, 2004 Rev Ed) O 18 r 19.

2.3.2 Legislation for Which No Chapter Number Has Been Assigned

Secondhand Goods Dealers Rules 2007 (G.N. No. S 551/2007).

2.4 Bills

Cite bills by title, year, bill number and year in parentheses, and section:

Official Secrets (Amendment) Bill 2001 (Bill 26 of 2001) cl 2.

2.5 Parliamentary Debates

Cite parliamentary debates by reporter italicized, date in parentheses, volume number, columns cited, and speaker and speaker's title in parentheses:

Singapore Parliamentary Debates, Official Report (14 November 2006) vol 82 at cols 772-784 (Tharman Shanmugaratnam, Second Minister for Finance).

2.6 Select Committee Reports

Cite select committee reports by title of report italicized, and in parentheses parliament session number, year, and date:

Third Report of the Special Select Committee on Nominations for Appointment as Nominated Members of Parliament (Parl. 7 of 2004, 10 November 2004).

3.0 Jurisprudence

3.1 Singapore Law Reports Citations

The official law reporter in Singapore is the Singapore Law Reports (SLR). When a Singapore case has been reported in the SLR, the SLR citation should be used. Cite cases by name of parties (italicized and separated by "v."), date of decision in square brackets, and SLR, by volume, page on which case begins, and page referenced (in square brackets):

> Chng Suan Tze v. Minister of Home Affairs and others and other appeals [1988] SLR 132 at [86].

> Tang Liang Hong v. Lee Kuan Yew and Another and Other Appeals [1998] 1 SLR 97 at [113].

3.2 Unreported Singapore Cases (Neutral Citation)

When a Singapore case is unreported, its neutral citation should be used citing parties separated by v., year in brackets abbreviated name of court and first page of decision:

> Beckkett Pte Ltd v. Deutsche Bank AG and Another [2007] SGHC 153.

> Odex Pte Ltd v. Pacific Internet Limited [2007] SGDC 248.

3.3 Older Singapore Cases (Pre-Independence)

For older cases (prior to Singapore's independence) reported in the Malayan Law Journal (MLJ) from 1932 to 1965, cite by name of parties (italicized and separated by "v."), year in square brackets, volume of MLJ and MLJ abbreviation, and page referenced:

> PP v. Tee Tean Siong [1963] 29 MLJ 201.

For older cases reported in the Straits Settlements Law Reports (SSLR) from 1867 to 1942, cite as above except no volume number will be included and the abbreviation for SSLR will be used:

> Khoo Keat Lock v. Haji Yusop & Ors [1929] SSLR 210.

III. SELECTED REFERENCES

The Singapore Academy of Law Style Guide Quick Reference (2007 July ed.), *available at* http://www.sal.org.sg/Lists/SAL%20Style%20Guide/Attachments/8/SAL%20Style%20Guide%20Quick%20Reference%202007%20Ed.pdf.

Kevin Y.L. Tan, THE SINGAPORE LEGAL SYSTEM (2d ed., National University of Singapore Press 1999).

U.S. Department of State, Background Note: Singapore, *at* http://www.state.gov/r/pa/ei/bgn/2798.htm (Apr. 2007).

S O U T H   A F R I C A

Republic of South Africa

COUNTRY PROFILE (COMMON LAW)

The Republic of South Africa is a democratic, secular state. The official languages of the Republic are Sepedi, Sesotho, Setswana, siSwati, Tshivenda, Xitsonga, Afrikaans, English, isiNdebele, isiXhosa, and isiZulu.

The first democratic elections in April 1994 marked the end of Apartheid. South Africa ceased to have parliamentary supremacy and became a constitutional democracy. The supreme law of the Republic of South Africa is the Constitution of the Republic of South Africa (Act 108 of 1996), which was adopted on May 8, 1996, and entered into force on February 4, 1997.

The President is the head of state. The National Executive is elected by the National Assembly from among its members and may not serve more than two terms.

South Africa has a bicameral parliament consisting of the National Assembly and the National Council of Provinces (NCOP). The National Assembly is elected by universal suffrage every five years under a system of proportional representation. It has between 350 and 400 members. The 90-member National Council of Provinces is composed of six permanent delegates and four special delegates appointed by the provincial legislatures of each of the nine provinces. Most legislation originates in the National Assembly (those concerning finance must originate there), though bills affecting the provinces may be introduced in the NCOP. The President either assents to and signs passed bills or refers them back to the National Assembly for review of constitutionality.

The national Constitution defines "spheres" of competence for the national, provincial, and local governments that are at once independent and interrelated. In addition to providing for their representation in the National Council of Provinces, the Constitution grants the governments of South Africa's nine provinces concurrent or exclusive authority over many substantial areas of public concern.

The local sphere of government consists of municipalities established for the whole of the territory of the Republic. Although there are different types of municipalities, the executive and legislative authority of each is vested in its Municipal Council. Members of the Municipal Councils are elected on the basis of proportional representation for a term of no more than four years.

South Africa's legal system is based on Roman-Dutch law and English common law. Although it exhibits features of both civil law and common law, its common law character predominates. The courts are independent and subject only to the Constitution and the law. They include the Constitutional Court, the Supreme Court of Appeal, the High Courts, the Magistrates' Courts, and other courts established and recognized in an Act of Parliament. The Constitutional Court consists of a President, a Deputy President, and nine Constitutional Court judges. It is the highest court in all constitutional matters and may only decide constitutional matters and issues connected therewith. Only the Constitutional Court may decide disputes between national and provincial organs of state concerning separation of powers, functions, and status of those organs; the constitutionality of any parliamentary or provincial bill; the constitutionality of any amendment to the Constitution; and whether Parliament or the President has failed to fulfill a constitutional obligation. Its decisions on these matters are binding on all other courts and all government officials or organs.

The Supreme Court of Appeal consists of a Chief Justice, a Deputy Chief Justice, and a number of Judges of Appeal determined by Act of Parliament. It may decide appeals on any matter and is the highest court of appeal, except on constitutional matters. The High Courts may decide any constitutional matter not under the exclusive jurisdiction of the Constitutional Court as well as any other matters not involving constitutional considerations. The Magistrates' Courts may not inquire into or rule on the constitutionality of any legislation or conduct of the President. Any order of constitutional invalidity of an Act of Parliament, a Provincial Act, or conduct of the President made by the Supreme Court of Appeal or a High Court has no force unless confirmed by the Constitutional Court. Decisions of the Supreme Court of Appeal are binding on all lower courts, and those of the High Courts are binding on the respective Magistrates' Courts.

The President, as head of the National Executive, after consulting the Judicial Service Commission and the leaders of the parties represented in the National Assembly, appoints the President and the Deputy President of the Constitutional Court. After consulting the Judicial Service Commission, the President appoints the Chief Justice and Deputy Chief Justice. The other judges of the Constitutional Court are appointed by the President from a list submitted by the Judicial Service Commission, after consulting the President of the Constitutional Court and the leaders of parties represented in the National Assembly. All other judges are appointed by the President on the advice of the Judicial Service Commission.

Several state institutions established to strengthen constitutional democracy are the Public Protector; the Human Rights Commission; the Commission for the Promotion and Protection of the Rights of Cultural, Religious and Linguistic Communities; the Commission for Gender Equality; the Auditor-General; and the Electoral Commission. These institutions are independent and subject only to the law.

Internet Resources:

South African Government:	http://www.gov.za
Constitutional Assembly:	http://www.constitution.org.za
Constitutional Court:	http://www.concourt.gov.za/
Supreme Court of Appeal:	http://www.law.wits.ac.za/sca/index.php
Labour Courts:	http://www.law.wits.ac.za/labourcrt/
Commission for Conciliation, Mediation & Arbitration (CCMA):	http://www.ccma.org.za
South African Law Commission:	http://www.law.wits.ac.za/salc/salc.html
Europa World Yearbook:	http://www.europaworld.com/entry/za
Department of Justice and Constitutional Development:	http://www.doj.gov.za/
Globalex — Researching South African Law:	http://www.nyulawglobal.org/globalex/South_Africa.htm
South African Journal on Human Rights:	http://www.server.law.wits.ac.za/sajhr/houscstylc.html

II. CITATION GUIDE

South Africa has no national uniform citation guide. The following reflects some accepted practices and suggestions.

1.0 Constitution

The "Constitution of the Republic of South Africa, Act 108 of 1996" is designated by "the Constitution." Cite to the subdivision referenced and the abbreviated title:

Section 1(a) of the Constitution.

This Constitution replaced the Constitution of the Republic of South Africa, Act 200 of 1993, known as the "Interim Constitution."

2.0 Legislation

2.1 Parliamentary Acts

Cite Parliamentary Acts by title (optional), number, and year:

Local Government Transition Act, 209 of 1993.

Note: Parliamentary Acts are published in the Government Gazette.

185

2.2 Provincial Acts

Cite Provincial Acts by number and year, followed by initials indicating the province in which they were enacted:

North West Local Government Laws Amendment Act, 7 of 1998 (NW).

Province initials include Eastern Cape (EC), Free State (FS), Gauteng (GP), KwaZulu-Natal (KZN), Limpopo (LP), Mpumalanga (MP), Northern Cape (NC), North Western Province (NW), and Western Cape (WC).

3.0 Jurisprudence

Cite cases by the names of parties, the year of the report, volume, report abbreviation, page number, and court:

Brink v. Kitshoff No 1996 (4) SA 197 (CC).

Note: There are no official reports of judicial decisions. However, the most commonly cited reporter is the South African Law Reports (SA).

3.1 Courts

South African Courts (and their abbreviations) since 1994 include:

Constitutional Court (CC)

Supreme Court

High Court of Appeal (A)

Magistrates' Courts

Courts established by Act of Parliament (special Income Tax Courts, the Labour Court and the Labour Appeal Court, the Land Claims Court, the Competition Appeal Court, the Electoral Court, Divorce Courts, "Military Courts," and Equality Courts)

Provincial Supreme Courts

III. | SELECTED REFERENCES |

CHASKALSON ET AL., CONSTITUTIONAL LAW OF SOUTH AFRICA (Juta, Kenwyn 1996).

THE LAW OF SOUTH AFRICA (Joubert ed., Butterworths, Durban 1976).

JOHAN DE WAAL, THE BILL OF RIGHTS HANDBOOK (Juta, Kenwyn 2000).

S O U T H   K O R E A

TAEHAN-MIN'GUK (REPUBLIC OF KOREA)

I. COUNTRY PROFILE (CIVIL LAW)

South Korea is a republic composed of nine Provinces (*do*) and seven Metropolitan Cities (*gwangyoksi*). South Korea's official language is Korean. Its legal system combines elements of the civil and common law traditions, as well as Chinese classical thought.

The South Korean Constitution, adopted on July 17, 1948, establishes the form of government. Executive power is vested in the President, who is the head of state. Prosecutorial authority belongs to the Executive. The President is directly elected by the people to a single five-year term. The Government consists of the Prime Minister, who is the head, and State Council. The Prime Minister is appointed by the President with consent of the National Assembly. Members of the State Council are appointed by the President based on the Prime Minister's recommendations.

Legislative power is vested in the unicameral National Assembly (*Kukhoe*). Of the 299 members of the National Assembly, 243 are directly elected by the people from single-member districts. The remaining 56 members are elected by the people on the basis of proportional representation. All members serve four-year terms.

Judicial power is vested in the courts, which include the Constitutional Court, the Supreme Court, the High Courts, and the District Courts. The Constitutional Court reviews the constitutionality of statutes and administrative acts and omissions upon referral from another court or in a petition directly to the Constitutional Court. A two-thirds majority is needed to declare legislation unconstitutional. Justices of the Constitutional Court are appointed by the President based partly on nominations by the National Assembly and the Chief Justice of the Court.

The Supreme Court is the highest court of appeal. Justices of the Supreme Court are appointed by the President with the consent of the National Assembly. District Courts include Family Courts and Administrative Courts. Other specialized courts include the Patent Court, the High Military Court, and the Ordinary Military Court. All cases can be appealed to the Supreme Court, although there are some legal restrictions.

Regional authorities have legislative, administrative, and taxing power over local matters.

Internet Resources:

The Supreme Court:	http://eng.scourt.go.kr/eng/main/Main.work
Ministry of Foreign Affairs and Trade:	http://www.mofat.go.kr/
Ministry of Justice:	http://www.moj.go.kr/
Ministry of Legislation:	http://www.moleg.go.kr/
Seoul National University Legal database:	http://law.snu.ac.kr/english/index.asp
Korean Studies Information Co., Ltd (not limited to legal material):	http://kiss.kstudy.com/Others/english/main.asp
DBPIA (not limited to legal material; Korean only):	http://www.dbpia.co.kr/index_b2b.asp
National Assembly Library:	http://www.nanet.go.kr/english/index.jsp

II. CITATION GUIDE

There is no official citation manual in either Korean or English.

0.1 Transliteration Issues

The McCune-Reischauer system has been the basic framework of official transliteration method in the Republic of Korea and is generally used to transliterate Korean into the Roman alphabet, though not strictly. For further reference, look at the Academy of Korean Studies webpage under http://www.aks.ac.kr/glossary/default.asp.

1.0 Constitution

The Constitution (Constitution of Sixth Republic, revised on Oct. 29, 1987) is written "*Daehanminguk Heonbeop*" [Constitution of the Republic of Korea] and may be abbreviated variously as "Heonbeop," "Const.", "S. Korean Const.", "R.O.Korea Const.", etc.

Cite to the abbreviated title followed by the article referenced, (with an optional reference to "S. Korea" or "R.O.Korea" if necessary):

Heonbeop [Constitution] Art. 111 (R.O.Korea).

S. Korean Const. Art. 47 (2).

Constitution Art. 47 para. 2 (S. Korea).

2.0 Legislation (*Beomnyul*)

Cite legislation by the name of the law or Code, its English translation (optional) (in square brackets), the article referenced, the law number, and "(R.O.Korea)" (optional):

> Court Organization Act (Law No. 3992, 1988) (R.O.Korea).
>
> Minsa sosongbeop, Art. 230 proviso item 3 (R.O.Korea).
>
> Minbeop [Civil Code], Art. 839-2 (R.O.Korea).
>
> Minsa chojeong gyuchik [Civil Mediation Rule], Daebeopwon gyuchik (Supreme Court Rule) No. 1120 (Aug. 21, 1990), Art. 3, amended by Supreme Court Rule No. 1275 (Dec. 28, 1993).

The abbreviations of the major Codes are:

Civil Code (Minbeop)
Code of Civil Procedure (Minsa sosongbeop)
Commercial Code (Sangbeop)
Criminal Code (Hyeongbeop)
Code of Criminal Procedure (Hyeongsa sosongbeop)

3.0 Jurisprudence

Although the elements and order vary, generally cite cases by the name of the court, date of the decision, category of decision (often abbreviated and added to the name of the court), and docket number. Reference to the official reporters may be optionally added:

> Supreme Court of Korea, July 22, 1975, 74 mu 22, Divorce Case, 23 Daebeopwon pangyeoljip [Supreme Court Case Reporter] 57 (1975, No. 2); Beobwon Gongbo [The Official Gazette of the Court] 1587 (1975).
>
> Seoul High Court, Decision of Feb. 14, 1973, Case No. 71 na 2764 [High Court Case Reporter, 1973 Civ. vol. 1, 91] (R.O. Korea).
>
> Supreme Court, Judgment of Feb. 9, 1988 (R.O.Korea).
>
> Seoul Family Court, Judgment Oct. 20, 1971, Divorce case (71 du 517).

S P A I N

España (Kingdom of Spain)

I. COUNTRY PROFILE (CIVIL LAW)

Spain is a parliamentary monarchy composed of 17 autonomous communities (*Comunidades Autonomas*) and two autonomous cities (*Ciudades Autonomas*). The State's official language is Castilian Spanish, while Catalan, Galician, and Basque are official in particular regions. Spain's legal system is based on the civil law tradition. It is a Member State of the European Union.

The Spanish Constitution, which took effect on December 29, 1978, establishes the form of government. Executive power is vested in the Monarch, who is the head of state but whose role is primarily ceremonial. The monarchy is hereditary. Executive power is exercised primarily by the President (*Presidente*), who is the head of Government, with the advice of the Council of Ministers (*Consejo de Ministros*). The President is nominated by the Monarch and elected by the Congress of Deputies (*Congreso de los Diputados*). Generally, the Monarch nominates the leader of the party or parties who form a majority of the Congress. The Monarch appoints and dismisses the other members of the Government (Vice Presidents, if any, and Ministers) at the President's proposal.

Legislative power is vested in the bicameral General Assembly (*Cortes Generales*), which consists of the Congress of Deputies (*Congreso de los Diputados*) and the Senate (*Senado*). The 350 members of the Congress of Deputies are elected by the people on the basis of proportional representation. Two hundred eight of the 259 members of the Senate are directly elected by the people, while the remaining 51 members are appointed by the regional legislatures. Members of both houses serve four-year terms. All legislation is introduced in the Congress of Deputies, although it may be initiated by the Government, Congress, Senate, Assemblies of Autonomous Communities, or popular initiative (at least 500,000 authenticated signatures). The Senate has the power to amend or veto legislation initiated by the Congress of Deputies, although the latter can later overturn any amendment or veto. Once passed by the National Assembly, legislation must be promulgated by the King in order to become law.

Within the terms of the Constitution, Statutes of Autonomy (*Estatutos de Autonomía*) are the basic institutional rule of each Autonomous Community, and the State shall recognize and protect them as an integral part of its legal system. The Assemblies of Autonomous Communities have legislative competence within their territorial and subject-matter jurisdiction.

Judicial power is vested in the courts, which are administered by the General Council of Judicial Power (*Consejo General del Poder Judicial*). There is a unified judicial power structure that rules on regional and state law of which the Constitutional Court (*Tribunal Constitucional*) is the highest court for constitutional matters. For all other subject matter, the Supreme Court (*Tribunal Supremo*) is the highest court. The National Audience (*Audiencia Nacional*) has jurisdiction to hear matters of national interest, such as extradition proceedings or crimes against the Crown. The Superior Courts (*Tribunal Superior de Justicia*) are the supreme authority for regional law.

Lower courts include Justices of the Peace (*Juzgado de Paz*), which hear very minor claims, and Courts of First Instance (*Juzgado de Primera Instancia e Instrucción*), which hear most civil claims in the first instance, judge minor criminal offenses, and investigate crimes subsequently tried in the first instance by the Criminal Court (*Juzgado de lo Penal*). The Provincial Audiences (*Audiencia Provincial*) hear appeals from decisions of both the *Juzgado de Paz* and the *Juzgado de Primera Instancia* and judges on serious crimes. Appeals from decisions of the Provincial Audiences are heard by the Supreme Court. Specialized courts include the Administrative Courts (*de lo Contencioso-Administrativo*), Labor Courts (*de lo Social*), Commerce Courts (*de lo Mercantil*), Gender Violence Courts (*de Violencia sobre la Mujer*), Court of Minors (*de Menores*), and Courts for Penitentiary Supervision (*de vigilancia penitenciaria*).

Internet Resources:

Government:	http://www.la-moncloa.es
Congress of Deputies:	http://www.congreso.es
Senate:	http://www.senado.es
Constitutional Court:	http://www.tribunalconstitucional.es

II. CITATION GUIDE

There is no uniform code of citation in Spain. Citation practices, however, are based either on the Spanish Official Gazette (*Boletin Oficial del Estado*) or on unofficial publications by private companies such as Aranzadi, Colex, La Ley, etc. The following is based on the Aranzadi standards.

1.0 Constitution

Cite the Constitution (*Constitución Española*) by article referenced and abbreviated title ("C.E."):

Art. 24 C.E.

2.0 Legislation

2.1 Laws, Orders, and Decrees

Cite legislation by abbreviated type of instrument, number and year [number/year], date [day, month], title, and the reporter in which the legislation is published by abbreviated title, year, and page referenced:

Real Decreto (R.D.) 1098/2001, de 12 de octubre, Aprobación del Reglamento General de la Ley de Contratos de las Administraciones Públicas, RCL 2001, 2594.

The two major Law Reports are RCL (*Repertorio Aranzadi Cronologico de Legislacion*) and BOE (*Boletin Oficial del Estado*).

A simplified citation format omits the Law Report as well as its year and page.

RD 296/1996, 23 febrero, que aprueba el Reglamento Orgánico del Cuerpo de Médicos Forenses.

The abbreviations of the main instruments are:

Ley ordinaria (L)
Ley Organica (LO)
Real Decreto (RD)
Real Decreto Ley (RD-Ley)
Real Decreto Legislativo (RDL)
Orden Ministerial (OM)

2.2 Codes

Cite codes by article referenced and abbreviated title:

Art. 12 C.C.

The abbreviations of the Codes are:

Código Civil (C.C.)
Código Penal (C.P.)
Código de Comercio (C.Com.)
Ley de Enjuiciamento Civil (LEC)
Ley de Enjuiciamento Criminal (LECr)
Ley Orgánica del Poder Judicial (LOPJ)
Ley de Procedimiento Administrativo (LPA)
Ley de Procedimiento Laboral (LPL)
Ley de la Jurisdicción Contencioso Administrativa (LJCA)
Ley de Orgánica del Régimen Electoral General (LOREG)
Ley de Orgánica del Tribunal Constitucional (LOTC)

3.0 Jurisprudence

Cite cases by name of the court (often abbreviated), location of the court, date of decision, and the reporter in which the case is published by title, decision number, and page referenced (in parentheses):

> STSJ Murcia (Social), de 1 de marzo 1991 (La Ley 7.8.91, min 2804).

Alternatively, cite cases by name of the court (abbreviated), full date [day, month, year], and "A" (for Aranzadi) and decision number (in parentheses):

> STS 15 abril 1992 (A 4421).

> STSJ Cataluña (social) 15 enero 1993 (A 2246).

3.1 Courts

The abbreviations of the courts are:

Sentencia del Tribunal Supremo (STS)
Sentencia Audiencia Nacional (SAN)
Sentencia Audiencia Provincial (SAP)
Sentencia Tribunal Superior de Justicia (STS)

3.2 Reports

When possible, cite to the *Repertorio Aranzadi de Jurisprudencia* (RJ).

3.3 Cases of the *Tribunal Constitucional*

Cite Constitutional Court cases by "STC," case number and year [number/year], date of decision [day, month], and number of the "point of law" (if any) referenced (*Fundamento Juridico, FJ*):

> STC 13/1986, de 22 octubre, FJ 9.

Exceptionally, the type of action (e.g., *recurso de amparo*) as well as the reporter in which the case is published (e.g., RTC for *Repertorio Aranzadi del Tribunal Constitucional*) may be provided.

III. SELECTED REFERENCES

CHARLOTTE VILLIERS, THE SPANISH LEGAL TRADITION: AN INTRODUCTION TO THE SPANISH LAW AND LEGAL SYSTEM (Ashgate/Dartmouth, Aldershot, Brookfield, USA 1999).

S W E D E N

Konungariket Sverige (Kingdom of Sweden)

I. COUNTRY PROFILE (CIVIL LAW)

Sweden is a constitutional monarchy composed of 21 counties (*län*) and 289 municipalities (*kommuner*). Sweden's official language is Swedish. Its legal system is based primarily on the civil law tradition, although it also incorporates aspects of the common law tradition. Sweden is a Member State of the European Union.

The Swedish Constitution, adopted in 1975, establishes the form of government. Executive power is vested in the Government (*Regering*), which consists of the Prime Minister (*Statsminister*), who is the head of Government, and the Cabinet. The Monarch, who is the head of state, plays a largely ceremonial and symbolic role. The Prime Minister is elected by the Parliament (*Riksdag*). Members of the Cabinet are appointed by the Prime Minister. The Government submits proposals to Parliament concerning legislation and the national budget. Parliament may dissolve the Government at any time.

Legislative power is vested in the unicameral Parliament. The 349 members of Parliament are elected by the people on the basis of proportional representation to four-year terms. Parliament enacts laws (*lagar*) based on the Government's proposals. It may delegate legislative power to the Government in certain areas. A regulation issued by the Government is called *förordning*.

Judicial power is vested in the courts. Sweden has a dual court system, which is composed of the civil and criminal courts and the administrative courts. In Sweden, the rule of precedent is relative, not absolute. The Supreme Courts include the High Court of General Jurisdiction (*Högsta domstolen*), the High Administrative Court (*Regeringsrätten*), the High Labor and Employment Court (*Arbetsdomstolen*), and the High Market and Competition Court (*Marknadsdomstolen*). Lower courts include General Courts (*Hovrätt* and *Tingsrätt*) and Administrative Courts (*Lansrätt* and *Kammarrätt*).

Internet Resources:

For an overview of Swedish law on the Internet: http://www.nyulawglobal.org/globalex/sweden.htm

Gateway to Swedish legal information with links: http://www.lagrummet.se

Parliament:	http://www.riksdagen.se
Government:	http://www.regeringen.se
Legislation in full text:	http://www.notisum.se

II. CITATION GUIDE

There is no uniform code of citation in Sweden. The University of Lulea, Sweden, recommends some basic rules of citation (*see* http://www.luth.se/depts/lib/utbildning/referenser/off.shtml) as well as the following guides: Peter Wahlgren, Wiweka Warnling-Nerep, & Pål Wrange, *Juridisk skrivguide* (Norstedts juridik, Stockholm 2002); and Ulf Jensen & Staffan Rylander, *Att skriva juridik* (4th ed., Uppsala 2006). The following represents some accepted practices.

1.0 Constitution

The four Constitutional laws may be abbreviated for citation purposes as follows:

Constitution Act: *Regeringsformen* (RF) SFS
The Freedom of Press Act: *Tryckfrihetsförordningen* (TF) SFS
Fundamental Law on Freedom of Expression: *Yttrandefrihetsgrundlagen* (YGL) SFS
The Act of Succession: *Successionsordningená* (SO) SFS

2.0 Legislation

Författning is a term that encompasses all types of legislation. Cite codes, laws, statutes, and decrees by type, year and number in the Swedish Code of Statutes (*Svensk Författningssamling* (SFS)) [year:number] (in parentheses), and title:

Lag (1994:1117) om registrerat partnerskap.

Lag (1987:232) om sambor gemensamma hem.

Förordning (1772:1104) angående sabbatens firande samt vissa helgdagars flyttning eller indragning.

3.0 Jurisprudence

Cite cases by abbreviated title of the reporter in which the case is published, year of decision, and page referenced:

NJA 1949 s. 609.

RH 1999 s.1.

RA 1998 s.1.

3.1 Reports

The names and abbreviations of major reports are:

Supreme Court: *Nytt Juridiskt Arkiv* (NJA)
Court of Appeals: *Rättsfall från Hovrätterna* (RH)
Highest Administrative Court: *Regeringsrättens Årsbok* (RA)

S W I T Z E R L A N D

Confédération Suisse;
Schweizerische Eidgenossenschaft;
Confederazione Svizzera
(Swiss Confederation)

I. COUNTRY PROFILE (CIVIL LAW)

Switzerland is a federal republic composed of 26 Cantons (*Cantons, Cantoni, or Kantone*), 20 of which are full Cantons and six of which are half Cantons. Switzerland's legal system is based on the civil law tradition. Its official languages are French, Italian, German, and Romansh.

The Swiss Constitution of 1874 was revised in 1998 and entered into force on January 1, 2000. Executive power is vested in the Government, which consists of the President, Vice President, and Federal Council (*Conseil Federal, Consiglio Federale, or Bundesrat*). The President is both the head of state and head of the Government. Members of the Federal Council are elected by the Federal Assembly, usually from among its own members, to a four-year term. The President and Vice President are elected by the Federal Assembly from among the members of the Federal Council to concurrent, one-year terms.

Legislative power is vested in the bicameral Federal Assembly (*Assemblée Fédérale, Assemblea Federale, or Bundesversammlung*), which consists of the Council of States (*Conseil des Etats, Consiglio degli Stati, or Standerat*) and the National Council (*Conseil National, Consiglio Nazionale, or Nationalrat*). The 46 members of the Council of States (two of whom represent each full Canton and one of whom represents each half Canton) are directly elected by the people in each Canton. The 200 members of the National Council are directly elected by the people on the basis of proportional representation. Members of both houses serve for four-year terms. The two houses of the Federal Assembly have equal powers in all respects, including the right to introduce legislation. All laws (except the budget) can be reviewed by popular referendum before taking effect.

Judicial power is vested in the courts. The only regular federal court is the Federal Tribunal (*Tribunal Fédéral, Tribunale Federale, or Bundesgericht*), which consists of 30 full-time judges and 30 part-time judges, all of whom are elected by the Federal Parliament to six-year terms. The Federal Tribunal is a court of limited jurisdiction. Its principal function is to hear appeals from civil and criminal decisions of the Canton courts. It has authority to review cantonal court decisions involving federal law and certain administrative rulings of federal departments, but it has no power to review legislation for constitutionality. All lower courts are organized within and by the Cantons.

The Cantons are sovereign subject to limitations imposed by the Constitution; they can exercise all rights that, according to the Constitution, are not transferred to the Confederation. The Cantons are thus in a position to define the tasks that they shall accomplish within the framework of their powers. The Municipalities are autonomous within the limits fixed by cantonal law. Accordingly, federal law takes precedence over conflicting cantonal law, and cantonal law takes precedence over conflicting municipal law.

The authorities within each Canton mirror the federal authorities in structure and assessment of powers. In every Canton, executive power is vested in a collegiate body, generally called the Council of State (*Conseil d'Etat, Consiglio di Stato*, or *Regierungsrat*). Each Canton also has a unicameral legislative body, generally called the Great Council (*Grand Conseil, Gran Consiglio*, or *Kantonsrat*).

Internet Resources:

Federal Confederation Authorities:	http://www.admin.ch
Official Collection of Federal Law:	http://www.admin.ch/ch/d/as/index.html
Systematic Collection of Federal Law:	http://www.admin.ch/ch/d/sr/sr.html
Federal Supreme Court:	http://www.bger.ch

II.   CITATION GUIDE

There is no uniform code of citation in Switzerland. The following represents the most common form of citation in German. Citations in French and Italian are different. For an overview of the commonly accepted standards of citation and legal research as well as a list of standard abbreviations, see Peter Forstmoser et al., *Juristisches Arbeiten, Eine Anleitung für Studierende* (2003), or unofficial recommendations by the University of Lausanne for German language citations available at http://www.unil.ch/webdav/site/eda/shared/zitierregeln.pdf.

0.1 Common Abbreviations

Common abbreviations in German include Article (Artikel or Art.), paragraph (Absatz or Abs.), and clause (Satz). The "Abs." and "Satz" symbols are optional.

1.0 Constitution

Cite the Constitution (*Bundesverfassung der Schweizerischen Eidgenossenschaft*) by subdivision referenced (see Section 0.1) and abbreviated title ("BV"):

Art. 62 Abs. 2 Satz 2 BV.

2.0 Legislation

2.1 Statutes, Laws, and Decrees

Cite statutes, laws, and decrees by title, short and/or abbreviated title (usually found in the official text) in parentheses, date (if not included in the official title), and official gazette (see Section 2.3) in which the statute, law, or decree is published by abbreviated title, year, and page referenced:

Bundesgesetz vom 9. Oktober 1992 über das Urheberrecht und verwandte Schutzrechte (Urheberrechtsgesetz, URG), AS 1993, 1798 ff.

Verordnung vom 26. April 1993 über das Urheberrecht und verwandte Schutzrechte (Urheberrechtsverordnung, URV), AS 1993, 1821 ff.

The official texts of the federal codes and statutes are available online (http://www.admin.ch/ch/d/sr/sr.html) or at the publication center of the federal administration in Bern (http://www.admin.ch/ch/d/bk/kav/index_de.html). The title page of each enactment gives all the relevant information needed for correct citations.

2.2 Codes

Cite codes by article and paragraph and short or abbreviated title. When cited for the first time, the code should be cited in full (see Section 2.1) or the full citation should be given in a footnote following the short title or abbreviation:

Art. 2 Abs. 3 Urheberrechtsgesetz.

Art. 2 Abs. 3 URG.

Alternatively, cite codes by abbreviated title, article, and paragraph referenced (in Roman numerals):

URG 2 III.

The abbreviations of major federal codes are:

Civil Code: *Zivilgesetzbuch* (ZGB), *Code Civil* (CC), *Codice Civile* (CC)
Law of Obligations: *Obligationenrecht* (OR), *Droit des Obligations* (CO), *Diritto delle Obbligazioni* (CO)

Criminal Code: *Strafgesetzbuch* (StGB), *Code Pénal* (CP), *Codice Penale* (CP)

2.3 Gazettes

The Constitution, federal codes and statutes, and decrees are published by the federal administration in German, French, and Italian in the following series:

Adjusted Collection of Federal Law: *Bereinigte Sammlung der Bundesgesetze und Verordnungen* (BS)

Official Collection of Federal Law: *Amtliche Sammlung der Bundesgesetze und Verordnungen* (AS)

Systematic Collection of Federal Law: *Systematische Sammlung des Bundesrechts* (SR)

The cantonal statutes are available in the cantonal state offices (*Staatskanzlei*). The cantons and some large municipalities publish their law in their own collections, and most can be found online (e.g., http://www.informationjuridique.admin.ch/index_de.html).

3.0 Jurisprudence

3.1 Unpublished Cases

Cite cases not published in an official reporter by the name of the court (the Federal Supreme Court, *Bundesgerichtsentscheid*, is usually abbreviated "BGE"), date of decision, and docket number (in parentheses, if available). If the decision has been published elsewhere, include a citation to the periodical in which the case is published. The exact paragraph of the decision may be cited by adding "E." (for *Erwägung*) and paragraph referenced:

BGE vom 23. Dezember 2003 (4C.224/2003).

BGE vom 3. April 1996 in ZBI 1997, S. 65 ff., E. 4.b.

In Switzerland, case law is an auxiliary source of law. Cantonal courts handle most of the cases dealing both with federal and cantonal law on the district and appellate court level. The Swiss Federal Supreme Court generally acts as a court of ultimate resort.

Typically, district court decisions are not published at all, and only select appellate court decisions are published (in cantonal law reviews). Select Federal Supreme Court decisions are officially published in the *Amtliche Sammlung*.

3.2 Published Cases

Cite cases published in an official reporter by abbreviated title of the reporter, volume, and page number referenced. If desired, the paragraph referenced may be included by adding "E." (for *Erwägung*) and paragraph referenced:

BGE 124 II 53, E.1a.

ATF 117 V 42.

3.3 Reports

Select Federal Supreme Court decisions are published in the *Amtliche Sammlung der Entscheidungen des Schweizerischen Bundesgerichtes* (cited as "BGE" in German, "ATF" in French, "DTF" in Italian). All decisions (since 2000) are available online (http://www.bger.ch). Decisions are published in German, French, or Italian, according to the language used in the litigation.

An important unofficial reporter of Federal Supreme Court cases — collecting officially published cases, select unpublished cases, and German translations of French and Italian decisions — is *Die Praxis des Schweizerischen Bundesgerichts* (abbreviated "Pra").

A number of law reviews, most highly specialized, also print cantonal and federal court decisions, often accompanied by explanatory and/or critical notes. Among the most important (and more general) are *Aktuelle Juristische Praxis* (AJP), *Schweizerische Juristenzeitung* (SJZ), *Journal des Tribunaux* (JdT), *La Semaine Judiciare* (Sem. Jud.), and *Repertorio di Giurisprudenza Patria* (Rep.).

3.4 Courts

Abbreviations of Federal Courts are:

Federal Supreme Court: *Schweizerisches Bundesgericht* (BGer), *Tribunal Fédéral* (TF), *Tribunale Federale* (TF)

Federal Supreme Social Security Court: *Schweizerisches Versicherungsgericht* (EVG), *Tribunal Fédéral des assurances* (TFA), *Tribunale Federale delle assicurazioni* (TFA)

Designations of cantonal courts vary from canton to canton; the most common are:

Appellate Court: *Obergericht / Kantonsgericht / Appellationshof*
District Court: *Bezirksgericht / Amtsgericht*
Commercial Court (some cantons only): *Handelsgericht*

T A I W A N

T'ai-wan (Republic of China)

I. COUNTRY PROFILE (CIVIL LAW)

Taiwan is a democratic republic with a civil law system primarily influenced by Japan, Germany, and the United States. The official title of Taiwan is "Republic of China" (ROC) (N.B.: "China" refers to the People's Republic of China (PRC)). Although there continues to be a dispute over Taiwan's sovereignty between the ROC and the PRC, most major nations maintain unofficial, semi-diplomatic relations with Taiwan.

The Constitution, adopted in 1947 for all of China, has been heavily revised since 1991 (with the last revision occurring in June 2005), in response to Taiwan's abandonment of its claim of governing mainland China.

The President, who is the head of state, has authority over the five administrative branches (*Yuan*): Executive, Legislative, Control, Judicial, and Examination. Executive power is vested in the Executive branch, which consists of the Premier and the Cabinet.

The National Assembly, a standing constitutional convention and electoral college, was established under the 1947 Constitution and held some parliamentary functions. In 1991, the people of Taiwan elected the Second National Assembly. This National Assembly amended the Constitution in 1994, paving the way for the direct election of the President and Vice President in March 1996. In April 2000, the members of the National Assembly voted to permit their terms of office to expire without holding new elections. Legislative power is now vested primarily in the unicameral Legislative Yuan.

The Judicial Branch administers Taiwan's courts. It includes a 16-member Council of Grand Justices, which has exclusive authority to interpret the Constitution and which also renders binding interpretations of statutes and regulations. The court system is composed primarily of the Supreme Court, High Court, and District Courts, all of which have general jurisdiction over civil and criminal matters. The District Courts have original jurisdiction over civil and criminal cases, and the High Courts have appellate jurisdiction to review District Court decisions and original jurisdiction for treason cases. The Supreme Court, as the court of last resort, has appellate jurisdiction to review all lower court decisions on questions of law. Parallel to these courts of general jurisdiction are the Administrative Courts (the Supreme Administrative Court and the High Administrative

Courts), which hear public law controversies, and the Committee on the Discipline of Public Functionaries, which presides over trials of civil servants accused of misconduct.

The Constitution provides for local self-government, which is conducted at three levels. At the highest level there are provinces (Taiwan and Fujian Provinces) and special municipalities (Taipei and Kaohsiung municipalities). Under the provincial level are county (e.g., Liyan County) and provincial cities (e.g., Tainan). Finally, there are rural and urban townships or county municipalities within the provincial counties. The heads of the local governments are elected by the people to four-year terms. Limited legislative powers concerning local affairs are exercised primarily by the municipal and county councils, which are elected by the people.

Internet Resources:

Office of the President:	http://www.president.gov.tw
National Assembly:	http://www.nasm.gov.tw
Executive Yuan:	http://www.ey.gov.tw
Legislative Yuan:	http://www.ly.gov.tw
Judicial Yuan:	http://www.judicial.gov.tw
Control Yuan:	http://www.cy.gov.tw
Examination Yuan:	http://www.exam.gov.tw
Ministry of Justice:	http://www.moj.gov.tw
Ministry of Economic Affairs:	http://www.moea.gov.tw
Ministry of Foreign Affairs:	http://www.mofa.gov.tw

II.   CITATION GUIDE

There is no uniform code of citation in Taiwan. The following represents an English transliteration of citation forms commonly used in textbooks and scholarly works.

0.1 A Note on Language

The official language is Mandarin Chinese, but Taiwanese is frequently used. The Romanization of Chinese in Taiwan uses *Tongyong pinyin*, which has been officially adopted by the national government, *Hanyu pinyin*, and Wade-Giles. Despite the official recognition of *Tongyong pinyin*, several Romanization systems are used concurrently by different levels of government, and within some levels of government, different systems are used for different purposes. This section primarily uses the traditional Wade-Giles system.

0.2 A Note on Dates

Dates are often cited using the Roman calendar along with the Min Gou calendar year in the following format: "Min Guo" (sometimes spelled "Min Kuo"), [year], "nian" (meaning "year"), [month], [day]. Reference may also be made to the year under the Roman calendar after the date or the citation (in square brackets).

1.0 Constitution

Cite the 1947 ROC Constitution (*Chung Hua Min Guo Hsien Fa*) by its abbreviated title ("Hsien Fa"), article, and section or paragraph referenced:

Hsien Fa [Constitution], art. 64, para. 1, subpara. 2.

Amendments to the ROC Constitution are consolidated as a separate text. Cite the additional articles added by amendment (*Chung Hua Min Guo Hsien Fa Tseng Hsiu T'iao Wen*) by its abbreviated title ("Hsien Fa Tseng Hsiu T'iao Wen"), article, and section or paragraph referenced:

Hsien Fa Tseng Hsiu T'iao Wen [Additional Articles to the Constitution], art. 9, para. 1, subpara. 2.

An official English translation of the Constitution and additional articles can be found at the English-language website of the Office of the President: http://www.president.gov.tw/en/.

2.0 Legislation

Cite codes, statutes, and regulations by title and subdivision referenced by title (optional), followed by article, paragraph, subparagraph and item, or part, chapter, section, subsection and item:

Min Fa, Ch'in Shu Pien [Civil Code, Family Part], art. 1052, para. 1, subpara 4.

Hsing Fa [Criminal Code], art. 38, para. 1, subpara. 4.

3.0 Jurisprudence

3.1 Interpretations of the Judicial Yuan and the Council of Grand Justices

Cite interpretations by the year (optional, using the Min Guo calendar, see Section 0.2 above), type of interpretation, and interpretation number:

1953.04.24 Yuan Tzu No. 15.

Yuan Cheh Tzu [Yuan Interpretation] No. 2926.

Shih Tzu [Interpretation of Council of Grand Justices] No. 446.

3.2 English Translations of Interpretations

Cite the English translation of an interpretation by interpretation number, translator, Constitutional Court Reporter by volume, abbreviated title, first page of the interpretation and page referenced, date of decision (optional), and year of publication of the reporter:

> Interpretation No. 499 [translated by Prof. Andy Y. Sun], 1 ROC Const. Ct. 1, 3 (decision rendered on March 24, 2000) (2000).

English translations of interpretations may be found on the website of the Judicial Yuan.

3.3 Precedents and Decisions

Cite cases by the name of the court, year (optional, using the Min Gou calendar, see Section 0.2 above), location of the court (for the Supreme Court only), jurisdiction (e.g., appeal, objection, traffic, etc.), case number, and case type (precedent or decision). The case is not precedent unless so indicated.

> Tsui Kao Fa Yuen 53 Nien T'ai Shang Tzu Ti 592 Hao P'an Li [Supreme Court 1964 Tai-Appeal No. 592 Precedent].

> Tsui Kao Fa Yuen 29 Nien Tu Shang Tzu Ti 1005 Hao P'an Li [Supreme Court 1940 Appeal No.1005 Precedent].

> Hsing Cheng Fa Yuen 46 Nien Ts'ai Tzu Ti 41 Hao P'an Li [Administrative Court 1957 Ruling No. 41 Precedent].

Note: For cases decided before 1949, it is important to provide the location of the Supreme Court, as its location changed periodically.

T A N Z A N I A

Jamhuri ya Muungano wa Tanzania
(United Republic of Tanzania)

I. COUNTRY PROFILE (COMMON LAW)

Tanzania is a republic composed of 26 regions. Tanzania's official languages are Swahili (also known as Kiswahili) and English. Its legal system is based on the common law tradition.

The Union Constitution (*Katiba ya Jamhuri ya Muungano wa Tanzania*), which was adopted in 1977, establishes the form of government. It was amended in 1984 to include a Bill of Rights and has been amended several times since. The 1992 amendments to the Union Constitution implemented a multiparty democracy in Tanzania.

Executive power is vested in the Government. The head of the Government is the President of the United Republic, who is also the head of state. The President is directly elected by the people to a five-year term. The Vice President is also directly elected by the people to a five-year term on the same ballot as the President. According to the Constitution, if the President comes from the mainland, the Vice President must come from Zanzibar, and vice versa. Members of the Cabinet, including the Prime Minister, are appointed by the President.

Legislative power is vested in the unicameral National Assembly (*Bunge*). Two hundred thirty-two of the 274 members of the National Assembly are directly elected by the people, 37 members are women, nominated by the President, and five are members of the Zanzibar House of Representatives. All members serve five-year terms. The National Assembly enacts legislation that applies to the entire United Republic as well as legislation that applies only to the mainland. The National Assembly may amend the Constitution by a two-thirds majority vote of both the Zanzibar and mainland representatives for certain provisions, and by a two-thirds majority of all representatives for other provisions.

Zanzibar is a semi-autonomous region governed by the 1984 Zanzibar Constitution. The President of Zanzibar, who is head of government for matters internal to Zanzibar, is directly elected by the people of Zanzibar to a five-year term. Zanzibar also has its own House of Representatives, which enacts legislation for Zanzibar for all non-Union matters. The 50 members of the Zanzibar House of Representatives are directly elected by the people of Zanzibar to five-year terms. The Union Constitution provides that any law promulgated by the House of Representatives that is under the jurisdiction of the National

Assembly is void, and vice versa. It further provides that any law enacted in Zanzibar that conflicts with the Union Constitution is null and void.

Judicial power is vested in the courts, which consist of the Permanent Commission of Enquiry (the official ombudsman), the Court of Appeal, the High Court, the District Courts, and the Primary Courts. The Court of Appeal consists of a chief justice and four judges. The High Court consists of a Head Judge (*Jaji Kiongozi*) and 29 judges appointed by the President and holds regular sessions in all regions. Constitutional disputes between the Union Government and the Zanzibar Government are referred to the Special Constitutional Court of the Union, which has equal representation from Zanzibar and the mainland.

The Primary Courts, which are courts of limited jurisdiction, hear petty civil cases and misdemeanors. Appeals of decisions of the Primary Courts are heard by the higher courts. The higher Courts are courts of unlimited civil and criminal jurisdiction. The Court of Appeals of the United Republic is the highest court.

Zanzibar has a separate judicial system, which includes a High Court, Kadhis Courts, and Magistrate Courts. Decisions of the Zanzibar High Court can be appealed to the Court of Appeals, except for those involving issues of constitutional or Islamic law. Islamic courts also operate in Zanzibar and have jurisdiction over cases involving Muslim residents in the areas of marriage, divorce, and inheritance.

Internet Resources:

Official site:	http://www.tanzania.go.tz
Information gateway:	http://www.tzonline.org
Parliament:	http://www.parliament.go.tz
Law Reform Commission:	http://www.lrct-tz.org

II. CITATION GUIDE

1.0 Constitution

Cite the Union Constitution by title and subdivision(s) referenced:

Constitution of the United Republic of Tanzania, Article 36(2).

2.0 Legislation and Other Non-Judicial Sources of Law

Cite legislation by title, year, act number, source, and subdivision(s) referenced:

Regulation of Land Tenure (Established Villages) Act, 1992, Act No 22 of 1992.

Income Tax Act No. 33 of 1974, ss 2(1), 2(b)(i), & 34(1).

Civil Procedure Decree, Cap. 8, s 15(c).

Rent Restriction Decree, Cap 98, the Laws of Zanzibar, s 24(1).

3.0 Jurisprudence

3.1 Reported Cases

Cite reported cases by the name of the parties (italicized), year (also represents the reporter volume, normally in square brackets), reporter in which the case is published by title and page referenced, and, if not clear from the title of the reporter, and the name of the court in parentheses:

> *Jimmy David Nyonya v. National Milling Corporation Limited* [1994] TLR 28 (HC).

> *Himid Mbaye v. The Brigade Commander* [1994] TLR 294 (HCZ).

3.2 Unreported Cases

Cite unreported cases by the name of the parties (italicized), case type, number and year, deciding court in parentheses, and "(unreported)":

> *R. v. Asha Mkwizu Hauli*, Crim Sessions Case No. 3 of 1984 (DSM) (unreported).

> *I G Lazaro v. Josephine Mgombera*, Civil Appeal No. 2 of 1986 (CA) (unreported).

3.3 Courts

Abbreviations of courts include:

DSM Magistrate Court (DSM)
Mainland High Court (HC)
Tabora Magistrate Court (Tabora)
Zanzibar High Court (HCZ)
Court of Appeals (CA)
(Former) Court of Appeals of East Africa (EA)

3.4 Reports

Reports include:

Tanzania Law Report (TLR)
Zanzibar Law Report (ZLR)
East African Law Report (EA)

III. SELECTED REFERENCES

HENRY BIENEN, TANZANIA: PARTY TRANSFORMATION AND ECONOMIC DEVELOPMENT (Princeton University Press 1970).

TANZANIA: DEMOCRACY IN TRANSITION (Immanuel K. Bavu et al. eds., Dar es Salaam University Press 1990).

JENNIFER WIDNER, BUILDING THE RULE OF LAW (Norton, London 2001).

T H A I L A N D

Ratcha Anachak Thai (Kingdom of Thailand)

I. COUNTRY PROFILE (CIVIL LAW)

Thailand is a constitutional monarchy composed of 76 provinces (*Changwat*). Thailand's official language is Thai. Its legal system is based primarily on the civil law tradition, but it is also influenced by the common law tradition.

The Constitution, signed by King Phumiphon in 1997, establishes the form of government. Executive power is vested in the Government. The King, who is the head of state, is the hereditary monarch. The King has power to convene the National Assembly, veto legislation, dissolve the House of Representatives, issue Emergency Decrees in relation to national security, issue Royal Decrees, declare war, declare and lift martial law, and conclude peace treaties. The Prime Minister, who is the head of the Government, is selected from among the members of the House of Representatives and is appointed by the King. In practice, the Prime Minister is usually the leader of the party that organizes a majority coalition in the House of Representatives. The Cabinet is composed of a Council of Ministers and a Privy Council.

Legislative power is vested in the bicameral National Assembly (*Rathasapha*), which consists of the Senate (*Wuthisapha*) and the House of Representatives (*Sapha Phuthaen Ratsadon*). The 200 members of the Senate are directly elected by the people to six-year terms, while the 500 members of the House of Representatives are directly elected by the people to four-year terms. Among other powers, the National Assembly controls the administration of state affairs, approves various issues such as succession to the throne, and declares wars. Only members of the House of Representatives may introduce bills and organic law bills. After the House of Representatives passes a bill or an organic law bill, it is sent to the Senate for consideration for a maximum of 60 days.

Judicial power is vested in the courts. The Constitutional Court is the highest court of appeals. Its jurisdiction, however, is limited to clearly defined constitutional issues. Members of the Constitutional Court are nominated by the Senate and appointed by the King. The Courts of Justice have jurisdiction over criminal and civil cases and are organized in three tiers: Courts of First Instance (*Sarn Pang* for civil matters, and *Sarn Aya* for criminal cases), the Court of Appeals (*Sarn Uthorn*), and the Supreme Court of Justice (*Sarn Dika*). In addition, Provincial Courts (*Sarn Changwat*) exercise unlimited original civil and criminal jurisdiction outside Bangkok. The Court of Appeals consists of three regional courts and a Bangkok court. The Supreme Court, which consists of 15 divisions, has jurisdiction to hear all appeals. Judges are appointed and removed by the King upon the recommendation of the Court of Justice of Judicial Commission. In Thailand's southern provinces, where Muslims constitute a majority of the population, Provincial Islamic Committees have specialized jurisdiction over family, marriage, and probate matters. Finally, specialized courts, such as the Central Intellectual Property and International Trade Court and the Central Bankruptcy Court, deal with particular commercial matters.

Internet Resources:

Government:	http://www.thaigov.go.th
Judiciary:	http://www.judiciary.go.th
Parliament:	http://www.parliament.go.th
Senate:	http://www.senate.go.th
Ministry of Justice:	http://www.muj.go.th
Ministry of Foreign Affairs:	http://www.mfa.go.th

II.   CITATION GUIDE

There is no uniform code of citation in Thailand. The following represents common practices.

1.0 Constitution

Cite the Constitution by title, statute number (in parentheses), and year:

Radthathammanoon (B.E. 2534) — 1997.

2.0 Legislation

Cite legislation by title (capitalized if in English), number, and year (in parentheses):

PATENT ACT, B.E. 2535 (1992) (Thai).

Por Sor 2535 [Patent Act B.E. 2535] (1992).

2.1 Official Publications

Laws may also be cited by their location in an official or unofficial gazette. Cite gazettes by volume, title (capitalized), page on which the law appears, number of the law, and date:

108 RAADCHAKIDJAA [ROYAL THAI GOV'T GAZETTE] pt.216 (B.E.2534, Dec. 9, 1991).

Thailand's Official Gazette is the *Ratchakitchanubeska*. An unofficial version (Thai text with English translation) is the *Raadchakidjaa* (Royal Thai Government Gazette).

3.0 Jurisprudence

Cite cases by name of the court, case number, and date:

Supreme Court Dika No.913/2536, March 26, 1993.

3.1 Reports

Reporters include the *Kamphiphaksa San Dika* and the *Kum Pipaksa Dika*.

III. SELECTED REFERENCES

BORWORNSAK UWANNO & SURAKIART SATHIRATHAI, INTRODUCTION TO THE THAI LEGAL SYSTEM, 4 CHULALONGKORN L. REV. 39 (1985-86).

T U R K E Y

Türkiye Cumhuriyeti (The Turkish Republic)

I. COUNTRY PROFILE (CIVIL LAW)

Turkey is a republican parliamentary democracy composed of 81 Provinces. Each Province (*il*; plural *iller*) is subdivided into Districts (*ilçe*) and Townships or Communes (*bucak*). Turkey's official language is Turkish. Its legal system is based on the civil law tradition.

The Constitution, promulgated on November 7, 1982, establishes the form of government. Legislative power is vested in the unicameral Turkish Grand National Assembly (*Turkiye Buyuk Millet Meclisi*). The 550 members of the National Assembly are directly elected by the people to five-year terms. The National Assembly may decide to hold new elections at any time before the end of its regular term. Under certain circumstances, the President of the Republic may also call for new elections. The National Assembly oversees the executive branch by means of questions (*soru*), oral questions with debate (*genel görüşme*), parliamentary investigations (*meclis araştırması*), parliamentary inquiries (*meclis soruşturması*), and interpellations (*gensoru*). It also controls the national budget. Rejection of the budget bill is considered an indirect vote for censure of the Council of Ministers.

Executive authority is vested in the Government. The President of the Republic, who is the head of state, is elected by the National Assembly to a seven-year term. The Council of Ministers (*Bakanlar Kurulu*) is composed of the Prime Minister, who is designated by the President from among the members of the National Assembly, and other Ministers, who are nominated by the Prime Minister and appointed by the President. The Council of Ministers must obtain a vote of confidence in the Assembly in order to operate. The executive branch enacts regulations, bylaws, and various other rules or supplemental legislation, a power that is referred to as the regulative power of the executive (*yürütme organının düzenleme yetkisi*). All presidential decrees must be counter-signed by the Prime Minister and the specific Ministers concerned. Many of the President's other powers require the participation of the Prime Minister and other Ministers concerned, who thus assume political responsibility for those decisions. One important power of the President that does not involve participation of the Council of Ministers is the dissolution of the National Assembly, effected when conditions set forth in the Constitution are met.

Judicial power is vested in the courts, which include the Constitutional Court, the High Court of Appeals (*Yargitay*), the Council of State (*Danistay*), the Court of Accounts (*Sayistay*), the Military High Court of Appeals, and the Military High Administrative Court. The Constitutional Court has exclusive jurisdiction to determine the constitutionality of laws, statutory decrees, and the standing orders of the National Assembly. The Constitutional Court also reviews constitutional amendments to determine whether they comply with procedural rules, tries impeachment cases, and determines the constitutionality of political party activity. It is composed of 11 regular and four alternate members. The President appoints the members of the Constitutional Court. Several of the members are appointed from the other courts. Other members are elected from administrative officials, lawyers, and teaching staff of institutions of higher learning.

Internet Resources:

Turkish Embassy: http://www.washington.emb.mfa.gov.tr

II. CITATION GUIDE

There is no uniform code of citation in Turkey. The Citation Regulations set out by the University of Istanbul are used by the legal community as a foundation for citation practices. The following represents the most accepted citation practices, but they are not adhered to by all authors.

0.1 Common Abbreviations

Common abbreviations in Turkish include article ("madde" or "m."), paragraph ("fikra" or "f."), and page ("s.")

1.0 Constitution

Cite the Constitution by title (*Türkiye Cumhuriyeti Anayasası*) or abbreviated title ("T.C. Ana." or "Ana."), and subdivision referenced (see Section 0.1):

Türkiye Cumhuriyeti Anayasası Madde 3.

T.C. Ana. m.3.

Ana. m.3.

2.0 Legislation

2.1 Statutes, Laws, Regulations, and Decrees

Cite statutes, laws, regulations, and decrees by short title or abbreviated title, and subdivision(s) referenced:

Vergi usul kanunu Madde 20 fıkra 3 [Tax Procedure Code, Article 20 paragraph 3].

VUK. m. 20 f. 3.

More formally, cite a code as a whole by title, law number, followed by the official gazette in which it is published by title, date and number, and date of enactment:

Türk Medeni Kanunu, Kanun No.: 743 R.G.: 04.04.1926 Sayı: 339, Kabul Tarihi: 17.02.1926.

Turkish Civil Code, Law No.: 743 Official Gazette [Resmi Gazete = R.G.], 4 April 1926 No. 339, enacted: 17 February 1926.

Other legislative sources of law use the same citation form as codes, including statutory decrees (*kanun hükmünde kararnameler*), regulations (*tüzük*), and bylaws (*yönetmelik*).

2.2 Codes

Cite codes by abbreviated name and article:

TTK.m.741.

MK.m.17.

The abbreviations of major Codes are:

Constitution: *Anayasa* (Ana)
Code of Obligations: *Borçlar Kanunu* (BK)
Code of Criminal Procedure: *Ceza Muhakemeleri Usulü Kanunu* (CMUK)
Code of Civil Procedure: *Hukuk Usulü Muhakemeleri Kanunu* (HUMK)
Execution, Enforcement of Judgments, and Bankruptcy Code: *İcra ve İflas Kanunu* (IIK)
Code of Administrative Trial Procedure: *İdari Yargılama Usulü Kanunu* (IYUK)
Civil Code: *Medeni Kanun* (MK)
Turkish Penal Code: *Türk Ceza Kanunu* (TCK)
Turkish Commercial Code: *Türk Ticaret Kanunu* (TTK)

3.0 Jurisprudence

Cite cases by name of the court, chamber number, the words "Esas No." (Case No.), year and number of the case, the words "Karar No." (Judgment No.), year and number of the judgment, and the reporter in which the case is published by title, year, number and page referenced (in parentheses). Elements may be abbreviated as shown below the full citations:

Danıştay 7. Daire, Esas No. 1987/501, Karar No. 1987/1471 (Danıştay Dergisi, 1988, sayı 68-69, sayfa 476) [Council of State Journal, 1988, No. 68-69, p. 476].

DS. 7. D., E. 1987/501, K. 1987/1471 (DD, 1988, S. 68-69, s. 476).

3. Hukuk Dairesi, 15.9.1986, Esas No. 7949, Karar No. 8017 (Yargıtay Kararları Dergisi, 1986 sayi 11, sh.1616) [Court of Cassation Journal, 1986, No. 11, p. 1616].

3. HD. 15.9.1986, E. 7949, K. 8017 (YKD, 1986, s.11 sh.1616).

III.   SELECTED REFERENCES

TUĞRUL ANSAY & DON WALLACE JR., INTRODUCTION TO TURKISH LAW (3d ed., Kluwer 1987).

BERNARD LEWIS, THE EMERGENCE OF MODERN TURKEY (Oxford University Press 1968).

ERGUN ÖZBUDUN, TÜRK ANAYASA HUKUKU (Yetkin Yayınları 1993).

MICHAEL N. SCHMITT & MEHMET NUR TANIŞIK, TURKISH LABOR LAW (Transnational Publishers 1995).

UNITED KINGDOM

I. COUNTRY PROFILE (COMMON LAW)

The United Kingdom is a constitutional monarchy composed of Great Britain and Northern Ireland. Great Britain consists of the countries of England, Scotland, and Wales. Each region is further subdivided into various municipalities, counties, and parliamentary constituencies. The United Kingdom's official language is English. Its legal system is based primarily on the common law tradition, although some parts of the legal system include elements of the civil law tradition. The United Kingdom is a Member State of the European Union.

The United Kingdom does not have a written constitution. Its constitutional law is based partially on common law and practice and partially on statutory sources such as the Magna Carta, the Bill of Rights, the Union with Scotland Act, and the European Communities Act.

Executive power is vested in the Government. The Sovereign, who is determined by a hereditary monarchy, is head of state, although this role is largely ceremonial. The Prime Minister, who is head of the Government, is appointed by the Sovereign from among the members of the House of Commons. Typically the Prime Minister is the leader of the majority party or coalition. Members of the Cabinet of Ministers are appointed by the Prime Minister.

Legislative power is vested in the bicameral Parliament, which consists of the House of Commons and the House of Lords. The 659 members of the House of Commons are directly elected by the people to five-year terms. Members of the House of Lords, none of whom are elected by the people, include approximately 500 life peers, 92 hereditary peers, and 26 clergy. The Prime Minister may ask the monarch to dissolve Parliament and call a general election at any time. Formally, legislation, which is proposed by the Government, must be approved by both Houses of Parliament and must receive Royal assent. In reality, legislative power is exercised almost exclusively by the House of Commons.

Judicial power is vested in the courts. However, the United Kingdom has three separate and distinct legal systems rather than a single unified system. England and Wales have a common law system, which incorporates a system of equity administered by the Court of Chancery. Although power has been devolved to Wales, its legal system is not distinct from that of England. Scotland has a mixed legal system, deriving principles from both Roman and English law. Finally,

Northern Ireland has a legal system somewhat different from that of England, including removal of the right to trial by jury for certain terrorist offenses.

The courts include the House of Lords, the Supreme Courts of England, Wales, and Northern Ireland, and Scotland's Court of Session and Court of the Justiciary. The House of Lords' legal functions are separate from its legislative functions. The Appellate Committee of the House of Lords is the final court of appeal in the United Kingdom and is composed of the Lord Chancellor and Lords of Appeal in the Ordinary. It hears civil and criminal appeals from the Courts of Appeal in England, Wales, and Northern Ireland, and civil appeals from the Court of Session in Scotland. Cases are heard by up to 13 judges, or Law Lords.

The Supreme Courts of England, Scotland, and Wales are composed of Courts of Appeal, High Courts of Justice, Crown Courts, and Magistrates' Courts. The Civil Divisions of the Courts of Appeal hear appeals from decisions of the High Courts and County Courts. The High Courts consist of three divisions: Chancery Courts, Family Courts, and Queen's Bench. The High Courts are courts of general civil jurisdiction. The High Courts sometimes hear appeals from decisions of the County Courts. The Magistrates' Courts and County Courts exercise limited civil jurisdiction.

Criminal jurisdiction is exercised in the first instance by Magistrates' Courts, in summary trials, and the Crown Courts, in jury trials. Appeal may be had to the High Court (Queen's Bench) or the Criminal Divisions of the Courts of Appeal.

The Judicial Committee of the Privy Council hears appeals from courts in United Kingdom Overseas Territories, a few Commonwealth countries, and the Channel Islands and the Isle of Man. It also hears admiralty and ecclesiastical matters and professional disciplinary proceedings.

In recent years, many governmental powers have devolved to the regions. National legislation reestablished the Scottish Parliament, created the Northern Ireland Assembly, and granted both bodies legislative competence over local affairs. Similarly, a National Assembly for Wales has been created and vested with governmental powers. Certain powers, including defense and foreign affairs, however, are reserved for and continue to reside with the House of Commons.

Internet Resources:

Parliament (United Kingdom):	http://www.parliament.uk
Northern Ireland Assembly:	http://www.ni-assembly.gov.uk
Scottish Parliament:	http://www.scottish.parliament.uk
National Assembly of Wales:	http://www.wales.gov.uk
Government Information Service:	http://www.open.gov.uk
Lord Chancellor's Department:	http://www.open.gov.uk/lcd

House of Lords judgments, from
   Nov. 1996:   http://www.parliament.the-
                                             stationery-office.co.uk/pa/ld1/
                                             ldjudinf
Acts of UK Parliament: http://www.hmso.gov.uk/acts.htm
Statutory Instruments
   (regulations):   http://www.hmso.gov.uk/stat.htm
Courts in England and Wales: http://www.courtservice.gov.uk
UK Official Publications: http://www.official-documents.co.uk

II.   CITATION GUIDE

There is no uniform code of citation in the United Kingdom. The following
represents a number of widely accepted citation norms. However, common
abbreviations (chapter, section, etc.) may vary.

1.0 Constitution

The United Kingdom has no single written constitution. Instead, constitutional
law is contained in a series of documents and in common law. Cite the most
important of those documents, which are listed below, by name of the source
and year, as well as regnal year (if any) (by year of the monarch's reign, abbreviated name of the monarch, and numeric designation of the monarch in Arabic
numerals [unless it is the first monarch with that name, in which case omit the
latter numeric designation]), and then chapter:

   The Magna Carta of Edward 1 (1297), 25 Edw. 1.

   The Petition of Right (1627), 3 Car. 1, c.1.

   The Bill of Rights (1688 or 1689), 1 Will. & Mary, sess. 2, c.2.

   The Act of Settlement (1700 or 1701), 12 & 13 Will. 3, c.2.

   The European Communities Act 1972.

   The Human Rights Act 1998.

2.0 Legislation

Cite a statute by short title, year, chapter number, section, and subdivisions
referenced (in parentheses):

   Companies Act 1985, c.6, s.6 (ii)(b)(iii).

Short titles may be abbreviated if used repeatedly in legal writing. Usually the title of the act is replaced by its initials, which should be indicated as follows when first used:

> Companies Act 1989 (CA 1989).

Older legislation may not have short titles. Thus, cite statutes enacted before 1962 by regnal year, chapter number, section, common name or a description of its subject matter, and year:

> 24 Geo. 2 c.24, s.23 (Minority of Successor to Crown) (1750) (repealed).
>
> 1 Edw. 6 c.11 (Repeal of 28 Hen. 8 c.17) (1547).
>
> Obscene Publications Act 1959, 7 & 8 Eliz. 2, c.66.

2.1 Statutory Instruments

Cite statutory instruments by full title, "SI," and year and number (year/number):

> Sex Discrimination Act 1975 (Application to Armed Forces etc) Regulations 1994, SI 1994/3276.

2.2 Treaties and Conventions

Cite a treaty or convention as described in Section 1.0 of Part II, on Treaties and Conventions, filling in the source information with the British treaty series by year, abbreviated title (Gr. Brit. T.S.), treaty number, and Command number:

> [Treaty information], 1950 Gr. Brit. T.S. No. 1 (Cmnd. 40), [date of entry, etc.].

3.0 Jurisprudence

3.1 Unreported Cases

Cite unreported cases by name of the parties [Claimant/Appellant v. Defendant/Respondent] (underlined), "(unreported)," name of court or tribunal, date of decision and transcript number (if available):

> Smith v. Jones (unreported) Court of Appeal (Civil Division) 3rd August 1993.

3.2 Reported Cases

Cite reported cases by name of the parties [Claimant/Appellant v. Defendant/Respondent] (underlined), volume number (usually indicated by a year in square brackets), reporter in which the case is published by abbreviated title and page on which the case begins, court (if not evident from title of the reporter) (in parentheses), and page referenced:

Ebrahimi v. Westbourne Galleries Ltd. [1973] A.C. 360 (HL (E.)).

Simmonds v. The Queen [1998] A.C. 286 (P.C.).

Mainwaring v. Trustees of Henry Smith's Charity [1998] Q.B. 1 (C.A.).

Cobra Golf Inc. v. Rata [1998] Ch. 109.

Ebrahimi v. Westbourne Galleries Ltd. [1973] A.C. 360 (HL (E.)) at pp.361-3.

Note: If the volume is indicated by a reference number and not the year, the year is enclosed in parentheses.

For criminal cases, the usual form is the Crown (abbreviated R., Rex, or Reg.) v. Defendant:

R. v. Lynch [1966] 50 Cr. App. R. 59.

3.3 Reports

There is no official law reporter in England. For cases prior to 1865, it is customary to cite the English Reports (E.R.). After 1865, cases should be cited to the Law Reports or Weekly Law Reports, which are produced by the Incorporated Council of Law Reporting in England and Wales.
The abbreviations of major Law Reports are:

House of Lords, Privy Council, and Appeals Division Cases (A.C.)
Chancery Division Cases (Ch.)
Queen's Bench Division (Q.B.)
King's Bench Division (K.B.)
Family Division (Fam.)

The following commercially published Reports are also available:

Weekly Law Reports (W.L.R.)
All England Law Reports (All E.R.)
Law Journal Reports (L.J.R.)
Law Times Reports (L.T.)

Note: In recent years, it has become the practice in England for cases relating to a specific area of the law to be reported in a special related reporter [e.g., Butterworths Company Law Reports (BCLC)]. In such circumstances, it is permissible to cite the case in this reporter if it is not contained in the Law Reports.

3.4 Judges' Names

Traditionally, references to extracts from the decision of a judge are identified by appending the word "per" and name of the judge to the end of the citation:

J.H. Rayner (Mincing Lane) Ltd. v Department of Trade and Industry [1990] 2 A.C. 418 per Lord Templeman at pp. 479-80.

It is customary to cite the judge's position as it was at the time that the decision was published:

Mr./Mrs. Justice: The Honourable Mr./Mrs. Justice (High Court)
Lord Justice: The Right Honourable Lord Justice (Appeal Court)
His/Her Honour: His/Her Honour Judge (Circuit Judge — Crown Court and County Court)

III. SELECTED REFERENCES

ROGER BIRD, OSBORN'S CONCISE LAW DICTIONARY (7th ed., Sweet & Maxwell, London 1983).

A. BRADLEY & K. EWING, CONSTITUTIONAL LAW AND ADMINISTRATIVE LAW (12th ed., Longman, London 1998).

HALSBURY'S LAWS OF ENGLAND (Lord Hailsham ed., 4th ed., Butterworths, London 1996).

PART 2

CITATION GUIDES FOR

INTERNATIONAL

ORGANIZATIONS AND

RELATED TRIBUNALS

SIGNIFICANT MULTILATERAL TREATIES

I. CITATION GUIDE

1.0 Treaties and Conventions

Generally cite treaties by official title, short title, or common title in square brackets (note: short title may alternatively be placed at the end of the citation), city of signature (optional) and date of completion in parentheses or set off by commas, parties to the treaty (for bilateral treaties), one or more official or unofficial sources (in the order described below; each source is cited according to its own standard), date of entry into force in parentheses or set off by commas, any relevant amendment information (if available), and subdivision referenced:

> International Convention on the Elimination of All Forms of Racial Discrimination (New York, 7 Mar. 1966), 660 U.N.T.S. 195, 5 I.L.M. 352 (1966), *entered into force* 4 Jan. 1969, Art 1.

> *Note:* In practice, the name of the city where the treaty was signed is often omitted. In such a case, the date of completion should be set off by commas:

> International Convention on the Elimination of All Forms of Racial Discrimination, 7 Mar. 1966, 660 U.N.T.S. 195, 5 I.L.M. 352 (1966), *entered into force* 4 Jan. 1969.

For citations in articles having a distribution to a mostly domestic audience, the first source should be a national treaty source from that country, followed by an intergovernmental treaty source (such as the U.N.T.S.), and an unofficial source.

For citations in articles having an international distribution, the first source should be an intergovernmental treaty source (such as the U.N.T.S.), followed by a national treaty source and an unofficial treaty source.

Cite treaties in volumized sources for United States consumption by volume of the reporter, abbreviated title, and page referenced:

> 660 U.N.T.S. 195.

Cite treaties in volumized sources for consumption outside the United States by abbreviated title of the reporter, volume, and page referenced:

> U.N.T.S., vol. 660, p. 195.

2.0 Treaty Sources

Note: Section 2.3 of many of the country profiles in Part I of this manual, as well as Sections 2.2 and 2.4 under some countries, lists their official treaty sources.

Intergovernmental Treaty Sources:

- United Nations Treaty Series (1946-date):
  - x U.N.T.S. xxx
- Pan-American Treaty Series (1949-date):
  - x Pan-Am. T.S. xxx
- European Treaty Series (1948-date):
  - Europ. T.S. No. x
- League of Nations Treaty Series (1920-1945):
  - x L.N.T.S. xxx

Unofficial Treaty Sources:

- International Legal Materials (1962-date):
  - x I.L.M. xxx (Year)
- Hein's United States Treaties and Other International Agreements (1984-date)
  - Hein's No. KAV xxxx
- Bevans (1776-1949):
  - x Bevans xxx
- Nouveau Recueil General des Traits (1494-1943):
  - x Martens Nouveau Recueil (ser. X) xxx
- Parry's Consolidated Treaty Series (1648-1919):
  - x Consol. T.S. xxx

U N I T E D   N A T I O N S

I. ORGANIZATION PROFILE

In the aftermath of World War II, representatives of 50 countries met at the United Nations Conference on International Organization in San Francisco to negotiate the existence of a new international organization to replace the defunct League of Nations. Working from proposals previously submitted by China, the Soviet Union, the United Kingdom, and the United States, the representatives negotiated and drafted the Charter of the United Nations. Forty-nine of the 50 countries signed the Charter on June 26, 1945, and the fiftieth, Poland, followed suit on October 14, 1945. On October 24, 1945, the United Nations (UN) came into existence with the Charter's ratification by a majority of its signatories, including the five so-called "permanent members" of the UN Security Council: China, France, the Soviet Union, the United Kingdom, and the United States. Currently, 192 sovereign states are members of the UN, representing nearly every country in the world.

According to its Charter, the UN has four principal purposes: to maintain international peace and security; to promote respect for human rights; to advance interstate cooperation and respect for international law; and to nurture international social and economic development. The UN works to promote these purposes through a family of agencies engaged in vast array of activities, ranging from providing emergency and disaster relief or promoting the peaceful use of atomic energy to protecting the environment or regulating air and sea travel.

Structurally, the UN has six main organs. Five of them — the General Assembly, the Security Council, the Economic and Social Council, the Trusteeship Council, and the Secretariat — are based at UN Headquarters in New York City. The sixth, the International Court of Justice, is located at The Hague in the Netherlands.

All UN Member States are represented in the UN General Assembly. "A parliament of nations," the General Assembly considers and passes resolutions related to pressing international concerns and UN action. Member States each have one vote. Decisions on key issues, such as international peace and security, the admission of new members, and the UN budget, require two-thirds majorities. Other matters are decided by simple majority. In recent years, a special effort has been made to reach decision through consensus rather than by formal votes. Excepting budget decisions, resolutions of the General Assembly are nonbinding on members; however, resolutions are perceived to carry certain moral and persuasive authority.

The UN Charter gives the Security Council primary responsibility for maintaining international peace and security. Unlike the General Assembly, resolutions of the Security Council are binding on UN members. The Security Council is composed of 15 members: five permanent members with individual veto power (China, France, the Russian Federation, the United Kingdom, and the United States) and ten non-permanent members elected by the General Assembly to two-year terms. When considering a threat to international peace, the Security Council first explores ways to settle the dispute in question peacefully. In cases of hostility or warfare, the Security Council attempts to secure ceasefires and may send a peacekeeping force, populated by military forces voluntarily contributed by Member States on a case-by-case basis, to maintain truces and keep opposing forces apart. The Security Council has the power to impose economic sanctions or order arms embargos, and the Security Council can authorize Member States to use "all necessary means," including collective military actions, to see that its decisions are carried out. The Security Council also makes recommendations to the General Assembly on the appointment of Secretaries-General and admission of new Member States to the UN. Nine votes (without the veto of a permanent member) are required for Security Council action.

The Economic and Social Council (ECOSOC), under the authority of the General Assembly, coordinates the economic and social work of the UN and all of its agencies, as charged under Chapter X of the UN Charter. As the central forum for discussing international economic and social issues, the ECOSOC plays a key role in fostering international cooperation for development. It also provides mechanisms for consultation with non-governmental organizations, thereby maintaining a vital link between the UN and civil society. The ECOSOC has 54 members, elected by the General Assembly for three-year terms. It meets throughout the year and holds a major session each July, during which a special meeting of Ministers, known as the Annual Ministerial Review (AMR), discusses major economic, social, and humanitarian issues, assessing progress on internationally agreed development goals (IADGs) arising out of major conferences and summits. The ECOSOC has authority over a range of subsidiary bodies on different issues areas, which meet regularly and report back to it. The Commission on Human Rights, for example, monitors the observance of human rights throughout the world. Other bodies focus on such issues as social development, the status of women, crime prevention, narcotics, and environmental protection. Five regional commissions promote economic development and cooperation in their respective regions.

The Trusteeship Council was established to provide international supervision for the 11 Trust Territories administered by seven Member States and to ensure that adequate steps were taken to prepare the Territories for self-government or independence. By 1994, all Trust Territories had attained self-government or independence, either as separate States or by joining neighboring independent countries. The last to do so was the Trust Territory of the Pacific Islands — Palau —

which was administered by the United States and became the 185th Member State. Its work completed, the Trusteeship Council now consists of the five permanent members of the Security Council. It has amended its rules of procedure to allow it to meet as and when the occasion may require.

The International Court of Justice, also known as the World Court, is the main judicial organ of the UN. Consisting of 15 judges elected jointly by the General Assembly and the Security Council, the Court decides disputes between countries. Participation by States in a proceeding is voluntary, but if a State agrees to participate, it is obligated to comply with the Court's decision. The Court also provides advisory opinions to the General Assembly and the Security Council upon request.

The UN Secretariat carries out the substantive and administrative work of the UN, as directed by the General Assembly, the Security Council, and the other organs. At its head is the Secretary-General, who provides overall administrative guidance. The Secretariat consists of departments and offices with a total staff of some 8,900 under the regular budget. Staffers are drawn from some 170 countries. Duty stations include UN Headquarters in New York as well as UN offices in Geneva, Vienna, Nairobi, and other locations.

A number of UN offices, programmes, and funds — such as the Office of the UN High Commissioner for Refugees (UNHCR), the UN Development Programme (UNDP), and the UN Children's Fund (UNICEF) — work to improve the economic and social condition of people around the world. They report to the General Assembly or the Economic and Social Council.

In addition, the International Monetary Fund, the World Bank, the World Health Organization, and 11 other independent organizations, known as "specialized agencies," are linked to the UN through cooperative agreements. These agencies are autonomous bodies created by intergovernmental agreements. They have wide-ranging international responsibilities in the economic, social, cultural, educational, health, and related fields. Some of them, like the International Labor Organization and the Universal Postal Union, are older than the UN itself.

All these organizations have their own governing bodies, budgets, and secretariats. Together with the UN, they are known as the UN family, or the UN system. They provide technical assistance and other forms of practical help in virtually all economic and social areas.

The specialized agencies and their mandates are:

ILO (International Labor Organization): Formulates policies and programs to improve working conditions and employment opportunities, and sets labor standards used by countries around the world.

FAO (Food and Agriculture Organization of the UN): Works to improve agricultural productivity and food security and to better the living standards of rural populations.

UNESCO (UN Educational, Scientific and Cultural Organization): Promotes education for all, cultural development, protection of the world's natural and cultural heritage, international cooperation in science, press freedom, and communication.

WHO (World Health Organization): Coordinates programs aimed at solving health problems and the attainment of the highest possible level of health by all people. It works in such areas as immunization, health education, and the provision of essential drugs.

World Bank Group: Provides loans and technical assistance to developing countries to reduce poverty and advance sustainable economic growth.

IMF (International Monetary Fund): Facilitates international monetary cooperation and financial stability, and provides a permanent forum for consultation, advice, and assistance on financial issues.

ICAO (International Civil Aviation Organization): Sets international standards for the safety, security, and efficiency of air transport, and serves as the coordinator for international cooperation in all areas of civil aviation.

UPU (Universal Postal Union): Establishes international regulations for postal services, provides technical assistance, and promotes cooperation in postal matters.

ITU (International Telecommunication Union): Fosters international cooperation to improve telecommunications of all kinds, coordinates usage of radio and TV frequencies, promotes safety measures, and conducts research.

WMO (World Meteorological Organization): Promotes scientific research on the Earth's atmosphere and on climate change, and facilitates the global exchange of meteorological data.

IMO (International Maritime Organization): Works to improve international shipping procedures, raise standards in marine safety, and reduce marine pollution by ships.

WIPO (World Intellectual Property Organization): Promotes international protection of intellectual property and fosters cooperation on copyrights, trademarks, industrial designs, and patents.

IFAD (International Fund for Agricultural Development): Mobilizes financial resources to raise food production and nutrition levels among the poor in developing countries.

UNIDO (UN Industrial Development Organization): Promotes the industrial advancement of developing countries through technical assistance, advisory services, and training.

IAEA (International Atomic Energy Agency): An autonomous intergovernmental organization under the aegis of the UN; it works for the safe and peaceful uses of atomic energy.

Internet Resources:

United Nations:	http://www.un.org
UN System Chart:	http://www.un.org/aboutun/ chart.html
International Court of Justice:	http://www.icj-cij.org
United Nations High Commissioner for Human Rights:	http://www.unhchr.ch
UN High Commissioner for Refugees:	http://www.unhcr.ch
International Criminal Court:	http://www.un.org/law/icc/ index.html
United Nations Development Programme:	http://www.undp.org
UN Educational, Scientific and Cultural Organization:	http://www.unesco.org
Food and Agriculture Organization of the UN:	http://www.fao.org
World Health Organization:	http://www.who.int/en/
International Labor Organization:	http://www.ilo.org
World Bank:	http://www.worldbank.org

II. CITATION GUIDE

1.0 Basic Treaties

1.1 UN Charter

Cite the UN Charter by title and subdivisions referenced:

U.N. Charter, art.2, para.4.

1.2 Basic Treaties

See Section 1.0 of Part II, on Treaties and Conventions, for a citation guide to major multilateral treaties deposited with the UN.

2.0 Documents

2.1 Official Documents

2.1.1 Security Council Resolutions (Security Council Official Record)

Formally, cite Security Council resolutions by resolution number [S.C. Res. #], source (the Security Council Official Record, abbreviated "U.N. SCOR"), U.N. document symbol, year of publication (in parentheses), and paragraph referenced (if necessary):

> S.C. Res. 1304, ¶ 1, U.N. SCOR, U.N. Doc. S/RES/1304 (June 16, 2000).

Alternatively, cite U.N. SCOR by volume, title, and page referenced. Also note that a descriptive title of the resolution may follow the number (in square brackets):

> S.C. Res. 687, 46 U.N. SCOR at 200, U.N. Doc. S/RES/687 (Apr. 8, 1991).

> S.C. Res. 743, 47 U.N. SCOR at 42, U.N. Doc. S/RES/743 (Feb. 21, 1992) [Establishing a United Nations Protection Force "Unprofor"].

Subsequently or informally, cite Security Council resolutions by number, date or year, and page or paragraph referenced:

> S.C. Res. 487 (June 19, 1981), ¶ 3.

2.1.2 General Assembly Official Records

The same general rules apply to General Assembly resolutions that apply to Security Council resolutions (with a few exceptions noted below). Note that the source in the General Assembly Official Record is abbreviated "U.N. GAOR." Formally, cite General Assembly resolutions as follows:

> G.A. Res. 1665, ¶ 1, U.N. GAOR, 16th Sess., Supp. No. 17, U.N. Doc. A/RES1665 (Dec. 4, 1961).

Formally, cite General Assembly resolutions in short form as follows:

> G.A. Res. 183, ¶ 6, GAOR, U.N. Doc. A/RES/54/183 (Feb. 29, 2000).

Subsequently or informally, cite General Assembly resolutions as follows:

> G.A. Res. 2270, ¶ 11 (Nov. 17, 1967).

2.2 Official Record Documents Other than Resolutions

Cite official record documents other than resolutions by title, source [session number, "Session," "Supplement No.", and supplement number], volume in parentheses, page referenced, UN Document symbol, and year in parentheses.

Report of the Human Rights Committee, GAOR, 58th Session Supplement No. 40 (Vol. I), at 100, U.N. Doc. A/58/40 (2002).

2.2.1 UN Yearbooks

Cite material in the UN Yearbook by title of the document (if available), year or volume, abbreviated title of the yearbook ("UNYB"), page referenced, and UN Document symbol (optional):

1980 UNYB, pp.312-314.

1962 UNYB at 108.

2.2.2 Yearbook of the International Law Commission

Cite material in the Yearbook of the International Law Commission (YILC) by title or abbreviated title of the yearbook ("Yearbook of the ILC" or "YILC"), year (in parentheses), volume number (see Note below for explanation), part (if applicable), page number, and paragraph referenced (if applicable):

YILC (1979) Vol. II, Part 2, 115, ¶ 3.

Volume numbers correspond to the following materials:

Vol. I: Summary records of ILC meetings.

Vol. II: Reports of the ILC session to the GA.

2.2.3 Documents Not Published in Official Records

Cite to any official UN document not published in official records by name of author(s) [last name only] or source (include the session if appropriate), title (optional, in quotation marks), UN document symbol, date of issue [day, month, year] (in parentheses), and page and/or subdivision ("para.", "s.", etc.) referenced:

Pellet, "Eighth Report on Reservations to Treaties," A/CN.4/535 (27 May 2003), pp. 10-14, paras. 34-48.

2.3 UN Publications for Sale

Cite UN publications (for sale to the public) by author and/or title, page(s) or paragraph(s) of the citation, the UN document number if available, the sales number (includes multiple numerical and alphabetic elements), and the year of publication. he author should be included only if it is not clear from the title of the document. The first element of the sales number (a letter) indicates the language of the publication; the second element (an Arabic number) indicates the year of publication (e.g., 04); the third element (a Roman numeral) indicates the subject of the publication or source (categories are listed online at http://www.un.org/Depts/dhl/resguide/symbol1.htm). The final element (an Arabic numeral) is a sequential number with no special meaning.

> U.N. DEP'T OF INT'L ECON. & SOC. AFFAIRS, U.N. MODEL DOUBLE TAXATION CONVENTION BETWEEN DEVELOPED AND DEVELOPING COUNTRIES at 243, U.N. Doc.ST/ESA/102, U.N. Sales No. E.80.XVI.3 (1980).

EUROPEAN UNION

I. ORGANIZATION PROFILE

In 1957, six countries — France, Germany, Italy, the Netherlands, Belgium, and Luxembourg — entered into the Rome Treaties, which provided for the creation of three new institutions: the European Economic Community (EEC), the European Coal and Steel Community (ECSC), and the European Atomic Energy Community (Euratom). The original Member States were joined by Denmark, Ireland, and the United Kingdom in 1973, by Greece in 1981, by Portugal and Spain in 1986, and by Austria, Finland, and Sweden in 1995, bringing the total number of Member States to 15.

Major changes to the political agenda and organizational structure of the Communities were introduced by four significant amendments to the Treaty of Rome on the EEC. The 1986 Single European Act provided the EEC with new powers in the fields of the environment, research, and development. The Act also attempted to create a framework for a common foreign policy of the Member States.

The 1992 Maastricht Treaty on the European Union further increased the scope of the EEC's powers (and renamed the institution the European Community (EC)), granting it some aspects of education, culture, public health, and consumer protection powers. The Maastricht Treaty balanced these new powers with the introduction of the principle of subsidiarity as a general principle of Community law.

Moreover, the Treaty of Maastricht provided for the creation of a new entity — the European Union, which was superimposed over the existing structure and whose task is to organize, in a manner demonstrating consistency and solidarity, relations between the Member States and between their peoples.

The European Union is based on three pillars. The first relates to cooperation in the fields of economic, social, and monetary policy. This remains the task of the EC. The second relates to cooperation in the areas of justice and domestic affairs. The third relates to the development and implementation of a common foreign and security policy, possibly leading to a common defense. The European Union exists mainly as a cooperative framework and does not possess any juridical personality as such. The last two pillars are thus independent from the original Treaty of Rome framework and do not, therefore, constitute Community law.

The 1997 Treaty of Amsterdam further enlarged the powers of the Community in areas of visas, asylum, immigration, and employment. The Treaty of Amsterdam also completely renumbered the articles of the previous Treaties.

Finally, the 2001 Treaty of Nice revised certain aspects of Community governance necessary for enlargement of the EU beyond 15 Member States, particularly the size and composition of various political bodies and the decision-making processes used. On May 1, 2004, the EU added ten Member States, incorporating much of Central and Eastern Europe. On January 1, 2007, Romania and Bulgaria jointed the EU, bringing the total number of Member States to 27.

Although the European Constitution failed in 2004, it led to the Lisbon Treaty of 2007, which incorporated many of the same goals. On June 12, 2008, Irish voters through referendum rejected ratification of the Lisbon Treaty, leaving the fate of the European Constitution as of publication of this guide in doubt.

Although the three Communities were established as separate organizations, their institutional structure has rapidly become uniform (although the treaty establishing the European Coal and Steel Community (ECSC) expired on July 23, 2002). Each uses the same organs, with the only variations lying in the powers exercised by the Communities in accordance with each of the Treaties. The primary organs are the European Parliament, the Council of the European Union (informally the Council of Ministers, or simply "Council"), the European Commission, the European Court of Justice, and the Court of First Instance. In addition to these institutions, the organs of the Communities also include the Court of Auditors and various specialized subcommittees. While not uniformly recognized as an organ of the EU, the European Central Bank, established in 1998, also plays a very important role in the implementation and management of the European Monetary Union. Additionally, the informal European Council (not to be mistaken with the Council of Ministers) consists of the Heads of State or Government and the Foreign Ministers of the various Member States, and the President and Vice President of the Commission. Since 1974, the European Council has met twice a year to define political guidelines for the European Union.

The Council of the EU is the principal decision-making body of the Communities. As stated in the EC Treaty, the principal role of the Council is "to ensure the co-ordination of the general economic policies of the Member States." In order to perform this task, the Council is entrusted with the power to enact Community legislation through regulations, directives, and decisions, and to adopt international agreements negotiated by the Commission. The Council is composed of 27 Ministers, one from each of the Member States, and a rotating six-month presidency. Qualified majority voting is the general rule under the EC Treaty, while unanimity or a simple majority is required in certain instances.

The European Commission is the organ of the Communities responsible for initiating European legislation and action and for overseeing the implementation of common policies and Union legislation enacted by Member States. The Commission is composed of 27 Commissioners, who serve five-year terms.

Commissioners are nominated by mutual agreement of the Member States and must be approved by the European Parliament. Each Member State currently is guaranteed at least one commissioner. Commissioners are independent of Member States' national governments. Although the Commission possesses a broad power of initiative when direct regulation is necessary — that is, it can issue a regulation that has a direct effect on the legal orders of Member States without any need for an internalization procedure — that power is generally limited to matters specifically mentioned in the Treaties. An important exception, contained in the ECSC Treaty, allows the Commission to make decisions that directly bind enterprises and to enforce these decisions by imposing fines and penalties. Acting in this role, the Commission may institute proceedings before the European Court of Justice against Member States it believes to be in breach of their obligations under the Treaties. Finally, the Commission is the main budgetary authority within the EU.

The European Parliament is the parliamentary organ of the European Union. The Parliament consists of 785 representatives, which are directly elected by the peoples of the Member States every five years.

The Parliament is involved in the legislative process through three main procedures: co-decision, assent, and consultation. The co-decision procedure, the most frequently used, involves power-sharing between Parliament and the Council. In the event of impasse, the proposed legislation is put before the "Conciliation Committee" — composed of equal numbers of Parliament and Council representatives — to attempt to reach an agreement on the text. The Parliament must approve all international agreements concluded by the Community in areas requiring co-decision or when such agreements have budgetary or institutional implications. In addition, the Parliament may also force the Commission to resign by a vote of censure.

The European Court of Justice (ECJ) is the common judicial body of the European Communities. The ECJ is composed of 27 Judges, one from each Member State, who are assisted by eight Advocates-General. There is also a Court of First Instance (CFI), which, like the ECJ, is composed of 27 Judges, one from each Member State. The CFI, however, has no permanent Advocates-General. Both ECJ and CFI Judges as well as the Advocates-General are appointed by agreement of the Member States to renewable six-year terms.

The ECJ's primary functions are to guarantee the uniform application and interpretation of Community law and to settle disputes between the various actors of the Community. The CFI helps the ECJ carry out these functions.

The Treaties and the Statute of the ECJ establish the specific division of jurisdiction between the two Courts. Generally, the CFI has jurisdiction over all direct actions and in areas of competition. The ECJ hears cases brought against Member States for failure to fulfill their obligations under the Treaties and responds to preliminary references. Preliminary references involve questions concerning the interpretation of Community law referred to the ECJ by Member

States' domestic courts. Finally, the ECJ has appellate jurisdiction over most CFI decisions with respect to questions of law.

Internet Resource:

Official website: http://europa.eu.int

II. CITATION GUIDE

Citation forms regarding the body of legislation from the EU change according to the country of publication. Some minimal rules have nevertheless been established by the Office of Official Publications of the European Union for citation to the Official Journal of the European Union, and by the European Court of Justice for the various Treaties of the European Communities and jurisprudence. Those are the rules stated here.

1.0 Basic Treaties

Because most of the Articles in the Treaties have been renumbered, it is important to determine which numbering system is used in a particular citation. A list of current and corresponding prior article numbers for the EU and EC treaties is located at http://curia.eu.int/en. Click on "Index," then on "Citation," and finally on "Articles of the EC Treaty" and "Articles of the Treaty on EU" as appropriate.

1.1 Treaties as They Stand after May 1, 1999 (Entrance into Force of the Treaty of Amsterdam)

Cite to the current Treaties and Treaties before May 1, 1999 by "Article," article referenced, and abbreviated title of the Treaty:

Article 234 TEC.

Article 85 TEC.

The abbreviations for the major treaties are:

Treaty on European Union: TEU
EC Treaty: TEC
ECSC Treaty: TCS
Euratom Treaty: TEA

Article 85 TEC.

When writing historically about pre-1999 articles, cite the EC Treaty and the Treaty on the European Union as they stood before May 1, 1999 by the above form, followed by a reference to the corresponding provision of the current version of the Treaty including, if appropriate, an indication that the article has been amended or repealed (in parentheses).

2.0 Official Documents (The Official Journal)

Any document issued by an institution of the European Union and published in the Official Journal must be cited by reference to the Official Journal (abbreviated "OJ").

Cite documents published on or after January 1, 1968, by title (optional), "OJ," series ("L," "C," or "S" — this subdivision did not exist prior to January 1, 1968), page referenced, and year:

Council Regulation 44/2001 on jurisdiction and the recognition and enforcement of judgments in civil and commercial matters, OJ L 12/1 (2001)

Council Directive 96/61/EC concerning integrated pollution, prevention and control, OJ L 257/3 (1996)

The Official Journal has three separate series, abbreviated as follows:

Legislation (i.e., Regulations, Directives, Decisions): L
Communications (i.e., Resolutions, Notices, Communications): C
Supplement to the Official Journal: S

3.0 Jurisprudence: European Court of Justice (ECJ) and Court of First Instance (CFI)

See subsection A.1.0 of Section III under Part III below, regarding Regional Courts.

4.0 Opinions

Under Article 300(6) of the Treaty on the European Union, the European Parliament, the Council, the Commission, or a Member State may obtain the opinion of the ECJ on whether an international agreement is compatible with the EU Treaty. Cite ECJ opinions by "Opinion," opinion number [number/year opinion request filed], agreement under review in parentheses and italicized, year of opinion (in square brackets), title of the reporter ("ECR"), volume, and page and paragraph referenced:

Opinion 1/78 (*International Agreement on Rubber*) [1979] ECR 2871, para 52.

Opinion 1/91 (*European Economic Area*) [1991] ECR I-6084.

5.0 Reports

The decisions of the ECJ and the CFI are published in the European Court of Justice and Court of First Instance Reporter (abbreviated "ECR").

Note that most if not all Member States also have their own private European law reports and journals, which have their own citation methods. Refer to country-specific methods of citation.

W O R L D   T R A D E
O R G A N I Z A T I O N

I.   ORGANIZATION PROFILE

The World Trade Organization (WTO) is an international organization consisting of 151 Member States (as of July 27, 2007) that deals with the global rules of trade between nations. The WTO's main function is to ensure that trade flows as smoothly, predictably, and freely as possible. It does this by administering trade agreements, acting as a forum for trade negotiations, settling trade disputes, reviewing national trade policies, providing technical assistance and training for developing countries, and cooperating with other international organizations.

The WTO was born out of the Uruguay Round negotiations (1986-94) of the General Agreement on Tariffs and Trade (GATT). The term GATT refers to both the multilateral agreement and the international organization that administers the agreement. The WTO provides a forum for future GATT negotiations and administers the dispute resolution system.

The WTO's top-level decision-making body is the Ministerial Conference, which meets at least once every two years. This body consists of representatives from each Member State and has full authority to make decisions on any matter arising from any of the Multilateral Trade Agreements (those agreements signed by all Member States). The Ministerial Conference is the chief policy-making body of the WTO, and any major policy change requires its approval.

Beneath the Ministerial Conference is the General Council, which meets regularly to carry out the functions of the WTO. This body is responsible for overseeing the WTO between Ministerial Conference meetings and consists of a representative from each Member State. The General Council has authority to act in all areas pertaining to Multilateral and Plurilateral Trade Agreements (the latter of which are not signed by all WTO Member States) and the WTO, except for major policy changes and decisions to alter the WTO treaties. The General Council, under different rules, also meets as the Trade Policy Review Body and the Dispute Settlement Body (DSB).

The Council for Trade in Goods (Goods Council), the Council for Trade in Services (Services Council), and the Council for Trade-Related Aspects of Intellectual Property Rights (TRIPS Council) report to the General Council. The Goods Council oversees the proper functioning of all Multilateral Trade Agreements affecting trade in goods, including interpretations of various GATT articles. The Services Council oversees the General Agreement on Trade in Services (GATS), which attempts to do for services what GATT has done for trading goods by establishing a multilateral framework for the reduction and elimination of barriers to international trade in services. The TRIPS Council oversees the TRIPS Agreement, which includes clauses ensuring nondiscrimination and most-favored nation (MFN) status. The Agreement also covers different kinds of intellectual property rights, such as copyrights, trademarks, and patents.

Six smaller bodies called committees also report to the General Council. These committees also consist of all WTO Members. The committees deal with issues such as trade and development, the environment, regional trading arrangements, administrative issues, investment and competition policy, transparency in government procurement, and trade facilitation. In addition, two more subsidiary bodies dealing with the Plurilateral Agreements regularly keep the General Council informed of their activities.

The WTO Secretariat services the WTO bodies with respect to negotiations and implementation of agreements. Based in Geneva, the Secretariat is headed by a Director-General. The Secretariat's main duties are to supply administrative and technical support for the various councils, committees, working parties, and negotiating groups, provide technical assistance to developing countries, analyze world trade, and explain WTO affairs to the public and media. In addition, the Secretariat provides legal assistance in the dispute settlement process and advises governments wishing to become WTO Member States.

The WTO's rules and agreements are the result of negotiations between Member States. Through these agreements, WTO Member States operate a nondiscriminatory trading system, which spells out their rights and obligations. Each Member State receives guarantees that its exports will be treated fairly and consistently in other Member States' markets. Each Member State also promises to treat imports from other Member States fairly.

Trade disputes are resolved under the Dispute Settlement Understanding. Member States may bring disputes to the WTO if they think their rights under the agreements are being infringed. The DSB is the body responsible for the dispute settlement mechanism. It has the sole authority to establish panels of experts to consider the case, and to accept or reject the panels' findings or the results of an appeal. The DSB monitors the implementation of the rulings and recommendations and has the power to authorize retaliation when a country does not comply with a ruling.

Internet Resources:

WTO	http://www.wto.org/
WTO Analytical Index (Jurisprudence by Agreement/ Article)	http://www.wto.org/english/res_e/ booksp_e/analytic_index_e/ analytic_index_e.htm
Appellate Body Reports	http://www.wto.org/english/ tratop_e/dispu_e/ab_reports_e.htm

II. CITATION GUIDE

1.0 Basic Treaties

1.1 Formal Citations

The general format for citing GATT/WTO treaties follows the standard set out in Section 1.0 of Part II, on Treaties and Conventions. For WTO agreements, however, reference to the official WTO publication—"The Legal Texts: The Results of the Uruguay Round of Multilateral Trade Negotiations"—is often added to the citation.

- GATT 1947:

  General Agreement on Tariffs and Trade, Oct.30, 1947, 61 Stat.A-11, 55 U.N.T.S. 194 [hereinafter GATT].

- Final Act Embodying Uruguay Round:

  Final Act Embodying the Results of the Uruguay Round of Multilateral Trade Negotiations, Apr. 15, 1994, THE LEGAL TEXTS: THE RESULTS OF THE URUGUAY ROUND OF MULTILATERAL TRADE NEGOTIATIONS 2 (1999), 1867 U.N.T.S. 14, 33 I.L.M. 1143 (1994) [hereinafter Final Act].

- GATT 1994:

  General Agreement on Tariffs and Trade 1994, Apr. 15, 1994, Marrakesh Agreement Establishing the World Trade Organization, Annex 1A, THE LEGAL TEXTS: THE RESULTS OF THE URUGUAY ROUND OF MULTILATERAL TRADE NEGOTIATIONS 17 (1999), 1867 U.N.T.S. 190, 33 I.L.M. 1153 (1994) [hereinafter GATT 1994].

- WTO Agreement or Marrakesh Agreement:

  Marrakesh Agreement Establishing the World Trade Organization, Apr. 15, 1994, THE LEGAL TEXTS: THE RESULTS OF THE URUGUAY ROUND OF MULTILATERAL TRADE NEGOTIATIONS 4 (1999), 1867 U.N.T.S. 154, 33 I.L.M. 1144 (1994) [hereinafter Marrakesh Agreement or WTO Agreement].

- Dispute Settlement Understanding (DSU):

  Understanding on Rules and Procedures Governing the Settlement of Disputes, Apr. 15, 1994, Marrakesh Agreement Establishing the World Trade Organization, Annex 2, THE LEGAL TEXTS: THE RESULTS OF THE URUGUAY ROUND OF MULTILATERAL TRADE NEGOTIATIONS 354 (1999), 1869 U.N.T.S. 401, 33 I.L.M. 1226 (1994) [hereinafter DSU].

- Agreement on the Application of Sanitary and Phytosanitary Measures (SPS):

  Agreement on the Application of Sanitary and Phytosanitary Measures, Apr. 15, 1994, Marrakesh Agreement Establishing the World Trade Organization, Annex 1A, THE LEGAL TEXTS: THE RESULTS OF THE URUGUAY ROUND OF

MULTILATERAL TRADE NEGOTIATIONS 59 (1999), 1867 U.N.T.S. 493 [hereinafter SPS Agreement].

- Agreement on Technical Barriers to Trade (TBT):

  Agreement on the Technical Barriers to Trade, Apr. 15, 1994, Marrakesh Agreement Establishing the World Trade Organization, Annex 1A, THE LEGAL TEXTS: THE RESULTS OF THE URUGUAY ROUND OF MULTILATERAL TRADE NEGOTIATIONS 121 (1999), 1868 U.N.T.S. 120 [hereinafter TBT Agreement].

- Agreement on Subsidies and Countervailing Measures (SCM):

  Agreement on Subsidies and Countervailing Measures, Apr. 15, 1994, Marrakesh Agreement Establishing the World Trade Organization, Annex 1A, THE LEGAL TEXTS: THE RESULTS OF THE URUGUAY ROUND OF MULTILATERAL TRADE NEGOTIATIONS 275 (1999), 1867 U.N.T.S. 14. [hereinafter SCM Agreement].

- Agreement on Safeguards:

  Agreement on Safeguards, Apr. 15, 1994, Marrakesh Agreement Establishing the World Trade Organization, Annex 1A, THE LEGAL TEXTS: THE RESULTS OF THE URUGUAY ROUND OF MULTILATERAL TRADE NEGOTIATIONS 275 (1999), 1869 U.N.T.S. 154 [hereinafter Safeguards Agreement].

- Agreement on Agriculture:

  Agreement on Agriculture, Apr. 15, 1994, Marrakesh Agreement Establishing the World Trade Organization, Annex 1A, THE LEGAL TEXTS: THE RESULTS OF THE URUGUAY ROUND OF MULTILATERAL TRADE NEGOTIATIONS 33 (1999), 1867 U.N.T.S. 410 [hereinafter Agriculture Agreement].

- Agreement on Import Licensing Procedures:

  Agreement on Import Licensing Procedures, Apr. 15, 1994, Marrakesh Agreement Establishing the World Trade Organization, Annex 1A, THE LEGAL TEXTS: THE RESULTS OF THE URUGUAY ROUND OF MULTILATERAL TRADE NEGOTIATIONS 223 (1999), 1868 U.N.T.S 436 (1994) [hereinafter Import Licensing Agreement].

- Agreement on Textiles and Clothing:

  Agreement on Textiles and Clothing, Apr. 15, 1994, Marrakesh Agreement Establishing the World Trade Organization, Annex 1A, THE LEGAL TEXTS: THE RESULTS OF THE URUGUAY ROUND OF MULTILATERAL TRADE NEGOTIATIONS 73 (1999), 1868 U.N.T.S. 14 [hereinafter Textiles Agreement].

- General Agreement on Trade in Services (GATS):

  General Agreement on Trade in Services, Apr. 15, 1994, Marrakesh Agreement Establishing the World Trade Organization, Annex 1B, THE LEGAL TEXTS: THE RESULTS OF THE URUGUAY ROUND OF MULTILATERAL TRADE NEGOTIATIONS 284 (1999), 1869 U.N.T.S. 183, 33 I.L.M. 1167 (1994) [hereinafter GATS].

- Agreement on Trade-Related Aspects of Intellectual Property Rights (TRIPS):

  Agreement on Trade-Related Aspects of Intellectual Property Rights, Apr. 15, 1994, Marrakesh Agreement Establishing the World Trade Organization, Annex 1C, THE LEGAL TEXTS: THE RESULTS OF THE URUGUAY ROUND OF MULTILATERAL TRADE NEGOTIATIONS 320 (1999), 1869 U.N.T.S. 299, 33 I.L.M. 1197 (1994) [hereinafter TRIPS Agreement].

- Agreement on Trade-Related Investment Measures (TRIMS):

  Agreement on Trade-Related Investment Measures, Apr. 15, 1994, Marrakesh Agreement Establishing the World Trade Organization, Annex 1A, THE LEGAL TEXTS: THE RESULTS OF THE URUGUAY ROUND OF MULTILATERAL TRADE NEGOTIATIONS 143 (1999), 1868 U.N.T.S. 186 [hereinafter TRIMS Agreement].

1.2 Subsequent or Informal Citations

GATT 1947, Art. III, para. 1(b).

GATT 1994, Art. XXIII, para. 1(b).

DSU, Art. 26.

SPS Agreement, Art. 5.7.

2.0 Documents

Cite all WTO documents by title (italicized), unique document symbol (explained in Section 2.1 below), date of issue and/or date of adoption (in parentheses), and page and paragraph referenced:

Transitional Review Mechanism Pursuant to Section 18 on the Accession of the People's Republic of China, G/ADP/W/436 (23 October 2003) p. 2, para. 5.

2.1 Document Symbols

All WTO documents are cited by a series of symbols (numbers and letters) separated by slashes, which uniquely identify the document. The order of the symbols designates the source of the document with increasing specificity.

The general order of symbols is: parent organ (or special body), subsidiary body, type of document, and any modification(s) to the document. In addition, some symbols are followed by a number indicating the chronological order of issue.

2.1.1 Document Categories

The major categories of WTO documents (and their symbols) are:

General/Administrative	**WT/** ...
Goods	**G/** ...
Services	**S/** ...
Preparatory Committee	**PC/** ...
Negotiating Group	**TS/** ...
Press Releases	**Press/** ...

2.1.2 Special Bodies

As an exception to the above principle, some categories are cited as the first element in the document symbol but do not reflect the major categories of WTO documents above. For example:

Committee on Government Procurement including Notifications:	**GPA/**
International Dairy Agreement:	**IDA/**
Council for Trade-Related Aspects of Intellectual Property Rights:	**IP/C/**
Committee on Trade in Civil Aircraft:	**TCA/**

2.1.3 Subsidiary Bodies

Common subsidiary bodies include:

Council:	... **/C/** ...
Informal Group:	... **/IG/** ...
Ad Hoc Group:	... **/AHG/** ...
Independent Entity:	... **/IE/** ...
Working Party:	... **/WP/** ...
Interim Committee:	... **/IC/** ...
Technical Sub-Committee:	... **/TSC/** ...

2.1.4 Types of Documents

Common general document types include:

Communiqué:	... **/COM/** ...
Report:	... **/R/** ...
Working Document:	... **/W/** ...
Minutes:	... **/M/** ...
Agreements:	... **/TC/** ...
Statements:	... **/ST/** ...
Notifications:	... **/N/** ...
Disputes:	... **/D/** ...

Information Series:	. . . /INF/ . . .
Questions and Replies to Notifications Submitted:	. . . /Q1/ . . .
Member submitted Document:	. . . /MEMBER/ . . .
Enquiries:	. . . /ENQ/ . . .
Replies to Questionnaires:	. . . /STAT/ . . .
Airgrams:	. . . /AIR/ . . .
Summary Records:	. . . /SR/ . . .
Provisional:	. . . /P/ . . .
Special Distribution:	. . . /SPEC/ . . .

3.0 Official Documents

Cite older documents published under GATT by title of the document, date, abbreviated title of the reporter (Basic Instruments and Selected Decisions, abbreviated "GATT B.I.S.D."), volume (in parentheses), page referenced, and year:

> *Treatment by Germany of Imports of Sardines,* Oct. 31 1952, GATT B.I.S.D. (1st Supp.) at 53 (1953).

4.0 Jurisprudence

See Major International Tribunals in subsection 3.0 of Section I in Part III below.

III.   SELECTED REFERENCES

THE LEGAL TEXTS: THE RESULTS OF THE URUGUAY ROUND OF MULTILATERAL TRADE NEGOTIATIONS (Cambridge University Press 1999).

JEANNE REHBERG, N.Y.U. LAW LIBRARY, WTO AND GATT RESEARCH GUIDE (2004), *at* http://www.law.nyu.edu/library/wtoguide.html.

J.H.H. WEILER & S. CHO, INTERNATIONAL AND REGIONAL TRADE LAW: THE LAW OF THE WORLD TRADE ORGANIZATION (2004), *at* http://www.jeanmonnetprogram.org/wto/Units/index.html.

WTO SECRETARIAT, GUIDE TO THE URUGUAY ROUND AGREEMENTS (Kluwer Law International 1999).

S H A R I A   L A W

1.0 What Is Sharia Law?

Sharia is the Arabic word used to refer to the corpus of law embodied in Islamic religious principles. Sharia, which literally means "way or path to the water," extends to all aspects of the public and private domain and has influence over all social, political, and religious facets of the society in which it is in force.

Sharia is derived from two principal sources:

(1) the interpretation of the teachings set out in the Qur'an; and

(2) the sunnah or the Hadith (the sayings and conduct of the prophet Muhammad).

At the outset the two schools of Islamic thought must be distinguished — the Sunni school and the Shia school. The distinction between the Sunni and Shia schools is outside the scope of this discussion. Suffice it to say for these purposes that the division initially emerged with respect to the succession of the Prophet Muhammad and has evolved from there. In the Sunni tradition there are two supplementary sources of Sharia law:

(1) ijma — the notion of consensus of the ummah (the community of believers); and

(2) qiyas — the notion of analogical reasoning employed to extend the application of rules in the Qur'an and the Hadith.

In the Shia tradition, instead of qiyas is the concept of 'aql (intrinsic human knowledge or intellect) as a source of law.

In addition to the sources noted above, the concept of Fiqh, meaning deeper understanding (and which is the embodiment of Islamic jurisprudence), complements and develops the Sharia. Fiqh is developed by interpretations of the Sharia in the form of fatwas (religious edicts of learned Islamic scholars over many centuries). Sunni scholars rely on the doctrines of ijma and qiyas, whereas Shia scholars rely on 'aql.

The following discussion elaborates on the primary sources of Sharia law.

2.0 Sources of Sharia Law

Primary Sources

In the Sunni tradition, there are five principal sources of Sharia law that exist, which include (in the order of importance):

1. *Qur'an* ("Recitation"): The Qur'an is the primary and holiest source of Muslim Law. It was revealed to Prophet Muhammad over 23 years and forms the bedrock of Islam and, in turn, Islamic law. The Qur'an comprises 114 chapters called "*Sura.*" Each Sura in turn comprises several verses called "*Ayah.*"

The legal significance of the Qur'an: When it comes to making a legal determination using the Qur'an, the text might fall into two categories: a text that is definitive or clear and unequivocal ("*Qati*") or one that might be subject to different interpretations ("*Zanni*"). The difference between the two is that while the Qati is subject to no other interpretation, the Zanni is open to using interpretative techniques and *ijtihad.* The best interpretation is that which can be obtained from the Qur'an itself, that is, by looking at the Qur'an as a whole and finding the necessary elaboration elsewhere in a similar or even a different context.

2. *Sunnah and Hadith*: The Sunnah, literally translated as "the path trodden," refer to the actions instituted by the Prophet Muhammad during his lifetime. In the Shia tradition the sunnah include the actions of the 12 Imams that succeeded the Prophet. The hadith refer to the traditions concerning the life and the teachings of the Prophet. There is some debate whether the hadith are a subset of the sunnah, and different schools of jurisprudence deal with this differently.

3. *Ijma*: The term "Ijma" refers to consensus of opinion of the community of believers. The concept is said to have emerged from a hadith of the Prophet in which he suggested that his believers never erred. It bears mention that there is some debate as to what the "community" is, namely, whether the community comprises only learned scholars or all of the ummah (the entirety of the community of believers).

4. *Qiyas*: Qiyas is the process of analogical reasoning that extends the reasoning inherent in the Qur'an and the sunnah/hadith to problems not specifically contemplated therein.

5. *'Aql*: Unique to Shia jurisprudence, 'aql refers to the concept of intrinsic human knowledge or intuitive logic. The reasoning that one undertakes when applying 'aql is deductive in nature.

3.0 Different Schools in Sharia Law

The four schools of Sunni Law include:

(1) *Hanafi*: Named after Imam Abu Hanifa, 702-767 CE

(2) *Hanbali*: Named after Imam Ahmed ibn Hanbal, 778-855 CE

(3) *Maliki*: Named after Imam Malik ibn Anas, 717-801 CE

(4) *Shafi*: Named after Imam Muhammad Idris al-Shafi, 769-820 CE

In the Shia tradition, the primary school of thought is that of the Ithna' Asheriyyah, or "Twelvers." According to the Ithna' Asheriyyah tradition, the fatwahs and teachings of the first three Sunni caliphs are to be disregarded (the fourth and last Sunni caliph is also the first Imam of the Shias), and the teachings and traditions of the 12 Imams that succeeded the Prophet are part and parcel of the sunnah.

4.0 List of Countries That Use Sharia Law

Listed below is a nonexhaustive list of countries that use Sharia law as a basis of law or identify Islam as the state religion:

ALGERIA	Article 2 of the Constitution of Algeria.
BAHRAIN	Article 2 of the Kingdom of Bahrain.
EGYPT	Article 2 of the Egypt Constitution.
IRAN	Article 1 of the Constitution of the Islamic Republic of Iran.
JORDAN	Article 2 of the Constitution of the Hashemite Kingdom of Jordan.
KUWAIT	Article 2 of the Constitution of Kuwait.
LIBYA	Article 2 of the Constitution of Libya.
MALAYSIA	Article 3 of the Constitution of Malaysia.
MOROCCO	Article 6 of the Constitution of Morocco.
OMAN	Article 1 of the Constitution of Oman.
PAKISTAN	Article 2 of the Constitution of the Islamic Republic of Pakistan.
QATAR	Article 1 of the draft Constitution of Qatar.
SAUDI ARABIA	Article 1 of the Constitution of Saudi Arabia.
SUDAN	Article 65 of the Constitution of Sudan identifies the sources of legislation by stating that "[t]he Islamic Sharia and the national consent through voting, the Constitution and custom are the source of law and no law shall be enacted contrary to these sources. . . ."

SYRIA	Article 3 of the Constitution of Syria states that Islam is the religion of the President and that Islamic jurisprudence is a main source of legislation. *Available at* http://www.servat.unibe.ch/icl/sy00000_.html.
TUNISIA	Article 1 of the Constitution of Tunisia, *available at* http://www.servat.unibe.ch/icl/ts00000_.html.
YEMEN	Articles 2 and 3 of the Constitution of the Republic of Yemen.

PART

3

CITATION GUIDES FOR

INTERNATIONAL AND

REGIONAL TRIBUNALS

1.0 International Court of Justice (ICJ)

1.1 ICJ Citations

1.1.1 ICJ Decisions (1945–Present)

Cite ICJ decisions in cases of controversy by title (italicized), name of the parties (in parentheses, italicized, and often abbreviated), type of hearing, type of decision (if applicable), "I.C.J. Reports" (sometimes abbreviated as "I.C.J. Rep." or "I.C.J.R."), year of the reporter, volume (in parentheses, if applicable), first page of the decision (if published), page and paragraph referenced (if applicable), and date of the decision (in parentheses):

> *Fisheries Jurisdiction (United Kingdom v. Iceland),* Jurisdiction of the Court, Judgment, I.C.J. Rep. 1973, 3 (Feb. 2).
>
> *Legality of Use of Force (Yugoslavia v. United Kingdom),* Provisional Measures Order, I.C.J. Rep. 1999, 826 (June 2).
>
> *Arrest Warrant of 11 April 2000 (Democratic Republic of the Congo v. Belgium),* Judgment, I.C.J. Rep. 2002 (I) (Feb. 14).

Types of decisions include: Order, Judgment, Jurisdiction Judgment, Merits Judgment, and Advisory Opinion.

1.1.2 Advisory Opinions

Cite advisory opinions of the ICJ by title (italicized), "Advisory Opinion," "I.C.J. Reports" (sometimes abbreviated as "I.C.J. Rep." or "I.C.J.R."), volume (by year), date of the opinion, first page of the opinion, and page and paragraph referenced (if applicable):

> *Legality of the Use by a State of Nuclear Weapons in Armed Conflict,* Advisory Opinion, I.C.J. Rep. 1996 (July 8), p. 66.

1.2 Permanent Court of International Justice (PCIJ) Citations (1922–1946)

Cite PCIJ decisions and opinions by title (italicized), name of the parties (italicized) (no parties are listed for advisory opinions), type of decision (if applicable), year of the decision (in parentheses), "P.C.I.J.", reporter series, case number, and page referenced (if applicable):

> River Meuse Case (Netherlands v. Belgium) (1937) P.C.I.J. Series A/B, no. 70.
>
> Société Commerciale de Belgique, Judgment (1939) P.C.I.J. Series A/B, No. 78.

1.2.1 List of Decisions

ICJ orders and decisions are available at http://www.icj-cij.org (click on "Decisions").

2.0 International Tribunal for the Law of the Sea (ITLOS)

Cite ITLOS decisions by title (italicized), name of the parties (in parentheses, italicized, and separated by "v."), type of the hearing (italicized), type of the decision (italicized), "of", date (italicized), title of the reporter in which the decision is published ("ITLOS Reports"), year, and page referenced:

> The M/V "SAIGA" (No. 2) Case (Saint Vincent and the Grenadines v. Guinea), Provisional Measures, Order of 11 March 1998, ITLOS Reports 1998, p. 24.
>
> Southern Bluefin Tuna Cases (New Zealand v. Japan; Australia v. Japan), Provisional Measures, Order of 27 August 1999, ITLOS Reports 2000, p. 3.
>
> The Mox Plant Case (Ireland v. United Kingdom), Provisional Measure, Order of 13 November 2001, ITLOS Reports 2001, p. 5.
>
> The "Camouco" Case (Panama v. France), Prompt Release, Judgment of 7 February 2000, ITLOS Reports 2000, p. 10.
>
> The "Grand Prince" Case (Belize v. France), Prompt Release, Judgment of 20 April 2001, ITLOS Reports 2001, 17.

3.0 World Trade Organization Dispute Settlement Body (WTO-DSB)

3.1 Panel Reports

Cite panel reports by "Panel Report on" (optional), Member State before the Panel (italicized), a dash (" — "), title of the dispute (italicized) including a short title (in parentheses and, optionally, preceded by "hereinafter"), document symbol ("WT/DS____/R"), date adopted, and page and/or paragraph referenced. Modification information may also follow:

> Panel Report on United States — Preliminary Determination with Respect to Certain Softwood Lumber from Canada (hereinafter "US — Softwood Lumber III"), WT/DS236/R, adopted 1 September 2002, ¶ 7.17.

Panel Report on *United States — Anti-dumping measures on certain Hot-Rolled Steel Products from Japan* (*"US — Hot-Rolled Steel"*), WT/DS184/R, adopted 23 August 2001 as modified by Appellate Body Report, *US — Hot-Rolled Steel*, WT/DS184/AB/R, adopted 1 January 2002, ¶ 7.54.

Subsequent citations may refer to the short title, document symbol, and page and/or paragraph referenced.

3.2 Appellate Body Reports

Cite appellate body reports by "Appellate Body Report on" (optional), Member State before the Appellate Body, a dash (" — "), title of the dispute (italicized) including a short title (in parentheses and, optionally, preceded by "hereinafter"), document symbol ("WT/DS____/AB/R"), date adopted, and page and/or paragraph referenced:

Appellate Body Report on *United States — Restrictions on Imports of Cotton and Man-made Fibre Underwear* (hereinafter *"US — Cotton Underwear"*), WT/DS24/AB/R, adopted 25 February 1997, p. 15.

Subsequent citations may refer to the short title, document symbol and page and/or paragraph referenced.

4.0 Human Rights Commission (HRC), Committee on Economic, Social and Cultural Rights (CESCR), Committee on the Rights of the Child (CRC), and Other International Human Rights Commissions

4.1 Communications

Cite communications by committee, title of the communication (italicized), communication number and year ["Communication no." number/year] (in parentheses), and official source if available (e.g., U.N. Document).

Human Rights Committee, *Mikmaq Tribal Society* v. *Canada* (Communication no. 205/1986).

4.2 General Comments

Cite general comments by committee, "General Comment" and comment number, subdivision referenced, session and date (in parentheses), and official source if available (e.g., U.N. Document):

Human Rights Committee, General Comment 23, Art. 27 (Fiftieth session, 1994), Compilation of General Comments and General Recommendations Adopted by Human Rights Treaty Bodies, U.N. Doc. HRI\GEN\1\Rev.1 at 38 (1994).

II. CRIMINAL TRIBUNALS

1.0 International Criminal Court (ICC)

Cite ICC cases by name of the parties (italicized, separated by "v."), ICC case number (ICC- . . .), document title (in English), and date in parentheses:

> *Prosecutor v. Ahmad Muhammad Harun*, ICC-02/05-01/07-2, Warrant of Arrest for Ahmad Harun (April 27, 2007).

> *Prosecutor v. Thomas Lubanga Dyilo*, ICC-01/04/-01/06-1495, Prosecution's Request for an Ex-Parte Hearing Pursuant to Rule 83 of the Rules of Procedure and Evidence (November 5, 2008).

If the document title of the cited case is in French originally, use the French title:

> *Prosecutor v. Thomas Lubanga Dyilo*, ICC-01/04/-01/06-1166, Soumission du représentant légal del la victime a/0105/06 suite aux difficultés d'accès au logiciel CITRIX (February 14, 2008).

2.0 International Criminal Tribunal for the Former Yugoslavia (ICTY)

2.1 Common-Form Citations

Cite ICTY cases by name of the parties (separated by "v."), "Case No." and case number, "ICTY," and date in parentheses:

> Prosecutor v. Vasiljevic, Case No. IT-98-32-A ICTY (Feb. 25, 2004).

2.2 Formal Citations

Cite ICTY cases formally by name of the parties, case number, type of decision, paragraph cited, and date:

> Prosecutor v. Duško Tadić, Case No. IT-94-1-T*bis*-R117 ICTY, Sentencing Judgment, ¶ 13 (November 11, 1999).

> Prosecutor v. Duško Tadić, Case No. IT-94-1-A and IT-94-1-A*bis* ICTY, Judgement in Sentencing Appeals, ¶ 4 (January 26, 2000).

> Prosecutor v. Miroslav Bralo, Case No. IT-95-17-A, Decision on Motions for Access to Ex Parte Portions of the Record on Appeal and for Disclosure of Mitigating Material, ¶ 17 (August 30, 2006).

PART III: INTERNATIONAL AND REGIONAL TRIBUNALS   II. CRIMINAL TRIBUNALS

3.0 International Criminal Tribunal for Rwanda (ICTR)

3.1 Common-Form Citations

Cite ICTR cases by name of the parties (separated by "v."), "Case No." and case number, and date (in parentheses):

> Prosecutor v. Serushago, Case No. ICTR-98-39-A (April 3, 2001).

3.2 Formal Citations

Cite ICTR cases formally by name of the parties, case number, type of decision, paragraph cited, and date:

> Prosecutor v. Ferdinand Nahimana, Jean-Bosco Barayagwiza, and Hassan Ngeze, Case No. ICTR-99-52-T, Judgment, ¶ 186 (December 3, 2003).

> Prosecutor v. Laurent Semanza, Case No. ICTR-97-20-T, Judgment and Sentence, ¶ 512 (May 15, 2003).

4.0 Hybrid Courts (International and Domestic)

4.1 The Special Panel for Serious Crimes of Dili District Court (East Timor)

4.1.1 Panel Decisions

Cite panel decisions by name of the parties (separated by "v."), "Criminal Case No.", followed by case number, year and "PD.Dil." (separated by backslashes), "of the Special Crimes Panel of Dili District Court," paragraph or page cited, and the date:

> Prosecutor v. Joao Fernandez, Criminal Case No. 01/PID.C.G./2000/PD.Dil. of the Special Crimes Panel of Dili District Court, ¶ 14 (Jan. 25, 2000).

> Prosecutor v. Carlos Soares Carmona, Criminal Case No. 03/PID.C.G./2000/PD.Dil. of the Special Crimes Panel of Dili District Court, p. 3 (Apr. 19, 2001).

4.1.2 The Court of Appeal Decisions

Cite appeals by name of the parties (separated by "v."), "Criminal Appeal No.", case number, year, "Arising from the Original" followed by a reference to the original panel decision, paragraph or page cited and the date:

> Julio Fernandes v. Prosecutor General, Criminal Appeal No. 7 of 2001, Arising from the Original Criminal Case No. 02/PID.C.G./2000/PD.Dil. of the Special Crimes Panel of Dili District Court, p. 2 (June 29, 2002).

4.2 Special Court for Sierra Leone (SCSL)

Basic Documents:

Agreement Between the United Nations and the Government of Sierra Leone on the Establishment of a Special Court for Sierra Leone

Statute of the Special Court for Sierra Leone

Cite SCSL cases by name of the parties (separated by "v."), "Case No." and case number, and date (in parentheses):

Prosecutor v. Foday Saybana Sankoh, Case No. SCSL-2003-02-PT (May 23, 2003).

Prosecutor v. Issa Hassan Sesay, Morris Kallon, Augustine Gbao, Case No. SCSL-04-15-AR65 (September 17, 2004).

4.3 "Regulation 64" Panels in the Courts of Kosovo

Basic Documents:

Regulation No. 2000/64 on Assignment of International Judges/Prosecutors and/or Change of Venue

Cite cases by name of the parties, case number, paragraph cited, and date:

Simo Mitrovic v. UNMIK, Case No. 06/07, ¶ 12 (May 8, 2008).

Brahim Sahiti v. UNMIK, Case No. 03/08 (April 10, 2008).

4.4 Extraordinary Chambers in the Courts of Cambodia

Basic Documents:

Agreement Between the United Nations and the Royal Government of Cambodia Concerning the Prosecution Under Cambodian Law of Crimes Committed During the Period of Democratic Kampuchea

Law on the Establishment of the Extraordinary Chambers, with the inclusion of amendments as promulgated on 27 October 2004 (NS/RKM/1004/006)

Please note: As of November 2008, only pretrial decisions have been made.

Cite cases by name of the parties, case number, type of decision, paragraph cited, and date:

Office of Co-Prosecutors v. Khieu Samphan, Criminal Case File No. 002/19-09-2007-ECCC/OCIJ (PTC11), Decision on Khieu Samphan's Request for a Public Hearing, ¶ 8 (Nov. 4, 2008).

III. REGIONAL COURTS

A. EUROPE

1.0 European Court of Justice (ECJ) and Court of First Instance (CFI)

Cite cases introduced before January 1, 1989 by "Case," case number [number/ year of filing], name of the parties (italicized and separated by "v."), year of decision (in square brackets), title of the reporter ("E.C.R."), volume (if necessary), and page and paragraph referenced:

> Case 120/88 *Commission v. Italy* [1991] E.C.R. I-621.

Cite cases introduced after January 1, 1989 by "Case," followed by "T" (for the Court of First Instance) or "C" (for the European Court of Justice) and hyphen, case number [number/year of filing], name of the parties (italicized and separated by "v"), year of decision (in square brackets), title of the reporter ("E.C.R."), volume, and page and paragraph referenced:

> Case T-224/95 *Tremblay and Others v. Commission* [1997] E.C.R. II-2215.
>
> Case C-242/95 GT-Link [1997] E.C.R. I-4449, ¶ 36.

Many authors include descriptions of the subject matter of the case following the parties' names (in parentheses), especially when a case involves common parties, such as Member States or EU institutions:

> Case C-350/92 Spain v. Council (Medicinal product certificates) [1995] E.C.R. I-1985.

1.1 Joined Cases

Cite joined cases as described in Section 1.0 above, preceded by the words "Joined Cases":

> Joined Cases C-34/95, C-35/95 and C-36/95 *Konsumentombudsmannen v De Agostini (Svenska) Forlag* [1997] E.C.R. I-3843.

2.0 European Court of Human Rights (ECHR)

The ECHR is an organ of the Council of Europe, which is an international organization distinct from the Communities or the EU, with a broad membership of more than 40 states.

2.1 Decisions after November 1, 1998 (Entry into Force of Protocol 11)

Cite cases decided on or after November 1, 1998, by name of the parties (italicized and separated by "v."), type of decision (in parentheses) (note: a judgment on the merits has no designation), or, if decided by the Grand Chamber, "[GC]," case number, section(s) referenced, date (optional), and abbreviated title of the reporter in which the case is published ("Eur. Ct. H.R."), year, and volume:

> *Brumarescu v. Romania* [GC], no. 28342/95, §§52-53, Eur. Ct. H.R. 1999-VII.

> *Hasan and Chaush v. Bulgaria* [GC], no. 30985/96, § 84, Eur. Ct. H.R. 2000-XI.

> *Messina v. Italy* (dec.), no. 25498/94, Eur. Ct. H.R. 1999-V.

> *Malhous v. the Czech Republic* (dec.) [GC], no. 33071/96, Dec. 13, 2000, Eur. Ct. H.R. 2000-XII.

> *Smith and Grady v. the United Kingdom* (just satisfaction), nos. 33985/96 and 33986/96, § 13, 25 July 2000, Eur. Ct. H.R. 2000-IX.

> *Akman v. Turkey* (striking out), no. 37453/97, Eur. Ct. H.R. 2001-VI.

Types of decisions (and their short forms) are:

Decisions on admissibility (dec.)
Preliminary objections (preliminary objections)
Judgments for just satisfaction (just satisfaction)
Judgments regarding revision (revision)
Judgments on interpretations (interpretation)
Judgments striking the case delivered by a Chamber (striking out)
Judgments regarding a friendly settlement (friendly settlement)

2.1.1 Unreported Decisions before November 1, 1998

Cite unreported cases decided before November 1, 1998, by name of the parties (italicized and separated by "v."), case number, section(s) referenced, date, and "unreported":

> *Party v. Party*, no. 31007/88, § 38, July 16, 1998, unreported.

2.1.2 Decisions of the Pre-1999 European Court of Human Rights (1959–1998)

Cite reported cases decided prior to January 1, 1999, by name of the parties (italicized and separated by "v."), "judgment of" and date, type of decision (if not a final judgment), reporter in which the case is published; for cases decided from 1959 to 1996 ["Series A no.", case number, page referenced, and section(s) referenced]; for cases decided from 1997 to 1999 ["Reports," year, volume, and page referenced], and section(s) referenced:

> *Ireland v. the United Kingdom*, judgment of Jan. 18, 1978, Series A no. 25, p. 65, § 161.

> *McCann and Others v. the United Kingdom*, judgment of Sept. 27, 1995, Series A no. 324, pp. 45-46, §§146-147.

> *Aerts v. Belgium*, judgment of July 30, 1998, Reports 1998-V, p. 1961, § 46.

> *Loizidou v. Turkey*, judgment of Mar. 23, 1995 (*preliminary objections*), Series A no. 310, p. 19, § 44.

3.0 The European Commission of Human Rights (1954–1998)

3.1 Decisions

Cite cases by name of the parties (italicized and separated by "v."), case number, "Commission decision of" and date, and reporter in which the case is published by abbreviated title, volume and page referenced, or "unreported":

> *N. v. Sweden*, no. 11366/85, Commission decision of Oct. 16, 1986, DR 50, p. 173.

> *Stewart-Brady v. the United Kingdom*, nos. 27436/95 and 28406/95, Commission decision of July 2, 1997, DR 90, p. 45.

> *Lupker and Others v. the Netherlands*, no. 18395/91, Commission decision of Dec. 7, 1992, unreported.

The reporters publishing the decisions include:

1958-1971: Collection of Decisions of the ECHR
1971-1998: Decisions and Reports (DR)

4.0 Court of Justice of the European Free Trade Agreement (EFTA)

Cite cases by "Case" and case number ["E"-number/last two digits of the year], name of the parties (italicized and separated by "v"), and reporter in which the case is published by year (in square brackets), abbreviated title of the reporter ("EFTA Ct. Rep.") and volume, or "not yet reported," and page or paragraph referenced:

> Case E-8/97 *TV 1000 Sverige v. Norway* [1998] EFTA Ct. Rep. 68, at paragraph 26.
>
> Case E-2/02 Technologien *Bau- und Wirtschaftsberatung and Bellona v. EFTA.* Surveillance Authority, judgement of June 19, 2003, not yet reported, at paragraph 37.

More information is available at: http://www.eftacourt.lu/pdf/E_2_03Decision.pdf.

5.0 Benelux Economic Union Court of Justice (*Benelux-Gerechtshof*)

Cite cases by title (italicized), "Benelux Court of Justice" or "Benelux-Gerechtshof," date, "Case" and case number, title of the reporter in which the case is published, volume, and location in the reporter (e.g., case number or first page of the case):

> *Christian Dior Perfumes*, Benelux Court of Justice, Dec. 16, 1998, Case A-95/4, Nederlandse Jurisprudentie 2001, No. 133.

B. THE AMERICAS

1.0 Inter American Court of Human Rights (IACtHR)

1.1 Judgments and Decisions

Cite cases by title of the court ("I/A Court H.R."), title of the case (italicized), type of decision ("Judgment," "Provisional measures," etc.), date (optional), series of the reporter in which the case is published, case number in the reporter, and the paragraph(s) referenced:

> I/A Court H.R., *Velasquez Rodriguez case*, Judgment of July 29, 1986, Series C, No. 4, para. 167.
>
> I/A Court H.R., *Bulacio Case*, Judgment of September 18, 2003, Series C, No. 100, paras. 116-118.

1.2 Advisory Opinions

Cite advisory opinions by title of the court ("I/A Court H.R."), title of the case (italicized), "Advisory Opinion," case number, date, series of the reporter in which the case is published, case number in the reporter, and paragraph referenced:

I/A Court H.R., *The Word "Laws" in Article 30 of the American Convention on Human Rights*, Advisory Opinion OC-6/86 of May 9, 1986, Series A, No. 65, para. 29.

1.3 Separate Opinions

Cite separate opinions by title of the court ("I/A Court H.R.") and "Separate opinion of [name of the judge]," followed by the case citation as indicated above:

I/A Court H.R., Separate opinion of Judge Rodolfo E. Piza Esoalante, *Enforceability of the Right to Reply or Correction (Articles 14.1, 1.1 and 2 of the American Convention on Human Rights)*, Advisory Opinion OC-7/86 of August 29, 1986, Series A, No. 7, para. 25.

C. AFRICA

1.0 Common Court of Justice and Arbitration for the Organization for the Harmonization of Corporate Law in Africa (OHADA)

Basic Documents:

Treaty on the Harmonisation of Business Law in Africa
Rules of Procedure of the Common Court of Justice and Arbitration

Cases are cited in French by name of the court, ("Arrêt No") and case number, date, and name of the parties (separated by "contre" or "c/"). Sections 1.1 to 1.3 give examples for various courts.

1.1 Cour d'Appel

Cour d'Appel d'Abidjan, Arrêt No 1036 du 30 Juillet 2003, (QUATTARA IDRISSA c/ Société COASTAL TRADING COMPAGNY dite CTC).

Cour d'Appel d'Abidjan, Arrêt No 981 du 15 Juillet 2003, (La SIB c/ M. HASSAN DRAMERA et Mme DEMBA NENE).

Cour d'appel d'Abidjan, Arrêt No 685 du 30 mai 2003, (Ecobank c/ Société Dalyna Voyages Travel Agency).

1.2 Tribunal Régional Hors Classe de Dakar

Tribunal Régional Hors Classe de Dakar, jugement du 26 mai 2003, Félicien SANCHEZ contre Elisabeth FONSECA.

Tribunal Régional Hors Classe de Dakar, ordonnance due mai 19 2002, Thierno MANE et autres contre SENELEC et SDE.

1.3 La Cour Commune de Justice et d'Arbitrage (CCJA, the Common Court of Justice and Arbitration)

CCJA, Arrêt no 005/2003 due 24 avril 2003 (BICICI c/ D.M. et BDM et fils), Le Juris-Ohada, no 2/2003, avril-juin 2003, p.14, note anonyme.

CCJA, Arrêt No 008/2003 due 24 avril 2003 (A.K. c./ H.M.), Le Juris-Ohada, no 2/2003, avril-juin 2003, note anonyme.

2.0 Court of Justice of the Common Market for Eastern and Southern Africa (COMESA)

Basic Documents:

The Treaty Establishing the Common Market for Eastern and Southern Africa

The Rules of Court of the Court of Justice of the Common Market for Eastern and Southern Africa

Cite cases by name of the parties (italicized and separated by "vs."), name of the court ("COMESA Court of Justice"), type of application, case number and year, and decision type and date (in square brackets):

Martin Ogang vs. Eastern and Southern African Trade and Development Bank and Dr. Michael Gondwe, COMESA Court of Justice, Consolidated Interlocutory Applications No. 1A/2000 and 1C/2000. [JUDGMENT OF 30/3/2001].

Bilika Harry Simamba vs. Common Market for Eastern and Southern Africa, COMESA Court of Justice, Reference No. 3/2002. [ORDER OF 25/10/2002].

3.0 African Court on Human and Peoples' Rights (ACHPR)

Basic Documents:

Protocol to the African Charter on Human and Peoples' Rights on the Establishment of an African Court on Human and Peoples' Rights

African Charter on Human and Peoples' Rights

REGIONAL COURTS   C. AFRICA

Envisioned by the African Charter on Human and Peoples' Rights concluded in 1981, the structure of ACHPR was not planned until the Protocol to the African Charter on Human and Peoples' Rights establishing the ACHPR entered into force on January 25, 2004. After the Organization of African Unity transformed into the African Union (AU), the AU determined that the ACHPR should be merged with the African Court of Justice. As the Protocol to the African Court of Justice has not come into force yet, the operation of the ACHPR has also been delayed. However, the AU has elected the first eleven judges to the ACHPR.

4.0 African Commission on Human and Peoples' Rights

Basic Documents:

African Charter on Human and Peoples' Rights

Cite commission communications by name of the parties (separated by "v." or "vs."), name of the Commission (African Comm. Hum. & Peoples' Rights), communication number, and date or "not dated" (in parentheses):

> Andre Houver vs. Morocco, African Comm. Hum. & Peoples' Rights, Comm. No. 41/90 (March 28, 1990).

> International PEN vs. Malawi, Ethiopia, Cameroon, Kenya, African Comm. Hum. & Peoples' Rights, Comm. No. 19/88 (August 30, 1989).

INDEX

independent organizations linked to
UN, 233
International Court of Justice, 231, 233.
See also International Court of
Justice (ICJ)
International Law Commission,
Yearbook of, 237
internationally agreed development
goals (IADGs), 232
Internet resources, 235
Office of the UN High Commissioner
for Refugees (UNHCR), 233
official documents other than
resolutions, 236-237
organization profile, 231-235
principal purposes, 231
publications for sale to public, 237-238
Secretariat, 231, 233
Security Council, 231, 232, 233
Security Council Official Record, 236
Security Council resolutions, 236
structure, 231
treaties, 235
Trusteeship Council, 231, 232-233
UN Children's Fund (UNICEF), 233
UN Development Program (UNDP), 233
yearbooks, 237
United Nations Conference on
International Organization, 231
Universal Postal Union (UPU), 233, 234
UPU. See Universal Postal Union (UPU)
Uruguay Round negotiations, 245
Final Act Embodying Uruguay Round, 247

Wales. See United Kingdom
WHO. See World Health Organization
(WHO)
WIPO. See World Intellectual Property
Organization (WIPO)
WMO. See World Meteorological
Organization (WMO)
World Bank, 233
World Bank Group, 234
World Health Organization (WHO), 233,
234
World Intellectual Property Organization
(WIPO), 234

World Meteorological Organization
(WMO), 234
World Trade Organization (WTO),
245-251
agreements
on Agriculture, 248
on Import Licensing Procedures, 248
on Safeguards, 248
Sanitary and Phytosanitary Measures
(SPS), on Application of, 247-248
on Subsidies and Countervailing
Measures (SCM), 248
on Technical Barriers to Trade (TBT),
248
on Textiles and Clothing, 248
on Trade-Related Aspects of
Intellectual Property Rights
(TRIPS), 249
on Trade-Related Investment
Measures (TRIMS), 249
WTO Agreement, 247
categories of documents, 250
citation guide, 247-251
Council for Trade in Goods, 245
Council for Trade in Services, 245
Council for Trade-Related Aspects of
Intellectual Property Rights (TRIPS
Council), 245
Dispute Settlement Body (DSB), 245, 246
Dispute Settlement Understanding
(DSU), 247
documents, 249-251
Final Act Embodying Uruguay
Round, 247
General Agreement on Tariffs and
Trade (GATT)
GATT 1947, 247
GATT 1994, 247
General Agreement on Trade in Services
(GATS), 245, 248
General Council, 245, 246
Goods Council, 245
Internet resources, 246
jurisprudence, 251
main function, 245
Marrakesh Agreement, 247
Ministerial Conference, 245
most-favored nation (MFN) status, 246